ALSO BY ANELISE CHEN

So Many Olympic Exertions

CLAM
DOWN

ONE WORLD • *New York*

CLAM
DOWN

A METAMORPHOSIS

ANELISE
CHEN

Published in the United States by One World, an imprint of Random House, a division of Penguin Random House LLC, New York.

ONE WORLD and colophon are registered trademarks of Penguin Random House LLC.

Some of these chapters have appeared, in slightly different form, in *The Paris Review Daily*.

This is a work of creative nonfiction. Some names and identifying features have been changed to protect the identities of certain parties.

LIBRARY OF CONGRESS CATALOGING-IN-PUBLICATION DATA
Names: Chen, Anelise, author.
Title: Clam down / by Anelise Chen.
Description: First edition. | New York: One World, 2025. | Includes bibliographical references.
Identifiers: LCCN 2024053923 (print) | LCCN 2024053924 (ebook) |
ISBN 9781984801845 (hardcover) | ISBN 9781984801852 (ebook)
Subjects: LCSH: Chen, Anelise. | Authors, American—Biography. | Women authors, American—Biography. | Human-animal relationships. | LCGFT: Autobiographies.
Classification: LCC PS3603.H4468 Z46 2025 (print) | LCC PS3603.H4468 (ebook) |
DDC 813/.6 [B]—dc23/eng/20241118
LC record available at https://lccn.loc.gov/2024053923
LC ebook record available at https://lccn.loc.gov/2024053924

Printed in the United States of America on acid-free paper

oneworldlit.com

1st Printing

Book design by Simon M. Sullivan

The authorized representative in the EU for product safety and compliance is Penguin Random House Ireland, Morrison Chambers, 32 Nassau Street, Dublin D02 YH68, Ireland. https://eu-contact.penguin.ie.

This book is for my family.

In the same way, A. realizes, as he sits in his room writing The Book of Memory, he speaks of himself as another in order to tell the story of himself. He must make himself absent in order to find himself there. And so he says A., even as he means to say I.

—PAUL AUSTER, *The Invention of Solitude*

In her own name she would have died of asphyxia. But once emerged from the membrane of self, spread out unto all the ways, coming to dwell at the brink of all sources.

—HÉLÈNE CIXOUS, *Vivre l'orange*

CLAM
DOWN

WHAT THE SCIENTIST SAID—

Before the Cambrian explosion, most creatures didn't live in the sediment. They lived on the sediment. These simple, soft-bodied animals mostly survived by consuming plants and microbes on the sediment surface as "mat scratchers."

So, you have the seafloor, which is like the recycling center of the ocean. Organic matter rains down, and where it's shallow, there's sunshine, and plants grow. All the pre-Cambrian animals were just happily eating that stuff.

It was like a garden! Each one pulling their own spinach, eating their own duff. There was no predation. Everyone lived harmoniously.

Then, all of a sudden, certain creatures developed vision, jaws, bilateral symmetry, a more efficient means of moving around. They evolved to eat others!

Soft-bodied animals on the sediment were vulnerable in this new environment. What did they do to adapt? One of the strategies they developed was to build hard parts like shells and spines. Another strategy was to get away. To do that, they started to dig into the sediment. Now, instead of a 2-D world, there is a 3-D world.

The Cambrian explosion was the biological Big Bang. An evolutionary arms race had begun between predator and prey. As a result, diversity boomed like at no other time in Earth's history.

The Paleozoic was one of the most chaotic eras of our eons. It was a "make it or break it" time.

Clam Down

She hadn't meant to become a bivalve mollusk, but it happened. Several nights ago, after a rib-bruising bike crash caused by momentary inattentiveness and conditions of reduced visibility (sobbing while cycling), the mollusk had briefly succumbed to an episode of hysteria, during which her mother kept texting her to "clam down." *Clam down*, she had commanded in that sober, no-nonsense way. At first, the clam looked all around her, like, *Who, me?* Until she realized that her mother was addressing *her*.

It made sense. Ever since the dissolution of her marriage, she *had* been consuming a lot of calcium carbonate. This was what clams and other shell-building animals used to make their shells. These days, she kept rolls of Tums in her bag, which got whittled down throughout the day with alarming speed. On her desk, beside her usual writing implements—pen, notepad—was a flip-top container that was more fun to feed from. It rattled percussively when she shook the tabs out into her palm. They were the tropical variety, in delicate pastel colors: flavors that felt like a getaway. Like all getaways, the balm was instant but brief, hence the need for repeated doses. Humans were not supposed to ingest more than six per day, but clams could eat them as needed. Both species possessed a stomach, and hers hurt most of the time.

Looking back, it hadn't been the first time her mother had issued that particular command. All summer, no matter what the mollusk had tried to convey, the response was much the same. *Clam down!* Had there been a recent, lengthy conversation about seafood? Or perhaps the typo was made fresh each time, her mother's subconscious pinning the bivalve as an ideogram for conduct during crisis. Indeed: The word *fire* in Chinese looked like a flame; the word *water* like a running stream; the word *peace* depicted a woman safe at home (notably a character in both daughters' names). Perhaps the word *clam* in English looked calm to her.

Everyone knows it's useless to tell an upset person to "calm down," but "clam down" was always a hoot. The first few times it happened, the clam (for now she was a clam) laughed and sent a screenshot to her sister, who was equally tickled. "She writes that to me all the time too!" They hahahahahaha'd into their text threads. Together, they recalled the document they once discovered on a shared Google Drive that turned out to be their mother's journal. This journal had read more like a captain's log than a confessional text, as it betrayed nothing about how their mother felt. Which was uncanny because this was a journal she kept during some of the family's most tumultuous years. In lieu of emotion, the journal was full of exhortatory language, with which she compelled herself to think positive, lose weight, and stay

claaaaaaaaaaaaaaaaaaaaaaaaaaaaaaaaaaaaaaaaaaaaaaammm

(Either their mother had fallen asleep while typing that sentence, or it was meant as a stage direction: READ WHILE SCREAMING.)

Oh, their mother's clam smile. That tight, insistent grimace that stretched from jowl to jowl. With it, she could smile her way out of anything.

Admittedly, the girls didn't know much about clams. Their early exposure to sea life had been restricted to the seafood section at the

99 Ranch Market, a kind of poor kid's aquarium. Upon being released from the car, they would rush over to the heaped bins to gently torment the sea creatures. They tapped on their shells with metal utensils until the animals snapped shut and shot out spurts of murky brine. Whether condemned to the seafloor or as food items to be poked and prodded by children, these creatures still had recourse against pain. If you shut yourself tight enough, nothing would happen to you.

A cursory Google search revealed that most people want to know whether clams are alive, or happy. Now the clam was at the library at the university where she worked, surrounded by books. No longer in denial about her true species, she was here to learn more about her evolutionary history.

She was reading from a book called *Animals Without Backbones*. Its cover featured a cartoon drawing of a squishy, undeniably phallic shape with googly eyes, amoebic and alert.

Clams belonged to the phylum Mollusca, which derives from the Latin *mollis* or "soft-bodied," the book explained. The molluscan body plan generally consists of a strong, muscular "foot" and a layer of tissue called the mantle that protects the viscera in the main body. Some mollusks, like clams, limpets, and snails, build protective shells out of calcium, while other mollusks, such as octopi, squid, and slugs, evolved to lose them. The shell-less mollusks, it should be said, are the intelligent species of the phylum, while she, a clam, "neither flees nor turns on its attacker but lies quiet and defenseless within its hard shell until this is split open, with a rock, to expose the soft, flabby, deliciously edible, bite-sized invertebrate within."

She flipped the page.

Despite being helpless and delicious, clams have nevertheless managed to persist through time, thanks to their simple, ingenious technology. What clams lack in intelligence they make up for in endurance. Clams are "particularly hardy" creatures, appearing in the fossil records as early as the Cambrian period some 510 million years ago. Which means that clams had survived the extinctions of other, superior creatures, such as dinosaurs and mastodons. Some clams are so tough they manage to dwell 17,400 feet down on the dark seafloor, enduring hydrostatic pressure of almost four tons to the square inch. And down there, they live on and on. The oldest living animal ever discovered was a deep-sea quahog named Ming the Mollusk, who was 507 years old when he was dredged up from the ocean floor.

As the clam read on, she began to feel cozy, validated. Perhaps it was the coffee, or the sun slanting in through dusty windows. These facts were doing a lot to legitimize her methods. By clamming down, her species had actually done quite well for itself. Hadn't this clamming down method worked well enough in her marriage? Instead of opening her mouth to spew seawater or sand, she swallowed whatever was bothering her and worried it under her tongue until it gleamed. She would coat the small agitation until it became round and pink and polished. Alone, she might examine the object, evidence of a job well done. *Look what I've made! Look what I'm capable of!* In this way, she could look at the problem without any lingering feelings. After all, she was an artist; she made beautiful things, and this was how she felt strong.

She was quickly learning about the perks of being a clam:

1.

Clams had sedimentary habits and dug happily into mud, feeling little, seeing little. They filtered detritus (on their phones) while burrowed under blankets. It was fine not to get out of bed.

Some of her most brilliant colleagues paid good money for what she could now summon at will: a sensory deprivation chamber that clamped a lid over you like a coffin and played soothing ocean sounds as you floated. They all swore by it. They reported feeling remarkably lucid and refreshed after only a single session inside it. Well, now she had a free pass with unlimited hours. Day or night, she could simply enter her shell and be subsumed by its stultifying caress.

2.

Clams are notoriously tight-lipped, which is where we get the expression: "She clammed up when forced to speak." Speaking was not the clam's forte, so in lieu of wordy explanations, she felt entitled to rely on stock phrases: *How are things? Good! How are you? I'm fine! Hanging in there!*

In couples therapy, however, such convenient phrases were somehow perceived as aggressive and unacceptable. She stared with laser focus at the therapist's cracked feet (she conducted sessions from a reclining armchair, in bare feet). *Why don't you say anything? Why can't you look at him? Are you scared, or ashamed?*

The clam didn't understand why the conjunction in that sentence wasn't *and,* but she did not open her mouth to object. Which turned out to be easier.

3.

Are you okay? her friends and colleagues asked whenever they saw saline issue forth, involuntarily, from her eyes. Clams, like most other mollusks, were generally lubricated in a shiny, protective fluid. From a human perspective, this phenomenon was disturbing, perceived as a form of emotional incontinence. For a clam, it was entirely normal. Whenever this happened, she flapped her hands in front of her face, as though to chase away pestering insects.

Don't mind me! Then, back in the privacy of her own room, she could finally release the miniature sea she contained. She finally understood the paradoxical necessity of hiding so one would no longer have to hide.

4.

Hardening up your exterior was something she'd learned in karate class as a child, lessening the pain of impending blows. Humans were soft, and anything could puncture them, even words. All summer long, she and her husband hurled the sharpest words at each other, wrenching revisions of a previously happy existence. *You've ruined every happy memory I have,* he spat. *You are a liar and a cheat.* Then he compared her to a certain presidential candidate who was often on the news for his lying and cheating. A muscle in her face twitched, but otherwise, she felt fine.

5.

Clams can't easily travel on their own, though scallops do manage to propel themselves by flapping their shells together, like wings. In a fit of desperation, she and her husband decided to take one final trip together, to see what they could salvage. They drove upstate. Predictably, they argued in the car. When they arrived at the cottage rental, she got out of the car and walked away.

She walked along the road's shoulder, trying her best not to look like a hitchhiker. This was not an intuitive place to stroll. She pumped her arms theatrically at her sides, as though engaging in a fitness activity. Knowing nothing about life up here, she thought maybe it was uncommon to see a woman walking down a narrow road. She walked purposefully, as though she had somewhere to be. The last thing she wanted was for someone to pull over and ask her what was the matter.

Each time a car zoomed past, her thoughts scattered like bits of paper. At the curve, a car slowed, honking gently. She wanted to scream, *Can't you see there's nowhere for me to turn off to?* These were country distances. Not traversable in blocks and minutes, but miles and eons. She needed something to reach for. A stop sign. A rock. Anything. The trees swayed anonymously. Up ahead, she saw a dirt path leading down to some kind of children's summer camp. When she reached it, there was a posted warning: *Private Property. Do Not Enter!* How nice it would be to sit down awhile next to this sign, next to this dirt mound and this colony of ants. She thought about getting dirt on her pants, and the ants, whether they might bite her if she sat down.

She turned around, back to the main road, and soon she approached a long hill. She began to climb, but found it so difficult that she turned back around to go down the hill, and then, filled with shame, she turned around, then back around, then around and back again, several more times. She was a ball without momentum, oscillating at the trough.

I have no follow-through, she thought. *I don't even have what it takes to have a nervous breakdown because I don't want to inconvenience myself.*

6.

On the last day of couples therapy, the therapist asked the clam to make a decision. How did she want to proceed? Lucky thing to be a clam, with poor vision and limited aperture. She didn't have to see the expression on her husband's face. *Separation first,* she mumbled. *Move away. No contact.* Her eyes, blurred with fluid, were riveted to the patterns of wood grain on the smooth rounded legs of the chair in which her husband sat, in his socks, and the wool fiber of those socks and the frayed cuff of denim covering the ankle and the tattoo on that ankle and the body that extended from that vector point—a person she was supposed to love. Communicating through nods, grunts, and improvised sign language, the three of them settled on a day, Friday, when the husband would vacate their apartment to allow her to pack up her things.

7.

She was a wild animal, so she ought to behave like one—careless, unsentimental, ruthless. On the prescribed day of the move, the clam had a sore throat and a fever. Unwilling to make excuses, she set out alone, climbed the six flights of stairs to their apartment, and closed the door behind her. Poking around, she gathered that he must have gotten sick too. Full-strength cold medicine had been left out in half-ripped packets. She took some of this, then tiptoed down the hall and nudged her office door open.

Everything was as she had left it. The hideous pink sofa with the coffee stain on the seat, her bulletin boards tacked with postcards from foreign places they'd once visited. The window was open and spots of rain were visible on the sill. She had always called this office her "chastity corner." If her door was closed, he was forbidden to enter unless it was an emergency, and he respected her wish with a fierce sense of loyalty. Even though the door had been a barrier against him.

She began cramming books into boxes without logic or discernment, wanting to finish the job quickly. She had imagined that the packing would be easy, as though she were going on a trip. Instead, each item represented a wager on whether she thought she would return. Would she take this box of rarely worn seasonal clothes? How about her childhood violin? She didn't intend to play it anytime soon, but if she intended on leaving for good, then she definitely wanted to have it. Her engagement ring could be left behind, but the printer . . . she had to take the printer. The printer was a necessary tool of her trade and she couldn't live without it! This uncomplicated desire for her printer chilled her to the core, as she considered the possibility that she might be more attached to her printer than to her husband.

8.

Clams carry their homes with them, so wherever they end up is wherever they live. They prefer not to live an itinerant existence, but they can survive it. She stood on the sidewalk, slick with sweat from carrying her boxes down six flights of stairs. The taxi driver was irked at the sight of her boxes, and gruffly shoved her belongings into the back. Then they were all deposited on the curb in front of her new Brooklyn sublet. A cold rain began to fall. The cardboard boxes darkened with moisture. If only she had a tarp, she thought. Only she didn't. She realized she was standing next to a giant dumpster, and that the distance to this dumpster was closer than the distance to the door of the loft. *Oh, this is nothing to get worked up over,* she thought. *My home is my body. That is all I need.* One by one, she dumped her boxes in the trash.

9.

The clam and her husband were sitting on a bench overlooking the East River. They had some final unfinished business to discuss. It was blustery and everything seemed to need staking, seemed to need another thing to clutch on to. A piece of trash blown against the trashcan was flattened against its surface like someone hugging a skyscraper in a hurricane. *Do you want to walk a bit?* They walked to the waterfront. Her hair was out of control. *Why'd you change?* he asked. *What happened to you?* She was struggling to roll her cigarette with numb, fumbling fingers. The last of her tobacco blew away. There it went. It was all blowing out of her hands.

The question, again. To speak or not to speak? Her research

rectified a misconception. As a child, she mistakenly believed that the clams that stayed shut even after their counterparts had been steamed to death were the ones worthy of emulation. When in fact, those were the dead ones, the ones you were supposed to throw away. She did not know, not then, that clams spend much of their lives with their mouths slightly ajar, like undersea mouth breathers. Their gills are located in the mantle cavity, through which oxygenated water can flow. Ignorance of this fact is why amateur cooks often suffocate their clams by placing them in cold bowls of water before cooking. Don't they like being in water? You can't mitigate your shellfish's suffering by providing a cheap facsimile of their projected wants.

Clams, like humans, needed to open their mouths to live.

Kafka's Metamorphosis

It was November. Upon waking, the clam stared at the domed brick ceiling of the loft, momentarily confused. *How did I end up here?* She felt misplaced, as though a bird had plucked her from the shore, dashed her upon some rocks, then forgot to eat her. Slowly, time, place, and situation reasserted themselves, clicking into place like some diabolical Rubik's Cube. *Oh, right.*

With a sigh, she turned off her stack of alarms, set to a grating, tropical island–themed ringtone, chosen for its cringe factor. *Might as well wake up and face the facts.* Mornings generally revealed a bright world wiped clean of the evening's dark thoughts; solutions materialized on their own; and she'd leap out of bed, ready for the day ahead. But she couldn't remember the last time she felt that way. She gazed mournfully out the window. Soggy weather. All over the country, or indeed, all over the world, people were waking up wishing things were different. Everyone, everywhere, had personal losses that felt too big to bear. Illnesses, bankruptcies, accidents, deaths, elections. Everyone, everywhere, was undergoing something or other.

Today, she had to go to the university to teach her creative writing class. The election had happened two nights earlier and the results had shocked everyone. In her role as instructor, she would have to conjure up a teachable something or other, and spout some comforting truths. But what was there to say? Crucially, what could *she* say? On social media, an award-winning poet had polled everyone to see how they would be addressing this "moment."

Should they recite poetry? Orwell? Lorde? The Brecht one about how speaking of trees at this time would be almost a crime? For some reason, the clam could only think of that Donald Barthelme story where, after a series of increasingly distressing deaths ("the trees, the salamander, the tropical fish, Edgar, the poppas and mommas, Matthew and Tony"), the students, frightened, demand nothing less than the ultimate assertion of the ongoingness of life: a live sex demonstration, an "assertion of value." Well, okay. Barthelme at least understood the absurdity of this profession. But unlike her more extemporaneously gifted colleagues, she knew she was not poised to provide any such assertion of value.

Yet! It was necessary to keep going. She knew that much. That was the takeaway from her recent rereading of Kafka's *Metamorphosis*. During her search for books that might shed light on her own transformation, it had seemed obligatory to read the transformation classic, about a young man who turns into a cockroach-like insect. When the clam had first read it in high school, she had interpreted it as a metaphor for the horrors of puberty. Upon this rereading, however, she realized that the story was also about the mandate of remaining a productive worker, even in the aftermath of catastrophe. The nightmare for Gregor Samsa is not that he has turned into a loathsome bug, but that in his bug form, he can no longer go to work. He wakes up and, contemplating the day ahead, thinks about train schedules and the harsh realities of his job. The ultimate horror for Gregor is not his chitinous exoskeleton or his waving bug legs, but the fact that his boss should have reason to admonish him. In one climactic scene, his family members and his boss all pound on the bedroom door, demanding to be let in, while Gregor wrangles the key with his dribbling mouth. *Let them see what I've become,* he thinks. *If this is no big deal to them, then I guess I'll go to work.* Being accused of shirking would be the ultimate shame. How absurd; how relatable! Gregor is not some resisting Bartleby declaring, "I would prefer not to"—he literally cannot participate in human society because he's a bug. Yet his infirmity does not excuse him from the duty of work; constitutionally unable to contribute to the family income, he becomes a true burden and pest. Thus, it seems Kafka is suggesting, there is no future left for Gregor except death.

The clam found the story hilarious, and she read the opening over and over again. In some sense, for a beleaguered writer, turning into a bug might not be a nightmare, but a fantasy. To be exempt from work because of one's monstrousness: free to stay in all day, to stare out the window, to daydream. Free to succumb to an internal wretchedness. The clam knew that Kafka wrote the story at the start of his tumultuous love affair with Felice Bauer, when he had felt stymied by his day job and intense pressure from his father to support the family. Kafka knew he would never be the kind of son his father had hoped for. In one reading, then, Gregor, as a projection of Kafka himself, becomes a bug to mirror back his true form: a disgusting, lowly creature at odds with what was expected of him. Perhaps the story was Kafka's thought experiment. What would it mean to give in to the alienation and unbelonging that one already feels?

Likewise—the clam thought—clamhood represented a similar kind of fantasy. Since her transformation, she was more convinced she could hold it together. She possessed self-control, stoicism, resolve. She had the ability to keep going. Whether there were certain aspects of clamhood that would render her unfit for modern life: that was still to be seen. But so far, she felt that being a clam was, overall, good. Clams put their heads down like obedient little bureaucrats and did the work without complaining or saying much. In fact, it seemed that since she outwardly presented as an amenable Asian woman, these characteristics were even expected of her. She didn't complain, she didn't ask for much, and she generally stayed out of the way. At worst, clams were a bit ridiculous, but ultimately, they were unthreatening.

If she were an insurance clerk from Prague, perhaps being a clam would be just fine. But in New York City, a jaguar or lion would certainly be preferable, a predator of strength and dignity. Or better yet, an animal with loud, exhibitionist tendencies—a parrot, perhaps. Why couldn't she have become an animal like that? Especially in her chosen profession as writer and professor, didn't she need to have a voice and be unafraid to use it?

A comparative study: A famous writer she was acquainted with had once been a child preacher, and was practiced at holding audiences in rapt attention. He was now doing the same thing as a public intellectual, in large auditoriums and lecture halls. *But I was the sort of child who didn't get spoken to at home; also English is my second language.* These were her excuses. *The less I spoke, the better. Out of earshot, out of trouble.* She broke out in a sweat and flushed red when challenged, and inchoate sentences often sputtered out when she was under pressure. When this happened in the classroom, she would quickly call on a student to help fill the gap of silence. It was a mystery how someone like her ended up with a job that required such verbal agility. She usually had to fight her nature, or fake it, or else.

At that, she heaved herself out of bed and hobbled down to the shared bathroom. *Time to wake up and face the facts!* This loft she was subletting, half squat, half reclaimed textile factory, was a kind of glorified college slum. It was more like a lifestyle or aesthetic. Everyone here did something art-adjacent, or held unconventional jobs that allowed them to exist at odd hours. If she encountered a roommate brushing their teeth at the kitchen sink, she would not know whether to say good morning or good night.

Luckily, no one was around this morning. She slipped into the bathroom and splashed palmfuls of icy water on her face. She considered herself in the mirror. A pink, swollen blob-face blinked back at her. She really should stop crying so much. And eating so much popcorn and ice cream. Without proper structure, she ate whenever she wanted, standing up or curled in bed, straight out of take-out containers, out of misery or out of boredom, often without the correct utensil. There was a German word for this—*Kummerspeck*—"sorrow bacon." It was like she was plumping up for some undefinable journey.

Once, she taught an entire class with a smear of tapenade on her forehead. *How did it get way up there?* She had no idea, and her students didn't tell her. They'd let her keep up the charade of imparting knowledge with a sandwich condiment on her face. Oh well. Humiliations never seem survivable until you go ahead and survive them, she thought. Being a clam was nothing. As long as one maintains a veneer of haughty disdain and unflappable certainty . . .

The clam plodded back to her chilly room. There was no heat in this loft, so they all lived bundled up, with scarves, hats, housecoats, and fingerless gloves, like impoverished characters in a nineteenth-century novel. The trick was to wear the same thing inside as you would wear outside. That cut down on the dressing time, because she was already wearing everything she needed to be wearing. She pulled on heavy boots, grabbed her bag, and headed out into the wind-whipped streets, toward the entrance of the subway.

The clam was nestled now between other warm, shower-scented commuters shuttling uptown. She felt, honestly, normal. They were all doing such a good job of carrying on. She smiled. That was the thing about this city. A bomb could go off on the adjacent platform and there would still be a large contingent scrambling to get on the train so as not to be late to work. *Clam down and carry on!* New York City possessed this practical immigrant nature, unflappable and bent on commerce. She kept her eyes softly focused on some middle distance. The man across from her was quietly reading a newspaper with the loud headlines splashed across the front page. Honestly, you could be an alien, a zombie, or a Sasquatch and probably get away with it in New York City, she thought. Nobody would even bother looking at you twice. Not even on a day like today. She imagined herself wearing a life-sized clam costume, like one of those walking tacos that advertised outside of restaurants.

The Total Failure of Narrative

"Class—as you may have gathered, today we will be discussing the failure of narrative," the clam began. Her eyes darted around the room. She was sitting at the head of a too-long conference table that reminded her of the interrogation room from another Kafka story.

"In this video we just watched, the author argues that . . . that . . . he says that . . . storytelling serves as our only defense against chaos. We sift through chaos to pick out certain details, then we string that together and call that a story . . ."

The clam cleared her throat and took another sip of water.

"After a plausible story is constructed, disorder seems to fall into order . . ."

Her actual speech was not coming out, in tone or mien, like any of the notes she had prepared, which sounded, in her head, authoritative and convincing.

"And what do we think, when he says that, that storytelling is innate? Part of who we are. We can't help doing it. We live by stories. Often, we have to summarize where we've been to figure out where we're going, right . . . ?"

Her voice cracked.

"Don't you agree? Who here agrees so far?"

Nobody raised their hand.

"Disagrees? Nobody? Okay, does anyone have any thoughts to the video we just watched?"

She surveyed her students' faces. Some had puffy eyes; others looked plain bored; still others sat with arms crossed, defiant. Were they judging her? She sincerely wished to excuse them, but here they all were, clinging to their responsibilities.

"Okay. Maybe we should pivot. Let's think together about the implied narratives bandied around in this election. What kind of story do these slogans imply . . . ?"

Without much confidence, she led the class through an exercise with various campaign slogans. *Yes We Can. I'm with Her. Make America Great Again.* They eked out a few feeble responses. Nobody was, as they say, in the mood. She pressed on. What is an accurate story? A responsible story? A harmful story? When we string events together and call that a story, how do we test its validity? What does it mean when we talk about a bedtime story? A fantasy or fairy tale? What about conspiracy theories?

At some point, she heard herself uttering the most insipid phrase: "It's time to mobilize our imaginations."

They can smell weakness, she thought. *They're circling like sharks for blood.*

A student or two wept. One said that all of this abstraction about narratives was hard to follow. Another, choking with emotion, said she felt oppressed by the singular narrative that was being promulgated by the school. Why describe it as a time of grief? That was not how all experienced it.

At the end of class, one of her most brilliant students stayed after to express her concern about their discussion, which she found to be ahistorical and damaging.

In therapeutic parlance, "I feel something, therefore it must be true" is a type of "cognitive distortion" called "emotional reasoning." After years of therapeutic analysis, the clam had learned to identify her distortive patterns with textbook precision. Like a scientist, she was constantly collecting "evidence" to "test" whether her feelings were "true." Don't start with feelings; start with observations. Gather the evidence. String it together. You feel inadequate. You feel like a fuckup. Are you? Your mind must not go searching for evidence that's not there.

Well, the evidence of today's class seemed to be right there.

The clam struggled down the long campus steps. It was so cold this evening. How did it get so cold suddenly? The classroom had felt stifling, her turtleneck threatening to strangle her. Now the chill blew in where the sweat had dampened her collar. *They're tweeting about my incompetence somewhere,* she thought. *I'll soon be fired. That's it. I'll lose this job and I'll never find another.*

She couldn't believe it, but in a few minutes, she would have to go and perform in a so-called faculty reading, which had been planned weeks in advance. It hadn't been canceled. It should have been; nobody ever wanted to go to a reading, especially not now.

In the auditorium, she saw her brilliant student and sat down. She had asked this student to provide the introduction weeks ago. They nodded at each other, then resumed looking down at their various reading materials. After a while, the student's friend arrived, and, not recognizing the clam for the instructor, leaned in and said, "I just got your text. I'm *so* sorry about what happened in your writing class . . ." to which the brilliant student seized up, with a frozen look of alarm. The friend visibly recoiled. "Oh! I didn't know." The clam forced a waggish smile, as though to say, *It's okay. I already know I'm ridiculous.*

After the poorly attended reading, the clam and two other faculty readers stumbled out into the cold night. Desperate for diversion, they went to dinner at Le Monde. One colleague was a poet who was decorated impressively in tattoos; the other was a young novelist endowed with big brimming eyes that made her impervious to criticism. Both were eager to hear how class went. The clam reported the events shamefully. She asked them whether they would try to talk about the election or steer clear.

"Steer clear," her novelist colleague said. The poet said he might share a few things on his mind, why not. Then, as he considered the menu, he reported how, once in class, a student had insulted him with some objection she'd made, and he'd snapped back, "You're the one who doesn't know anything! Think before you speak!" In the same breath, he interrupted the waiter to ask whether the ingredients were organic.

"Look, I know I'm such a stereotype," he went on, folding up the menu. "Look at me. I get to be an asshole." He leaned back in the chair. "But we're all adjuncts," he reminded them. "We already have no power. The least you can do is say what you think. Whether people get upset or not. Don't you have a right to say what you think?"

The clam really didn't know. Most of the time, she skirted controversy at all costs.

Dinner wrapped up. She was heading back to Brooklyn, on the subway again.

She clicked off her phone and took out her notebook.

Gather the evidence.

She thought she should try to do an exercise like the one she had assigned earlier to her students. Write it all down without any judgment. What happened? How did I end up here? Don't try to find a continuous narrative. Piece it together later.

Age twenty. Showed up for office hours, which he was holding at a café on University. Sat down, took out my notebook and a bag of candy I bought from Andronico's. *Do you want some?* I asked. He made an urgent motion for me to put it away, and said in a sharp voice of reproach, *I have a good relationship with this café, and ask that you not consume outside food on these premises.* A sting of shame. What was appealing about this interaction? I often returned to the memory with a feeling of exhilaration, even after we began dating.

Age twenty-three. *No. You are not working at that bar. Do you know how dangerous it is to walk home alone at night?* I screamed and protested like the young woman I was. As a compromise, he picked me up every night from the bar when I got off work, often at two or three in the morning.

Age twenty-eight. *You're different now,* Shelma said while we were screen printing T-shirts at her nonprofit. *Ever since you got married* . . . she trailed off. *But this is how I am,* I defended myself. *You don't understand what my goals are. I'm trying to become a writer.* Later that night, I returned home and told him I would cut off my friendship with her.

Age thirty-one. He cursed himself after spilling a jar of something. *You never fucking learn!* he screamed at himself. I sat there pushing my oatmeal around in the bowl. *I know you'll remember that I threw a tantrum,* he said, furiously wiping the spot with a rag. He said, *Don't punish me for showing emotions that you prohibit yourself from expressing. Don't hate me for doing what you're scared to do.*

The clam stopped and read over what she had jotted down. It wasn't making any sense, this accounting of the past. She was just listing random incidents that had been brought up in couples therapy.

She turned to a fresh page.

Was becoming a clam a kind of wish fulfillment, or was it a curse that *prevented* her from acting out, from getting angry? Part of her craved the catharsis of emotional excess, but clams didn't get angry. Clams wouldn't dare.

During that fight upstate, when she had gotten out of the car and walked away, she remembered how that rage had felt brand-new, bright white, as clean and precise as a surgeon's incision. Suddenly her mind was made up. It had felt enlivening, like courage, or absolution. But then, standing at the bottom of the hill, she remembered how one of the rare times her mom ever threw a tantrum, she'd gotten in the car meaning to disappear for good, but backed out so fast she crashed into the mailbox post. The car crumpled like a can of beer. Her mom hadn't even made it out of the driveway. There must have been a moral to that oft-told story, since all stories have one simple goal, to mark out zones of possibility or impossibility. Clams were not cut out for grand gestures. Theatricality was not in their nature.

Clam down, her mom would text her, as she had done so many times before. *Clam down ok girl?* Go back where the bed was nice, the towels fresh on the rack, and the husband waiting, repentant, on the porch. A clam needed nothing but mud and water. A clam dug in and stayed.

But a prouder person would walk up this hill, she thought. If only she could make herself. She closed her eyes and tilted her head back. The light pierced through her eyelids, exploding in red shapes. The rage was changing color already. She saw the blood coursing through her body, and saw it slow. Lightheaded, she opened her eyes and saw the sunlight flecked on leafy branches, and the blue sky beyond that. The rage was gone.

Lutetian Limestone

The clam never celebrated holidays before she got married. Her parents had worked through all of them—Thanksgiving, Christmas, even Chinese New Year—so when she went to college, she did the same. She was a bakery girl, and always took the holiday shifts for overtime pay. She'd watch the parking lot empty, pack up the unsold panettone, then go home and eat an entire cake on her own. After her marriage, however, holidays became big affairs that required travel and planning. These were holidays as celebrated in the movies, with stockings and decorations and board games by the fire. She thought it was incredible that these rituals weren't made up. As she was feeling such attendant pressure to insert herself correctly into the scene, her cheeks would be sore by the end of the holiday from all the aggressive smiling.

This year, newly liberated from her husband's family obligations, the clam had nowhere to be on Thanksgiving. This should have been a relief, but the omnipresent holiday decor assaulted her senses. The smell of cinnamon repulsed her, as did the sight of falling leaves, cornucopias, turkeys, cobwebs, ghosts, and that stupid cursive that had become the font of choice for selling pumpkin lattes and a vague notion of cozy well-being. The American holiday cycle was such a sick aberration, she thought. Autumn was supposed to be a winding down of the year, when animals prepared to go into hibernation, not this frenetic jetting to and fro between forced celebrations and hysterical, high-pitched shopping. The pressure to couple up was intense, the expectation to *be somewhere* intimated each time someone asked, *Where will you be going for the holidays?* Was this the onus behind cuffing season? Settle for *any* body. No one wanted to endure the holidays alone if they could help it.

"Does that mean you'll do a Friendsgiving then?" her loft-mate Anton ventured one day while they were washing up their dishes at the sink. They had both walked out of their rooms at the same moment with their dirty dishes, their intention regretfully obvious. Now it was an awkward dance of yielding and waiting with dripping soap hands while the other finished rinsing. Decidedly not a picture of domestic bliss. Although Anton remained her favorite roommate because he, too, kept rigid hours of monastic discipline and always did his dishes. He was the only one they ever saw sprinting down the hall with the gigantic bag of dripping garbage. Everyone else just stuffed and stuffed, blithely certain that someone else would take care of it.

Was Anton her soulmate? Look at those nimble, sturdy hands, foaming and lathering! Perhaps her heartbreak occurred only to clear the way for *this* man, Anton the monk.

"Are you going to a Friendsgiving then, now that you don't have any family obligations?" Anton repeated.

"I don't know . . ." she said in a noncommittal way, in case he wanted to invite her somewhere. "I wasn't planning to, but I'm open to suggestions . . . !"

She had mewled this last part in a bizarre singsong voice. She got chills when she heard that coming out. "Sorry, I think my voice cracked there? I haven't spoken to anyone all day!" she announced. "No, I'm unaccounted for. What about you?"

"Me, I'm going to New Jersey with my girlfriend!" he chirped.

So—Anton had a girlfriend. Why didn't she know that? The world was dizzying with its injustice.

"Mm. That sounds nice," she said. "Actually, my best friends are in Paris. I'll probably go see them."

"Paris! That's amazing. I've always wanted to go. My brother says it's magical."

"Oh, I treat Paris like it's another crappy borough, like Brooklyn. It's really nothing special. Not like going to *New Jersey*."

The clam ran back to her room and slammed the door. *I will never eat again so I will never do dishes again so I will never see Anton again,* she thought. *I will never leave this room. Jesus, why the hell did I have to say that?*

Open the browser. JFK to CDG. Mike and Shelma told her she was always welcome to visit them in Paris whenever. *I'm being so brave and spontaneous,* she thought. *I'm going to buy this ticket without asking permission.* She flinched upon seeing the ticket price, then charged it all to a credit card. She reviewed the receipt. Nine days. She couldn't believe it. The dread rolled in.

Immediately upon landing, she knew Paris was the wrong city to flee to. As she dragged her rolling suitcase down the cobbled boulevards, she realized she'd been to this city so many times with her husband that their memories had accreted into the landscape. Each time she looked up, she saw something that triggered involuntary recall. There was Chez Prune, along the Canal Saint-Martin, where they had once dined. That art bookstore. That cheese shop next to the produce stall next to the laundromat. Every green bench was one they could have sat upon, every cooing pigeon one she could have once stopped to admire.

She wove her way through a marché aux puces in the Marais, willfully ignoring the objects he would have once expressed interest in. This ornamented paper clip, that lion head bookend. The clothes that would have appealed to him, or probably would appeal to him still. She tried to extricate herself from the meandering masses. Everyone was so happy. Couples linked by the elbows, young people crouching over to inspect glasses so old they'd become new again. The flea market, she realized, was where you went to consume the material remains of the dead, all their watches and clothes and furniture. She never before thought of the longevity of clothes. The way a coat lived on and on. *Even my clothes will outlive me,* she thought abruptly, recalling how the last time she was here in Paris, she had worn the same exact clothes. You think you're doing something innocent by collecting staples in your closet, but soon these clothes solidify into a style and that's it. Your sartorial life is a one-way thing and now you can't change.

Every decision you make has a lasting consequence, think about that, she thought as she walked down the narrow alleys shadowed by stark rows of Haussmann-era buildings, toward Mike's flat. These buildings were made of Lutetian limestone, the stone that built Paris, quarried right here since Roman times. Limestone was a sedimentary rock, composed of the calcium remains of mollusks, corals, and microscopic creatures that had lived and died in this formerly shallow sea. The white stone was a memorial. She ran a hand along the cool surface, some parts smooth, other parts rough and pocked. At least forty million years of sedimentation and pressure created this stone. Excised from the subterranean depths and lifted up to the surface, Paris forced you to look all this memory in the eye, at street level. That was why she couldn't stop remembering.

Bring too much memory up to the surface and collapse becomes imminent. She knew that after centuries of quarrying in place, Paris was barely supported underneath. Hundreds of miles of man-made tunnels, many poorly buttressed, had collapsed and swallowed entire city blocks. The metro stop at Denfert-Rochereau, for instance, near the Barrière d'Enfer, or Gate of Hell, was one such collapse site. One unassuming day in the late eighteenth century, horse carriages, pedestrians, an entire apartment building, were swallowed whole. The city's extensive labyrinth of catacombs was nearby as well, underground ossuaries crammed full of the skeletal remains of millions of Parisians. Their bones were stacked in an incredible density down below. *Couldn't these bones eventually morph into a kind of limestone?* the clam wondered. All these lives, once singular, reincorporated through time into a single consolidated mass. She would be in this limestone too.

Her only recourse was to keep moving. She could plaster over her past memories with this new memory in which the territory belonged to her alone. Her past memories would be buried with this newer, fresher memory, or at least made more faint, even if, in this new memory, she was crying. But even this scene—woman, clam, crying—happened so many times in Paris, in real life and in the movies, that it, too, was part of the city, part of what made Paris so distinctly itself.

"**W**hy'd you buy this sack of cranberries?" Shelma yelled from the kitchen. "Anelise already brought cranberry sauce!"

"I thought we could make *fresh* sauce!" Mike yelled back. "Do you know how impossible it is to find fresh cranberries in Paris?"

"So now we're going to have *two* sauces? She almost got detained at JFK bringing your stupid cans of sauce!"

"The grocer had to put this aside for me! Don't take what I do for granted!"

The clam reclined on the couch and marveled at Mike and Shelma, her beloved friends from college. They stomped around, waving and gesturing. These two truly loved each other. They never failed to command admiration with their constant bickering. Even after years of marriage, they had managed to preserve a fresh sense of hostility and defiance, which, at least in playground terms, was the same thing as seduction. Couples who didn't fight in front of others were either dishonest or hiding something, she thought. These two were so secure in their love, there was no need to keep up appearances.

"Why are you here?" The clam heard Mike addressing her all of a sudden.

"Why am I here? I'm here to see you guys."

"You know you only come see us when something's happened to you."

This was true; she couldn't even be offended by this statement. She tended to be neglectful of her friends until she needed help.

She lived too hard and banged up her knees, and then she had to be looked after. Returning to them was always a return to safety.

"Last time you showed up, you gave me a week's notice. Same with this time. Out of the blue. Just, Guess what, I'm coming!"

"Why can't I come see you guys because I feel like it?"

"Because it's always something. We know you. What are you trying to escape this time?"

"I mean . . ." She lowered her eyes.

"Yes. You're separated, or soon to be divorced," he scoffed. "La di da."

The clam fumed. Mike was like a brother, so they said these things to each other all the time, but for once! Why were these two always so *unshockable*! When she'd told them the news, they had looked at each other, and Mike—she thought—had rolled his eyes, like a bet had been made that one of them won. They had always anticipated everything or had experienced everything themselves, so whatever happened *to her* was never a surprise *to them*. Why did they have to be so goddamn *advanced*?

"Fine. I'm traveling by myself to prove I'm not a sedimentary creature."

"Sedimentary? You mean sedentary."

"Same thing."

"It's too late. The moment you decided to become a writer, you became sedentary. We didn't know this was what we were choosing when we became writers. I mean, just look at me."

She looked at him. He was sitting there sipping a warm beverage, hair and beard untidy, an acupressure Thera Cane propped against the wall. She had just learned about his new morning routine. He had so many aches and pains from being hunched over his books and laptop, he had to start every morning with a series of calisthenic exercises. Then he would drink coffee, but not too much, his stomach wasn't what it used to be. Suddenly it seemed they had grown so old. The decade flew by in a flash—when did it happen? Wasn't it yesterday they were chugging forties in someone's dorm room, laughing with open, unlined faces?

"God. How did we end up here?"

He shrugged. "You make one decision, and the rest follows. How does that koan go? At the potter's wheel, form increases, possibilities decrease."

"Softness goes to hardness."

"What did I miss?" Shelma had emerged with glasses and a bottle of wine. "Don't worry, I'll never leave him," she said, patting Mike's head. "He makes me laugh." Then, "Hey, you're used to our arguing, right? Some people feel uncomfortable about it."

"It's fine," the clam said.

The three of them drank the wine and reviewed their menu for the next day—the roast turkey, also a rarity here, would have to be picked up from the butcher's—while the clam asked about the other guests who would be in attendance. "Oh, Emily from college," Mike said, the one the clam always went to great lengths to avoid. It was because of Emily's foreign language fluency and casual scarf wearing. Also, Emily was the kind of charmed and easily bored girl to whom one had to confess everything to keep her engaged. Which was how the clam once found herself on Sproul Plaza, eighteen or nineteen years old, telling Emily about contracting a (treatable!) STD from her apparently cheating boyfriend.

Great, the clam thought. One person with a proven track record for rooting out information she was loath to share. Who else? Mike listed other friends of theirs that she didn't recognize. And then he said, "Helene. Remember Helene?" He gave her a look.

Helene was Mike's friend from Paris who had visited New York earlier that spring. After the clam met her, they watched the Charlie Kaufman movie *Anomalisa* together, and then the two women had, for whatever reason, spontaneously decided to drive to Cincinnati for some ironic fun. Their plan was to eat Cincinnati's "famous chili" and visit its "world-famous zoo." What ended up happening was the clam white-knuckle driving through a violent rainstorm, while Helene in the passenger seat questioned her unceasingly about her marriage.

A writing mentor . . . !

But he was a grad student, technically?

Helene seemed only to want to have conversations about transgressive l'amour, as befitted her French heritage.

Do you and your husband still have terrific sex? Do you believe in passionate awakenings?

The windshield wipers had flung back and forth (non! non! non!) against the bullets of rain pelting down on all that flat, drenched nothing out there. The clam tried her best to deflect the questions, but had little bandwidth left—she was focused on not crashing at eighty miles per hour—and had, implausibly, nauseatingly, told the truth.

After that trip to Cincinnati, Helene returned to Paris. Their road trip had been like a one-night stand, but the oversharing, confessional version. They had experienced some illicit thrill from their forced, stuck-in-the-rental-car intimacy, but out in ordinary life the lights were too bright and they didn't know what to do with the information they now had. The clam guessed that Helene had satisfied her curiosity and the information would dissolve as other unimportant trivia in her brain. And that would be the end of it.

"Yes, Helene is coming. Are you ready? Don't run away this time," Mike warned. "By the way, you never ever told *us* the story about the other guy. You told *Helene* but *not us?*"

The Other Guy. How did they know about The Other Guy? So, her confessions to Helene had not remained secret! She hadn't mentioned him to Mike and Shelma as part of this saga, was trying not to think about him herself. She didn't want this detail to be part of her story. The Other Guy's emergence in her life made no sense to her. It was easier to pretend he didn't exist.

But now it was clear they already knew she was being tormented by this mysterious man. What was his name? They couldn't re-member. Or did they ever know it? Their eyes glazed over.

"Ah, so, hmm, well . . . he . . . um . . . remember that guy I've been talking to?"

"Who?"

"That person. That guy."

"Do we *know* him? What does he do?"

"He . . ." (Faltering.)

"Who? Is it Geoff?"

"God, no! Not Geoff!"

"Can you give me some initials? It's so annoying, I can't follow the story this way!"

She could not, not then, bring herself to give them any identify-ing details. She could not say *G* for *Geoff* or *geologist* or *guitarist* or *grad student*. To do so would be to confirm the reality of his con-tinuing presence in her life. She could not describe his looks, or explain how they met, or pull up his Instagram account to show them. She understood that innocent crushes were supposed to be exciting, and people normally couldn't wait to share with their friends. This was a rare storytelling event for them and they wanted to be entertained. Just tell them!

"Yeah, so what's going on with you and *Geoff*?" Shelma asked.

The clam chuckled uncomfortably. Part of her wanted more than anything to divulge all, but how to begin? It would be like taking off all her clothes in public. It was a big gesture that one had to be intentional about; it would require a leap of faith, or drugs, or at least more wine.

"How about you give us simple yes-or-no answers," Mike sug-gested. "Is it the guy you met at that writers conference a few years back?" The clam made a face. "No?"

The clam did not move her head to nod yes or shake it to say no.

"Is the sex amazing?" Shelma added. "Yes? No?"

"Come on, give us something!" Mike protested.

The clam was horrified. She did not like this game. She felt every muscle taut to snapping.

"The sex?" the clam stammered.

"This affair hasn't been *consummated* yet," Mike announced. They were taunting her. She felt batted around and wanted to cry.

"Show us his picture," Shelma demanded. "Is he hot?"

"I'm sorry, I just can't," was all she could manage. "It would be like if I showed you a profile of a celebrity."

"What does that even mean?"

The clam thought about what she'd said. "I guess it means, if you saw him, you'd think this guy is so out of my league, it's like he's a celebrity. Like he's the hot guy in the movie while I'm the ugly girl who has no chance."

"Oh my god. That answer makes me so sad," Shelma said.

"That's just her posture," Mike said. "She likes to be in this abject state."

"Well. He must be giving you something. You can't have a one-sided infatuation if no one gives you anything. He must be throwing twigs to the flame."

Twigs? No. We're not talking kindling. This is logs. Forests. The clam gulped her wine down. Okay. Here is an opportunity to let loose! Go crazy! Why not be like, fuck it all? One thing she did not allow herself to do was cheat. But she was delusional by virtue of omission. She didn't dare mention this guy during couples therapy, during all their exacting negotiations for change. She had always maintained that the need to separate was about something else—her freedom. It wasn't until the last possible minute, the last, last possible minute, that she revealed his existence.

She thought about pulling up his picture on her phone. Let her friends read the text exchanges and let them interpret his intentions. No. Looking at him made her eyes hurt, it made her queasy. He looked like a popular Hong Kong action film star of her youth.

"Honestly, though. Why did you tell Helene about The Other

Guy but not us?" Mike said after a while. "You're not even close to Helene!"

The clam tried to remember what she may have confessed in the car, to gauge how much of the story had likely been relayed in this warped game of telephone.

Last summer, I was reading Torpor *by Chris Kraus—do you know that book? I had a shock of recognition when I read a part that went something like: "What kind of monster would marry someone so much younger?" I actually sat straight up from the couch as though I needed to confront him right there. It made me question his motives. It made me question everything.*

What was different about The Other Guy?

I liked how I felt sitting next to him at the bar. How we must have looked like a couple. It seemed so much easier. He joked about us living together as creative partners. Platonic roommates. We ended up texting all the time. Last thing before bed. First thing in the morning . . .

"Don't blame Helene for this," Mike said. "You should give credit where it's due and thank her that you're single again!"

"When are you going to see him next?" Shelma asked.

The clam didn't want to talk about it. The guilt stuck like peanut butter in her throat. "It's not about that guy," she kept insisting to them, and to herself most forcefully of all.

"But anyway," they were saying, with genuine gravity now, "you seem to have a *history* of disastrous romances."

"Why?"

"We don't know why. Shouldn't you be asking yourself why? Why do you constantly make yourself out to be the monster in your own story? But the primary question is"—and they both said this in exasperated tones—"*Why should you feel bad for giving yourself what you want?*"

After they finished their wine, the three of them went out into the night. Why did Parisians eat so late? She felt it was time for bed.

The restaurant they were taking her to was near the Gare de l'Est, and there was such movement in this part of town, whizzing motorbikes, the clicking of heels. They arrived at Chez Casimir. It was one of these rustic French establishments that hadn't yet been gentrified by Brooklyn tastes. The tables were covered in red checkered oilcloth, and they were serving giant hunks of cheese on knotted wood platters, with fresh bread overflowing in baskets. Mike spoke to the waiter, who regarded them with a flabbergasted expression. "Incroyable!" He clicked his tongue and wagged a finger.

"Why does he look so put upon?" the clam whispered. Shelma lifted her shoulders noncommittally.

They got a cramped table next to the kitchen, but from her seat she spied a chef wearing that quintessential tall chef's hat, hacking into a beast of a fish. *This is so good,* she thought happily. *I'm having a fulfilling and rewarding experience entirely on my own, without him.*

"Is this okay?"

"This is great."

As they looked over the menu, from the corner of her eye, she saw something that made her startle. An overturned scallop shell, likely fished out from the garbage heap to serve another term as a utilitarian object. Its insides were stubbed gray with cigarette ash. Oof. She felt singed at the sight of those burn markings. Suddenly the thought of eating shellfish or using them as ashtrays seemed unconscionable.

"I'll have the coquille Saint-Jacques," Mike said, as though reading her mind. "What will you have?"

She frowned and chose some kind of cheese thing.

"Scallops are called coquille Saint-Jacques?" she asked. "What's the deal with Saint-Jacques?"

"The French name *everything* after saints," he averred with an indulgent flourish. "Even cheese."

"Hey. Do you think *I'm* a little bit clam-like?" she asked them. "Scallop-like, mollusk-like? Closed up or whatever."

"Hmm. Yes ... maybe ..." Mike said. "We never see you unless you feel like it."

"Before, you weren't," Shelma piped up. "You used to be down for anything."

"Oh, I get it," Mike said, pointing accusingly at the clam. "You're doing that thing again! You're trying to make yourself feel bad. *You're* the clam, *you're* the one with the problem. *It's all your fault!*"

"But I'm the one who . . . what about . . . the vows and all that . . . ?"

Shelma actually laughed at this.

"I mean, I liked your ex, don't get me wrong," Mike added. "When you guys first got together, I think you were craving structure and a way to temper some of your destructive habits? Maybe you were looking for a father figure, kind of. But now you've outgrown those needs. That's normal."

"But congrats, you're finally free! Good job! You can start dating again!" Shelma said excitedly. "Most people never leave. Most people stay and stay. You did the brave thing."

"Dude, can you imagine your Tinder profile? You'll be able to write, *I'm recently divorced, in my thirties, and in my experimentation phase*. You're going to get so many dates!"

Lying on their pull-out couch later that night, the clam googled "coquille Saint-Jacques" and learned that the scallop's name derives from the worship of St. James, who was said to have performed a miracle by saving a drowned knight. When the knight reemerged from the sea, he was covered in shining scallop shells. The scallop is now the symbol for the Camino de Santiago, or St. James's Way, one of the oldest pilgrimage paths in Europe. It went for hundreds of miles, and some people spent years walking it.

Those who completed the pilgrimage could pin a shell to their cloaks as evidence of arrival, and were granted a lifetime of forgiveness. Unsurprisingly, in modern times, the walk was a magnet for divorcées.

She scrolled through the various articles, suddenly captivated by the idea of walking this shell-lined path. She imagined it like an airplane runway lit up at night, or the rows of lights that guide you helpfully out of the theater when you need to use the bathroom. She understood why divorced people found the pilgrimage appealing. It was a simple, clearly marked, one-way path to transformation and forgiveness, which sounded like exactly what she needed too. Though her friends would probably object to this. They seemed irked by her guilt, which they interpreted as self-loathing martyrdom.

She clicked off her phone and took out her notebook, opening to where she had left off last time in her accounting.

Start again.

Age thirty-two. G invited me to take a trip with him to Texas. Before I accepted the invitation, I actually asked the husband for permission. *Why are you asking me?* he answered irritably. *I don't control you. It's not Saudi Arabia.* But I knew why I asked. By asking, I was taking my own responsibility out of my hands and putting it into his. I couldn't even take ownership of my own desire. Ridiculous to think that it would have ended any other way.

It was late now; the street was quiet. Exhausted, she closed her notebook, turned off the light, and fluffed up her pillow. She could hear the gentle snoring of either Mike or Shelma in the other room. It was always like a return to childhood when she reunited with her friends, a pair of strange surrogate parents. She followed their breathing.

Earlier, when she'd observed them fighting—why was she all of a sudden so impressed by that? Perhaps the fighting had represented something. *I am distinct from you. I want this and you want that.* Arguing was an exercise in power, she realized. They were marking out territories and negotiating treaties because they knew they were equally matched in firepower. One side couldn't easily overcome the other without a fight. It took courage to stake out a contested desire, one that would make you potentially undesirable to the other person, one that would be seen as a provocation. Whereas she always sought to avoid conflict by absorbing the interests of the other party. Most of the time this worked, but then her husband often accused her of being borderless, of not knowing when one person ended and she began. She merged others' interests with her own, picked it up as she went along, like that Japanese video game of the sticky ball that rolls over random terrain, picking up sheep and skyscrapers indiscriminately. In this way, it was easy to get along with—even love—whoever was in her vicinity, regardless of her own feelings. Her inexplicable desire for The Other Guy—was this desire also not her own? Was she mirroring something back to herself? Which desire was genuine? The desire for her husband, the desire for The Other Guy, or the desire for freedom?

Imagine not having to choose, and sticking to a path prechosen for you. That would be so easy. She stretched out on the couch. Beyond the balcony windows—no stars out there tonight. She read that early pilgrims had once called the footpath that eventually became the Camino de Santiago *La Voie Lactée*, or the Milky Way, because the celestial path above seemed to mirror the earthbound path they were traversing below. Pilgrims looked up whenever they felt lost. She called to mind the stars, the fields, the wildflowers, and the butterflies that she had seen in the online photographs earlier. There was the road and the Galician hórreos of crumbling stone and the mossy pads growing on them. The tall grasses waved. There was the sun, so much sun, and rain, so much rain, and there was a ripped poncho, and she was sitting down in the middle of the road because she couldn't keep going with the sore knee and blisters and the burned skin on her shoulders peeling off in sheets. It was as though she were molting right there, against her will, into something else. She was walking down the last hill and the sea glimmered in the distance. She got up to it and touched the lapping water and stood a moment at the edge. What happens now? She woke with sun in her eyes. Mike was already up doing his stretches. She touched her arms and face; she was still the same.

Rule 30 Exhibits Chaotic Behavior

A few hours later, the clam was walking to the butcher shop to pick up the dinner turkey, her self-assigned task this afternoon so as to avoid being trapped on the couch between Emily and Helene. She kept her head down in the rain. How does anyone manage to be happy in a gray, dreary place like this? She moved numbly toward the boucherie, rehearsing her lines over and over. *Walk, walk, walk,* the clam thought, pulling her lumpy coat around her. All she had to do was go in, use the ridiculous textbook French that nobody would ever use in real life (*Why hullo, kind sirs, might you be in possession of our goodly pheasant?* she imagined them hearing her say) and hand over the paper ticket that she was shredding to a fluff inside her pocket.

Nearing the butcher's shop, she still felt unprepared for the interaction so she paced around the block. After a few laps, she flung herself inside and mimed her best impression of a turkey. The man at the counter shouted over the din, "It's not ready!" It was very busy. She exited, ashamed. She didn't ask how much longer it would take. Ten minutes? Three hours? She walked away, planning to return later.

Now she had time to kill. So far this trip, she hadn't crossed the Seine at all. Because she had once picnicked with her husband along the Seine, that whole word, *Seine,* felt contaminated like a chemical spill. So she'd stayed put on this bank, not wanting to go over there. But soon, before she recognized where she was going, she had walked as far as the Place de la Bastille.

Well, if she made it as far as the Bastille, then she might as well cross over to the Left Bank! She hailed a cab. "Vous allez où, madame?"

"Deyrolle!" Yes. She would go to Deyrolle to buy *The Print*! That was where the cab was taking her now. Years ago, during one of her stints here, she had purchased an expensive print of trees commonly found in North Africa. The poster was in Arabic, a remnant of France's colonial exploits, but she found it extraordinarily beautiful. She bought the print against her better judgment, considering the cost; it was one of her only contributions to their apartment's decor. She hadn't seen it since that day she'd packed to leave. She didn't take it then because she thought it wasn't one of the items she could take. But now, she felt she needed to see it again, to buy it for herself this time, to claim ownership of this one small desire.

Outside the cab window: Don't look at the Sorbonne campus or that hotel over there, where you'd once gone as a plus-one to one of his academic conferences, and everyone looked at you in that presumptive way. That was before you were able to say you *wrote* without feeling so ashamed you'd cry. Don't look at that street where Roland Barthes was struck by a laundry cart. It's an unlucky corner. Don't look at the bookstores. Don't look at the old writer cafés, tourist traps where the bathroom attendants charged you ten euros. Which you gave. Don't think about all the times he accompanied you on your stupid "Writers of Paris" walk, when you had been in such despair about your novel that you needed to physically manifest yourself into some literary landscape. He'd done all of that for you, and you had not kept up your end of the bargain. Don't look. Don't look.

The clam stood across the street from Deyrolle, her back pressed against the stone portico like a second-rate detective. She was scoping it out. Should she go inside? It seemed like a silly errand.

The pacing earlier had left her feeling cold and dizzy, so she rummaged in her bag to retrieve the bread she'd bought at the boulangerie, a "pain énergie," which had sounded promisingly like Red Bull in bread form. Perfect. She unwrapped the club of wheat and began gnawing.

Deyrolle was the famous taxidermy shop on 46 Rue du Bac that, since its founding in 1831, had lured legions of artists and writers to its cabinet of curiosities. Crammed full of treasures from the natural world, it exhibited minerals, fossils, butterflies, and beetles, in a raucous celebration of the marvelous. Surrealists André Breton and Salvador Dalí once believed that the store provided a conduit to the subconscious.

The clam looked up at the store windows, where several of the taxidermy animals were positioned. At least on this corner of Rue du Bac, it was unremarkable to see a group of animals gazing languidly out the window. The ostrich, leopard, and albino peacock looked as though they were taking their afternoon tea.

Will you look at that, she imagined the albino peacock saying, with an aristocratic inflection straight out of a BBC period drama. The starry, tufted crown on the peacock's head gave it the look of an aging princess. *I daresay. Some kind of clam girl.*

The clam smiled. It was fun to imagine that these taxidermy animals might recognize her as one of their own. The taxidermy leopard might reply, *Indeed! Half mollusk, half woman! She looks like those exquisite corpses the Surrealists used to draw.*

The exquisite corpse creatures were freakish hybrids, not quite this and not quite that. Breton once said of the drawings that they helped to "fully release the mind's metaphorical activity." One person would draw one part of the body then fold the paper over, and another person would draw another part, and the creature would emerge from their collective consciousness. For the Surrealists, it was preferable to enter into meaning not through reason or logic, but through metaphor, intuition, and chance.

Revived, the clam crumpled up the paper wrapper, brushed crumbs off her face, and readied herself to go inside. At the entrance, she paused for a young father who was jamming a serious stroller through the door. Nowadays, she thought, Deyrolle was just a precious boutique tailored toward yuppies and their small children, and featured in cloying, nostalgic movies by Woody Allen. But it used to be an enchanted place. She, too, had imbued this place, this whole boulevard, with magic potential. Maybe it still possessed some magic. All she had to do was go in and buy the poster, she told herself. An easy enough assignment.

Inside, the clam wandered aimlessly around the store, waiting for the poster aisle to free up. In the meantime, she checked in with the display of taxidermy animals. She knew that some of these animals were available for rent, if one ever needed a taxidermy for a wedding or a séance. She remembered someone told her that the animals were identified by name. Paulette the Polar Bear's hourly rate was higher than Fabien the Ferret's, for instance. She knelt down next to the albino peacock she'd seen earlier by the window.

Hi, Albertine, the clam said in her head. *Can you tell me what's happening to me?*

Albertine the Peacock shivered elegantly.

You are drowning in a sea of feelings that you can't easily translate into words, Albertine responded.

Totally, the clam said. *You get me. What would it take to open up?*

That's up to you. What would you say if you could?

I would like a moral universe to be imposed.

In essence, you want to be punished for what you've done.

You could put it like that.

And since no one is going to punish you, you're going to do it to yourself in story form.

Is that what I'm doing?

In myths and fables, young women are turned into animals to render them mute. Think of Ovid's Metamorphoses. *Jupiter rapes Io and then transforms her into a cow. Callisto, also raped by Jupiter, is turned into a bear. Philomela is raped by Tereus, who cuts out her tongue to silence her. She is turned into a nightingale. In Ovid's day, the victim was typically the one who was punished by becoming an animal, you see.*

The clam nodded in agreement. In these stories, the animal form erupted, usually in the aftermath of intense emotion, such as inappropriate love that has exceeded conventional bounds. Whenever there was too much of something—anger, lust, jealousy, pride—transformations precipitated.

But you say your mother may have been the one to transform you, eh? Now it was Walter the Snowy Owl speaking. He was soaring above them, hanging from a plastic wire. *That, my dear, is yet another trope. In fairy tales, animal transformations are often catalyzed by the spells of witches and mothers. The handsome prince offends the evil stepmother in some way, so to punish him, she turns him into a frog. Luckily, the secret to disenchantment is usually* true love. *True love leads to redemption, restoration, and recognition.*

The clam thought about it. *In other words, when I find true love, I'll turn back into myself?*

Depends what kind of story this is!

The clam wandered into another aisle, pausing before a toucan with a polished plate in front of it: "Toco." Toco Toucan would have a car-horn type of voice, like the spokesbird of a certain breakfast cereal she used to eat. Above them, Barry the Giraffe droned on in a monotonous, booming, giraffe-splainer voice. *Your pearly insides are inaccessible to the outside.* He was quoting from a Francis Ponge poem. *Strictly speaking, a mollusk is nothing but a muscle. A hinge. A door-closer . . .*

Turning the corner, she reached the large cabinet that displayed the seashells, which seemed so beautiful to her suddenly. There was a potency to their form that was reaching deep inside, a new resonance. They brought to mind the eroded shell fragments her dad had once collected, heaped on plates around the house, furred with dust over the years. If her dad were the kind to accept gifts easily, she would've bought one for him. But she knew he would find these glossy purchased souvenirs abhorrent.

Wasn't this *Conus textile*? She leaned in to inspect the tag, but couldn't find it. She had learned recently about a cone snail shell with atypical markings, which Wikipedia had included in the entry for cellular automaton. Cellular automata were simple rules that could be repeated over and over to create a pattern. Rule 30 created an unpredictable, textbook example of chaos that mathematicians often used for encryption purposes. It also closely resembled this pattern now printed on *Conus textile*'s shell.

The clam looked at the shell and felt amused—*Conus textile* was messy and chaotic—her spirit mollusk! This snail built its shell, line by line, secreted through the mantle, a fleshy hood that separated the internal organs from the outside. The newest layers of shell were the ones closest to the main body, while the oldest parts of shell were farthest away. The mantle, filled with nerves that collect to clusters of ganglia, was the closest thing the mollusk had to a brain. Therefore, whatever it thought, it secreted, and the secreted story became the shell, the testimony.

Thinking of this process, she was somehow reminded of those printers from the nineties in her dad's office. The paper had a perforated border of punched holes that spooled the paper through the printer's gears, which she would tear off and fold into a paper spring. The shuttle worked laboriously back and forth, slowly imprinting each black dot. On the level of each row of dots, it was impossible to see the whole. One had to be patient and wait to see what it was creating in aggregate. She used to stand next to the printer and watch it printing lines of incomprehensible code. Her dad said it was a program she would never understand.

Maybe this was where she was stuck, on the level of the line. How could she possibly know, at this moment, the pattern of her shell? Her shell held her together. But because this shell was her own shell—she lived inside it, it contained her—she couldn't see beyond it. Contents can't see outside the parameters of their own packaging; it would be like questioning your mind with your own mind. All she could do was add to her shell, one line at a time, in layers, like writing. Then she would be able to look back, one day, to see what she was creating.

Her phone was buzzing in her pocket. Oh, no, she looked. It was Mike, most likely wondering where she'd gone. She'd already spent too long here. It was time to return to the others.

She hurried now to the aisle with the botanical prints and assertively wedged herself between the people who were there. "Pardonnez-moi!" She quickly rifled through all the crates and saw it, the tree print covered in a plastic casing.

She lifted it up. *Mirror, mirror, on the wall.* In the plastic reflection, she saw an image of her and her husband, in their old bedroom. They are roving from wall to wall, and he is saying, *But where should we hang it?* There isn't much room in their small apartment. Then he says to her, in an attitude of great largesse, *When we move to our next place, you can have a room that you can decorate in any way you want.*

Her phone buzzed again—and this time she answered it.

"Where are you?"

Marvelous Monsters

A
few days later, on the plane back to New York, the clam typed "Leonora Carrington" into her phone's search bar. When she had returned to the party with the turkey, and handed it over to Mike, he'd asked why she needed to go to Deyrolle so badly. (She was too embarrassed to mention the tree print, which she couldn't allow herself to buy, after all that.) She explained that she was interested in animal stories. Mike, the inveterate literature professor, asked if she'd ever read the animal fables of Leonora Carrington, the youngest Surrealist who was often forgotten. In one of her stories, a snarky hyena wears a human face to attend a debutante ball; in another, a girl's beloved rocking horse comes to life, only to be destroyed by the girl's father.

Reading on her phone, the clam learned that Carrington, born in Lancashire, England, had grown up in a stifling upper-class home. After her domineering father sent her to various convent schools, the rebellious, incorrigible Carrington, around nineteen years old, ran away to join the Surrealists. Soon, she began a relationship with the artist Max Ernst, twenty-six years her senior. Carrington was the classic example of the fetishized "femme-enfant," or woman-child muse. Despite their notable age difference, the couple shared a productive period of artistic flourishing, eventually moving to a secluded farmhouse in the Rhône Valley, where they immediately set about painting strange, hybrid creatures.

It was at this farmhouse in Saint-Martin-d'Ardèche that Carrington painted her famous *Self-Portrait (Inn of the Dawn Horse)*. In the portrait, a woman sits in a blue armchair in a high-ceilinged manor room, and extends a hand toward a female hyena, whose breasts are engorged with milk. Behind the seated woman, a white rocking horse is mounted on the wall, its posture mirroring the white horse galloping freely just beyond the window. Movement and stasis; freedom and confinement. Carrington was still trapped inside, immobilized, even if her animal alter egos were free to gallop. The couple's idyll didn't last long. In 1939, at the outbreak of the war, Ernst, a German citizen, was considered an enemy alien and imprisoned in a French internment camp. After his second arrest, Carrington, wracked with guilt, descended into madness. Emerging from the ordeal, she wrote that perhaps she had "an unconscious desire to get rid for the second time of my father: Max, whom I had to eliminate if I wanted to live."

Back in Brooklyn, the clam went to the library, picked up Leonora Carrington's collected stories, and read them in quick succession. Mike had been right to characterize the stories as playful with a steady undercurrent of violence. Carrington's animal characters weren't cute or cuddly; they were intimidating, cruel, and unapologetic in their wildness. And they were often hybrids, as in her paintings: half woman, half animal. If coming-of-age implied domestication, then perhaps for Carrington, the radical thing for a woman to do was hold on to her animal nature.

Carrington's Irish nanny had regaled the young girl with Celtic folktales, which likely included the example of the selkie, a seal-like creature. In these stories, a man will encounter a naked selkie bathing and secretly hide her seal suit, preventing her from returning to the sea. He compels her to marry and start a family. The selkie yearns forever for her lost youth. Even if the selkie wife is satisfied, the husband must take great care in hiding her suit, because if she had a choice, she would immediately return to the sea. In this formulation, marriage is a compromise at best, and a kind of hostage situation at worst.

(Male selkies, on the other hand, are depicted as seductive, oversexed lovers who emerge from the sea to gratify lonely wives whose fishermen husbands have been gone too long. Between these trysts, the male selkies happily return to the ocean.)

From there, the clam went on to survey a handful of Chinese animal transformation stories, curious whether they concealed similar messages of romantic partnership. In "The Snail Girl," a penniless farmer rescues a snail from his fields and takes it home to keep as a pet. Over the next few days, the farmer comes home to find his house nicely swept and dinner made. Confused and eager to discover this mysterious visitor, he comes home early and peeks through the window. He sees his rescued snail step out from her shell and transform into a beautiful woman. Caught, she promises that if he agrees to marry her, she will be satisfied with very little, just like a snail.

In the case where the animal is formidable and deadly, the animal wife must pretend otherwise. In "The White Snake," a white snake spirit falls in love with a mortal man and changes herself into a submissive woman. She dotes on him and cares for him, and they share a happy existence. Unfortunately, an evil monk convinces the husband that his wife is other than she claims and urges him to feed her a potion that unveils her true snake form. Upon seeing her as a gigantic white snake, the husband faints, or in some versions of the story, he dies. Then, of course, there are the famous huli jing fox spirit stories, about foxes who shapeshift into scheming seductresses to destroy entire dynasties.

In all of these stories, the clam noted, there's an element of deception and double consciousness. In order to be in a marriage, these stories suggest, a woman must contort herself into something other than what she is naturally, because what lies underneath is something hideous and incompatible. Hans Christian Andersen's "The Little Mermaid," published in 1837, is perhaps the ultimate example of the female lover who willingly deforms her own body in the name of love. Struck by love, the little mermaid seeks assistance from the sea-witch, who agrees to give her legs, at a steep price. Every step the little mermaid takes will feel as though she is treading on sharp knives, and the mermaid will also lose her beautiful voice. *Are you prepared to suffer all this?* the sea-witch cackles. The little mermaid, young and stupid, drinks the potion, loses her voice, and spends the rest of the story mincing on her pained feet before her oblivious prince, who duly falls in love with another woman. Unable to earn his love, the little mermaid commits suicide by jumping into the waves.

The clam was so excited to read this fairy tale. She was familiar with the Disney version of "The Little Mermaid," but Andersen's original was deliciously dark and depressing, a cry of anguish. There was no better allegory for describing the agonies of love. Hadn't the clam suffered all the same torments during her infatuation with The Other Guy? The catching of the throat, the dumb smile. Endlessly dancing and performing some version of yourself that you think might be more appealing.

Some now read "The Little Mermaid" as an allegory of unrequited homosexual love. Like the little mermaid, Andersen also loved to dance and had a beautiful soprano voice as a child. He used his artistic gifts to court the favor of the local bourgeoisie, including Jonas Collin, who would become his longtime patron. According to Rictor Norton, Andersen became hopelessly smitten with his benefactor's son Edvard Collin. About a year before the publication of "The Little Mermaid," Andersen professed his feelings to Collin: "I long for you as though you were a beautiful Calabrian girl," he wrote in one letter. "My sentiments for you are those of a woman," he wrote in another. When Andersen learned that Collin was to be engaged, he wrote "The Little Mermaid" as his response.

Now the clam was watching the Yorgos Lanthimos film *The Lobster* on her laptop, in bed. She was eating popcorn again. Her research had led her, at last, to this modern transformation fable. The premise was simple: In the film's dystopic world, everyone was required to couple up based on simple, superficial traits. Those with limps were paired together, as well as those with frequent nosebleeds. These couplings were facilitated at an upscale hotel where singles could dance, dine, play tennis, and enjoy other leisure activities. Hotel "guests" had forty-five days to find a mate, though more days could be earned by hunting down single "loners" who escaped into the woods. If the guests were still unsuccessful by the end of their stay, they would be wheeled into a forbidding surgical room and transformed into an animal.

The film's hyper-rational, conformist citizens have made a bargain based on the assumption that there is no worse fate than falling prey to the animalistic urges that accompany love. To manage such violent passions, these people have opted instead for rules, order, and bureaucracy. Their system is designed to maintain a vise-like grip on unwieldy emotions. Those who do not couple up under these parameters are no better than animals, so they should be transformed into animals. But in the end, humans still lose control. The brutality of passion is replaced by another kind of brutality—the brutality of order.

Of course, the two main characters, played by Colin Farrell and Rachel Weisz, find love precisely where they shouldn't—in the loners' woods. Even here, in the margins, order must prevail. As punishment, Rachel Weisz is blinded by the loners' leader, and Colin Farrell must decide whether he will also blind himself to continue to "match" his match. This is a test of love. In the last scene, he hovers a steak knife over one quivering eyeball.

Taking stock, the clam thought now while lying in bed, if there's a progression from *Metamorphoses* to "The Little Mermaid" to *The Lobster*, it's this: The female characters in Ovid never have a choice in love—they are raped against their will and still suffer the consequences by being turned into an animal. Andersen's little mermaid is at least able to choose whom she loves, even if she, too, must suffer. In contrast, the characters in Lanthimos's paternalistic world are only allowed to choose within a prescribed range, in order to not suffer too much. But the clam realized that she didn't want to live in Lanthimos's world. She wanted to choose freely, recklessly, to feel the full range of what was possible, the elation as well as the pain.

Well, if that's the case, the clam thought, if suffering in this formulation is a kind of privilege, then why not make a stand for freedom? Why not test it out?

Let's plumb the depths of this thing.

She texted The Other Guy. A few hours later, he texted back—

You requested that we talk?

I have a proposition. Could I call you?

Why? Am I in trouble?

Why would you be in trouble?

I don't mean specifically, I mean cosmically.

Maybe I missed something important.

What could you ever do that would make me mad?

It's a relief to know I'm not in trouble.

So I can call now?

Didn't I always say that it wouldn't be intolerable if you called me?

Let's hear your proposition, go.

The Proposition

Too terrified to actually voice call, she unveiled her proposition over text, which she elaborated carefully like a business plan. She proposed that perhaps she should move to Houston so they could see each other more often. She thought this was a conservative proposal, since he often joked that they should live together. Nothing was holding her to New York anymore, she said. Then she added, using this exact phrasing, that she would like to be in "proximity with his body."

After she texted this last line, he stopped responding, so she quickly qualified that this could be a "once-a-month proposition," as in, they could be in each other's proximity, maybe, once a month?

Minutes, then an hour, went by. She made excuses, spun theories, chastised herself for bad timing. She'd caught him in the middle of something. His phone had died. He was so shocked he'd swerved his car into an embankment and now he was crawling out from the wreckage. It appeared that his Facebook Messenger status alternated from inactive to active, back and forth, which suggested he was texting other people and checking his phone intermittently. He was alive, then, interacting with others but not with her. The insult of his silence began to creep in, but she bargained, *If he texts back in the next hour, I'll forgive him. I won't even be mad.*

A discomfiting thought: Had she grossly misinterpreted his intentions all this time? Maybe he really did see her as just a friend, and this last, somewhat suggestive text about his body was the equivalent of grinding up against someone at the club without permission. She was not an incautious person. What evidence did she have for believing there was something more between them?

A few months ago, when she'd texted to say she would be out of reach for a while, he'd responded right away. They quickly arranged a time to talk. She sat on some park bleachers as a softball game progressed. She was saying that she couldn't talk to him anymore, not until things became . . . clearer. She couldn't say it outright then, but she had to remove him from the equation if she wanted to save her marriage. In other words, their daily texting had to stop. *But what's wrong with being friends?* he'd countered, with what she'd interpreted (at the time) as indignation. He saw nothing wrong with the nature of their relationship. So it had been a one-sided infatuation all along, she told herself. All at once, his tone seemed to suggest, he didn't want to lose her, but of course he would, out of decency, respect her wishes. Because he was this impeccable, beautiful person, she thought, he would certainly comply and support her however he could.

But there was no reason to start immediately, so they'd spent the rest of the hour talking: what he was listening to on his long commutes, who had been remaindered on the four-dollar poetry cart, a recap of the latest issue of a magazine they loved. When the conversation wound to a close, she thought, *Tomorrow I'll wake up without a message from him, and I'll have no one to tell my jokes to.*

Are you still going to go to New Mexico then? He was asking her about the writers' residency she had just been accepted to. She said she wasn't sure anymore.

But you're still coming to see me in Texas tomorrow, right?

Oh, of course! She played along. *I'll get on the Greyhound . . .*

No, that's too slow. I think that'll take several days. But if you do go to New Mexico, we could go exploring together. I'll come stay with you . . .

Did friends say this to each other? Maybe it was all within the range of normal behavior. She had wanted so badly to say, *Just tell me where to go. I'll drop everything. I would happily follow you to any country, to any garage in any shitty place.*

Afterward, she was buoyant, giddy; she felt she had infinite energy; she could be kind to everyone; she could walk back to the apartment and be gentle with her husband. Perhaps that was what this other man had always offered, a drug or a dream she could use up until the next encounter. Was it greedy to want this all the time? She never felt as alive as she did with him. Whenever he came to New York, they'd spend all day together, visiting museums, walking and talking very fast, gossiping about their friends, summarizing complicated books on moral philosophy and articles they had read, drinking too much coffee. They dove into this bookstore, then that one, analyzing book covers, reading their over-the-top blurbs aloud, and invariably he would lose something important, his wallet, his phone, and they would have to backtrack their steps. *It's because I'm so happy to see you!* he would exclaim, and she believed him. When they walked together it felt natural to link arms; they sat on benches squished together like kids in the back seat of the car, sharing melted ice cream, theorizing about socks. Should they buy socks? They would go to the store to buy socks, or search for matching sweatsuits, to show up as a united front. She remembered watching him zip up a neoprene hoodie. Her legs wobbled. How could anyone look so good wearing a piece of workout gear, the stickers and tags still attached? She rubbed the synthetic material on his chest, giggled, then fled, embarrassed, to check herself in the mirror.

He maintained a respectful silence in the months following that particular conversation, but then one day he showed up in New York (again), and (she couldn't help it, promise or no promise) they picked up where they'd left off. They arranged to meet in the East Village, bought a pint of ice cream from an Indian grocery, and sat on a bench, talking, fireflies igniting around them. Weeks of pent-up language spilled out, and they talked and walked from Manhattan to Brooklyn; the next day, he went over to her new loft sublet to check it out. He flopped onto the bed, kicking his legs, and said he was happy for her. *You're going to flourish here,* he said. *Just like we were really flourishing on that bench.*

The clam summarized this recent history to herself again, with the usual obsessive detail. She felt as though she were searing it into her brain. She typed a question into the search bar: *How do you know if he likes you?* The price of entry for the various online quizzes that popped up was only all of your personal information, so she used a repertoire of fake email aliases at ClamChen@me.com.

The results all told her the same thing. If he's into you, you should know right away. You've already lost if you're taking these quizzes to help interpret his "clues" and "signs."

This wasn't helpful. They didn't know the kind of man she was dealing with. She believed that his signs were more meaningful (and ambiguous) than the average man's. What did it mean when he sent her, for instance, a few weeks ago, with no context, a drawing of a pie? Did this mean "sweetie pie"? Was he standing next to a pie and thinking of her? Had they eaten pie together recently? (No. She remembers everything.) Did he want to spend the holidays with her? Did he want to have a piece of her pie?

"Know your worth," the articles said. "You are a high-quality woman. Do not beg for scraps."

But clams are extremely resourceful, she thought, great at filtering water for particles and nutrients. It only takes one small interaction—one grain of sand, one pie—to fertilize her imagination. As a clam, she was designed to beg for scraps.

Like that, the middle of the night became early morning. And then she fell asleep.

Learning to Say "I"

The moment she woke, she clawed crazily in the sheets for her phone and found it blank. No messages. *He's trying to save me from myself,* she reasoned. *Okay.* Tinder immediately presented itself as the next logical step. In order to find true love in this modern era, she thought, one had to be proactive and bravely broadcast one's romantic eligibility to other eligible subjects within a ten-mile radius, relying on a pithy statement of impenetrable irony and a series of slightly misleading photographs. Those were the rules of the day! *If not now, when?* she thought as she set up her account, almost giddy. She scrolled through her photo reel, her legs propped on several pillows.

She needed a photo. Just one. She knew the exact kind of photograph she was looking for even as she knew that she would be unlikely to find it. An impromptu one taken during a hike, a dance party, lounging in a swimsuit, et cetera. The curation of these activities was as important as how one looked doing these activities. Any photo that included her husband was automatically disqualified. And why was she always ducking out of view? At the very least, she needed to have a photo of herself just smiling and looking directly at the camera. Unbelievably, it seemed the only time she took selfies was when extremely intoxicated, usually in the bathroom of a bar. Those kinds of shiny, red-faced photos definitely sent the wrong signal.

Take a selfie now? Impossible, the way she looked this morning.

She finally settled on a photo that fulfilled all the criteria and seemed ethical enough as a visual representation of her. It was a photo of her driver's license, zoomed in and with all the personal information cropped out. She'd taken a picture of her license months ago to send to the couples therapist. The pixelated, cropped black-and-white portrait reminded her of those distorted image tests you have to pass on websites to prove you are human. "Can you see a face in this square? Click yes or no." This would do. Now she just had to add some text.

If you started dating again, can you imagine your Tinder profile? she recalled Mike saying. *You'll be able to write, "I'm recently divorced, in my thirties, and in my experimentation phase."*

She typed out this sentence, annoyed. Noncommitment was the millennial malaise. Everyone was already deeply disenchanted, disillusioned, disabused; nobody was a fool.

"On here looking for true love and enchantment," she wrote. "Hope you'll be able to help."

The profile went live. A sick feeling rose up, but she squashed it down. What if someone she knew swiped into her? She imagined her students lying about their ages (she had set the filter to age thirty-two and up), seeing her, screen capping it, and sharing it among themselves. She imagined her ex-husband's friends swiping into her, screen capping it, and sending it to him as evidence of her continued perfidy.

The app invited her to begin perusing its contents. She didn't know which swiping direction meant what. Her muscle memory told her that if you wanted to see more information, you scrolled vertically, but each time she did this, a bright blue star erupted on the screen. "You have Super Liked Tommy!" Jesus, she thought, she definitely did not want to Super Like that guy, but in her attempts to undo, she sent out a flurry of aberrant signals left and right. After a few panicked moments of this, she got a new screen. "It's a Match!" and then, unbelievably, a lewd message from the matched man.

Astonishing, she thought.

She clicked off the phone and tried not to think of how exposed she was making herself by being on this app. The everyday horror of this system was breathtaking. How had everyone surrendered to this system so readily, and with such resignation? It was just like in *The Lobster*—when humans tried to solve a problem, they usually ended up creating a new, different problem.

Luckily, it was going to be a busy day. She put on her headphones, packed her bags, and got ready to go. "Work work work work work work . . ." the song repeated. Today, she had to pick up her writing class's final papers from her campus mailbox, and then she had to rush to Koreatown to interview the famous Japanese novelist Yoko Tawada for *The Village Voice*. Whenever she could, she wrote freelance articles that paid a few hundred dollars, which wasn't nothing, and she couldn't afford to turn her nose up at it.

It was luck that Yoko Tawada happened to be in New York to promote the English translation of her novel *Memoirs of a Polar Bear*. The clam was eager to meet her—if a little nervous. She specifically chose the book to review because it was yet another animal story, narrated from the perspective of three generations of polar bear artists. This novel was unlike anything the clam had ever read. The first part was narrated by a "grandmother" polar bear who fled the Soviet Union to live in exile in the West; the second was about her daughter Tosca, a circus performer who fell in love with her human trainer; and the third was about the son that Tosca abandoned, none other than Germany's most famous polar bear, Knut.

Reading under layers of blankets, the clam had been delivered to a dreamy state in which she only half understood what was happening, but she could feel the emotional resonance of it. Among other things, the novel seemed to be a commentary on otherness, exile, and migration. But it also seemed to be an expression of impossible love. All three generations yearned for an unattainable ideal: a member of another species, an imaginary homeland, a parent not one's own. The question the clam most wanted to ask Yoko was whether writing from an animal perspective was simply a way to capture the grief one felt when estranged from one's love, as in "The Little Mermaid." Unfulfilled longing made the world strange and the self stranger.

After the short interview, the clam would have to rush to the Financial District for her other job as a copywriter for a toy company that made DIY puppets for Montessori schoolchildren. Of all her miscellaneous gigs, this was the one that paid the most. The job entailed assembling colorful felt pieces in the proper order and documenting what she did in language. This week, she was working on a series of woodland creatures—a bear, a fox, a deer, a rabbit, and some red-capped mushrooms. "First, sew the fox's eyeballs on its head. Then, sew on the rosy cheeks. Then, sew on the mouth in the shape of an X. Finally, stuff in the stuffing."

Did it require a graduate degree to do this? She had typed out the phrase "stuff in the stuffing" so many times this week, it was beginning to take on an inappropriate tinge of sex.

As usual, the clam arrived unnecessarily early to Yoko Tawada's hotel. When the receptionist said, "I'll call up and tell her you've arrived," the clam jumped and said, "No, no! Don't rush her! I'll be right back." She went outside, looking for something to do for the next half hour, and wandered into a donut shop. She ordered two black teas, thinking maybe she would give one to Yoko later. Did this violate some kind of journalism code? She returned to the hotel lobby with her two teas and sat in a cramped alcove next to a plastic Christmas tree bleating a techno version of "Jingle Bells." *This is literally the worst place to have an interview,* she fretted. She scooted the chair to a quieter corner, but it hardly helped. She always arrived too early no matter what she did; it was a way to lessen her anxiety, but it always had the reverse effect.

The elevator door opened and closed. When the clam looked up from her notes, she was startled to see that Yoko was already standing before her. Yoko was smiling, wearing a stylish black leather jacket with slim jeans that made the clam ashamed of her own sloppy outfit.

It was something about the curve of Yoko's smile, the angle of her upper lip, that reminded the clam of the universal way bears are depicted in cartoon form—the clam immediately saw a resemblance to the felt puppet bears she had been assembling all week.

"Are you here to interview me?" Yoko asked.

"Yes! That's me! Thank you so much for taking the time . . ."

The clam relaxed, and they both sat down. Yoko had already brought coffee down from her room.

Yoko only had thirty minutes, so the clam had to speak quickly. The clam's first question was about writing from an animal perspective: a predictable, possibly vexing question, because Yoko had immediately laughed, like, *Oh, this again.*

"For me, I wanted to look at human beings from the outside," Yoko said. "Already, I observe the European language from outside as a Japanese. To see human beings from the outside, I must be an animal."

Yoko went on to explain that, initially, her interest had been to write about Knut's mother, the circus performer Tosca. When Knut was abandoned by Tosca, the German public immediately criticized Tosca for having no "mother instinct," when in fact she had been trained in the circus and forced to perform unnatural behaviors her entire life: balancing on balls and jumping through hoops. The bears had to learn to walk on two feet. Like Tosca, the novel seemed to suggest, our own human behaviors had been trained into us as habits we could no longer escape, so much so that what felt "natural" to us was in fact the most unnatural of behaviors. Shopping for packaged food in a grocery store instead of hunting for salmon, for instance. Or sitting at one's desk to write an autobiography.

Throughout the novel, the "natural" and the assimilated were constantly called into question, the clam agreed. The polar bears had to conform to human society to survive. They were exotic members of the "minority perspective," but they had to assimilate, learn their new adopted language, and speak their testimony to become legible to others. In one scene, a bookseller directs the grandmother polar bear to Kafka's animal stories, including "A Report to an Academy," about a wild monkey who shares his tortured, depressing journey toward becoming a civilized monkey. It is a transformation that happens under duress, in captivity. As a German-speaking Czech Jew, perhaps Kafka felt similarly compelled to perform an identity that was imposed upon him.

Next, the clam asked Yoko whether there was something "unnatural" about the first-person voice, since the baby Knut initially struggles against his instinct to speak in the third person. When he does so, he is taunted by the other bears for speaking in baby-babble.

At this, Yoko grinned and rubbed her hands together.

"Ah! The first person is something special. In the Middle Ages, in European languages, people spoke not with 'I' but 'we.' The first person is new and modern. Before that, we felt ourselves not as the center of the world, but part of the world. Animals do that too. They don't think in the first person, but in the third."

The clam felt an idea forming: the possibility of expressing yourself without centering the self . . . to speak in the third person, as part of something larger. A top-down view, like seeing yourself from the perspective of a map. Could the clam do that, too, in writing? Not from inside out, but from outside in.

"The way that animals, and the dead, communicate is not like how we humans communicate," Yoko emphasized. "But I wanted to show—translate—that there is communication happening."

"How do animals and the dead communicate?" the clam asked.

"Through dreams, behavior, and memories in the unconsciousness," Yoko answered.

The clam found this idea so arresting she paused from her note-taking.

"Animals *know* certain things without *learning*, without *language*," Yoko continued. "When a dog shakes in fear to a loud sound— why does he do that? Does he know in language? No. But he has a memory in his body. Maybe he was beaten by a previous owner. Maybe it is his instinct. That is memory and knowledge, but it is not learned through language."

"So we carry knowledge in our bodies that we haven't learned consciously? But we learned it somehow . . . ?"

Abruptly, the timer sounded; thirty minutes had flown by. The clam knew Yoko had to leave, so now was the time to ask the question she had come here to ask: Did the novel have a theory of love? What was the novel trying to say about love?

Yoko smiled and nodded again, like she understood.

"If the love is natural, you don't need to say. In Japan, mothers never say 'I love you.' There is no sentence for that. Maybe you can translate it, but people will think you are crazy. What do you mean, 'I love you'? Mothers do all the things, from feeding to touch and care. It comes through actions. That's love. The word 'love' is used in the case when you are not sure if you are loved. You want to confirm. But if it's natural, you don't need to say."

The clam was scribbling notes as a decoy. Words weren't the only way to communicate. Explicit verbal expressions of love weren't the only proof. Dreams and touch, that counted too.

Yoko said she had to go. The two women stood, shook hands, and said very politely, "Thank you, thank you, thank you." The clam felt the urge to do an action like kowtowing. But they were upright and professional, so good, the both of them, at performing their roles.

"Thank you." The clam trailed wistfully after Yoko. "Words cannot express how thankful I . . ."

The elevator door closed.

Human Languages Are Too Vague

If love is natural, there's no need to say the words. The clam was thinking about Yoko's answer again. Actions spoke louder than words. Although she and The Other Guy were literate people with graduate degrees, their communication had never been straightforward. She could never say exactly what she wanted to say, and everything he said became a kind of code to crack. They spent years sending confused signals to each other. They called themselves "friends" and insisted that this simple word defined their relationship. But the physical cues never added up. What did the furtive glances mean? She had thought, back then, that all these signs meant they were both in love but one of them was married and so it all had to be buried. The pieces seemed to fit into that kind of narrative.

But what did it really mean, now that she was a free agent and had made her proposition clear, that he had chosen silence?

Two weeks had passed, and still not a word from him. She drafted an email—*I should be clearer about what I want. What I want is to exist somewhere in your vicinity all the time. . . . Let me know if our needs/wants are coterminous*—but she wasn't yet sure if it was meant to be a final goodbye or an ultimatum. *I'll go look for another portal if you don't want to be the portal . . .*

She revised the email so many times it was beginning to lose meaning. Human communication *was* a farce. Emitting one's phero-mones took no language. Body chemistry, touch. Modes of com-munication in the animal world were instinctual and honest, unlike the contortions of verbal language. She gave up on the email and left it unsent. Not responding got the job done better. Not responding was its own definitive statement.

But hadn't he sent her signs for her to believe what she believed? She thought back to one of the last trips she had taken with him. Still under the guise of friendship, they had gone camping together near where he lived in Texas. The campsite they chose was along a dammed river, though the reservoir was uncharacteristically low and mucky because of the drought. "Used to be you could haul Moby Dick through that water," the park ranger muttered before locking up the gates for the night.

Alone at the camp; the moon was out. They poured bourbon into a thermos, filled another with water from the spigot, packed cigarettes, and headed down to the levee overlooking the river. She had her phone out for light, but he said, "No, turn the flashlight off. Let's try to find our way there in the dark."

"I'm going to trip and fall," she protested. He offered his hand. She stiffened and instead chose to hold on to his forearm, like a grandmother would. They shuffled along, a mistake, a glitch in the choreography. After a while, their eyes adjusted to see the path, and they unclasped.

The stone levee was a white gash in the darkness. They sat next to each other with their legs lightly touching, dangling over the edge, the parched river many feet below, the moon coning over the water. She felt aware that this was exactly the kind of scene that would show up in a romantic movie, and that they were just going through the motions, shaping this scene, playing their roles, though both understood that there would be no culmination to the proceedings. There couldn't, or at least, not yet. They were saying, suggesting, in some roundabout way, *We don't know why we're here in Texas together, but whatever this is, it isn't wrong.*

He was grumbling, perhaps obviously, she thought, about his

recent breakup with a young art student she'd met a few times. He said that she didn't have enough talent or ambition. She wasn't serious.

"It's not like she has goals. She's not trying to become a novelist."

"Maybe you just prefer being single," she offered emptily. "You're convinced that you make better art that way. Isn't all creative energy libidinous?"

"Maybe," he said, lazily stretching out on his back. He put his head on her thigh to use as a pillow. "But what about you?" he asked, and she was quick to deflect.

"I'm different. My husband made my entire life possible. I wouldn't be anything without him. I'm not . . . I haven't been a real person."

It had gotten cold; what sounded like coyotes howling in the distance made the hairs on her neck stand on end. She was mumbling something about being young, barely out of undergrad when she made the decision to get together. "I'm just starting to feel that it's all wrong . . ." She trailed off, feeling like a defrauded investor in the seconds before his life would vanish, gazing up at the screen with a faint grin of dumb optimism.

She tried to imagine herself meeting a young student in some café, then taking the girl back to her place as he had done with her all those years ago. Back then, she'd found his boldness alluring. In his place, she realized how lonely he must have been. Easing his loneliness had been an act of her own self-expression. At first, she told herself that if it didn't work out, she could always leave. Her only miscalculation was the degree of her own commitment. She hadn't recognized that in herself yet.

Well, that's that, she thought, shaking away the memory. Once again, the understanding between them was incorrect, the communication insufficient.

"Human languages are too vague," quibbles the god Apollo in the novel *Fifteen Dogs* by André Alexis. Apollo's view is that humans have no special merit but think themselves superior, and he wagers that the gift of human intelligence will only guarantee that animals become as unhappy as humans. Hermes, the god of communication, insists that the human way of exchanging symbols is their great asset, because it makes them so much more amusing. He gestures at the humans sitting around them in the bar: "Just listen to these people. You'd swear they understood each other, though not one of them has any idea what their words actually mean to another. How can you resist such farce?"

The clam texted her friend Sam a screenshot of her email draft to The Other Guy. She always resisted texting Sam when she felt sad, guilty to be reaching out in this needy state. She didn't think that was a fair balance for a friendship. But Sam said she was happy to hear what was going on.

I just needed a witness.

Hm. Are you actually going to send this?

Should I?

You do know that you don't have to be rejected to be alone, right? You can just be alone. It's like going to the movies by yourself and enjoying it.

You don't think I should send it.

Why don't you try to have some fun? You're allowed.

Perhaps the clam should go on a Tinder date to "take the edge off," she suggested. Sex would require no language—was better without language. Sam assured her that this was just necessary to do sometimes. Throw yourself into your body, come back to center. Pick a guy, any random guy who didn't seem like an axe murderer, and take it from there.

So now the clam was in the dressing room of Urban Outfitters, picking out a new outfit to wear to her date. She had selected an oversized hoodie, ripped jeans, and some kind of faux fur jacket. The outfit made her look like Justin Bieber. Gleeful, she had dug out her phone to send Sam a picture when she saw the message.

Her heart dropped into her crotch.

It was The Other Guy. He had texted his location—LaGuardia Airport. No further details. But why was he in town? Why did he want her to know he was in town? There was no accompanying text. No explanation for what this gesture meant.

"What does this mean?" she immediately texted Mike.

"Gurl, it's his *Moonlight* drive," he texted right back.

"What?"

"You know. The Barry Jenkins movie. He realizes what he's missing and he's coming to declare his love."

The clam was stunned. Was he really coming to declare his love? She stood there a moment, hyperventilating. She looked in the mirror. But . . . was it possible? This morning, when she looked, her face had seemed the same fleshy blob. Now a strong jawline had reasserted its place, and her neck grew slenderer as she moved. She touched her cheek. So it was already happening. *I'm about to transform,* she thought. This was it.

"So you'll see him tonight?" Sam texted.

"Tonight unless anything changes," she added. "I mean, unless he cancels. I mean, it's within his character profile. I really wouldn't be surprised."

Three dots emerged on Sam's end, then disappeared. The clam watched the three dots come and go, come and go. The dots formed and dissolved, like waves. A thought ebbed, a thought was reconsidered. The clam wished she could see the underside of that thought.

What the Moonlight Does

*H*e *had* wanted to meet. An hour later, he sent her another text with a link to an avant-garde play downtown. When she arrived, he waved her over to a seat he'd saved next to him.

"What did I miss?" she whispered. He leaned in, smiling. He looked, she thought, like someone in love. A high-octane smile that seemed only possible on small children, a jumping-up-and-down kind of smile, with all the pyrotechnics of uninhibited joy behind it.

"You missed the part quoting Melville," he said into her ear. "When one finds oneself with a life not worth living: it's monastery, suicide, or one goes to sea. *Is* that Melville? I confess I've never read *Moby-Dick* because the print is so small."

She laughed, unnerved, wondering what this meant. After the play ended, he pulled her across the hall to introduce her to some of his friends. Did this have a meeting-the-parents kind of vibe? Was he attempting to bring her into the fold, signaling to others that the two of them were a unit now? She thought this was it, their happiness would finally become solidified, its borders obvious and encompassing.

They mingled, then they followed his friends to a party they were hosting. By the time the two of them said their goodbyes, she was buzzed. It was late, the hour of breaking off, peeling away, entering private spaces in the dark. Look at us leaving together! They left in what she thought was a showy way; he had this kind of bravado. Was he, possibly, proud? He wasn't afraid to be seen in public with her, and that meant something? She was filing away all of these signs and clues for later processing with Sam.

Out in the street, they kept laughing, leaning into each other as though they had just endured some impossible thing together and gotten out alive. He held out his palm and, missing the cue, she handed over a pack of cigarettes.

"Can I tell you something?" she began to say.

She was drunk; she suddenly felt she didn't have anything to lose. The words were already bursting out of her.

They sat down on a cool stone slab, lit theatrically by a street-light. They seemed to be looking at each other meaningfully. She was just going to say it.

"Wait. You don't have to say what you're about to say," he interrupted.

She couldn't believe she'd been preempted.

"Do you even know what I'm about to say?"

"I think I do. I can only be a friend."

"But I can't separate the two things in my head," she said.

"What two things?" His expression was forlorn.

"Wasn't this supposed to be your *Moonlight* drive?"

"What?"

She shook her head.

"Can I at least walk you home?"

"What's the point?"

The conversation had lasted no time at all. She said she needed to go. She had to get away. She didn't dare to look at him. "Well, let me know when you're ready to be friends again," he said sadly. Those were the last words she remembered. She was crying now. When they approached the subway entrance, she saw that he went down the side of the platform heading toward Queens, the same direction she needed to take. Instead, she went down the other end of the platform in the wrong direction and rode it all the way to Ninth Street until she was sure he would be far away. She put on her noise-canceling headphones and played her music as loudly as she could stand it. Her face must have been something. She got off at the station to switch platforms but slipped on ice and tumbled down the steps. Her knees were badly scraped. A stranger stopped and asked if she was okay, saw her wild smile, and lurched away.

Animals in the sea spawn based on external cues. They watch the moon and monitor the water temperature carefully. When conditions are just right, they spew their sex cells straight into the water for a night of orgiastic mating. The moon serves as aphrodisiac and North Star. The moon tells you when to open and where to go, and sea creatures hold in their bodies a memory of the moonlight and its directives.

In Leonardo da Vinci's notebooks, he once recorded the behavior of a crafty crab that would wait until the full moon for a certain mollusk to open her mouth. Then, he would shove a stone or stick into the open crevice so that she would not be able to close it. That way the crab could happily, and without risk, eviscerate the hapless mollusk. The moral of the story? Don't open your mouth and place yourself at the mercy of an indiscreet listener. Don't ever make yourself vulnerable by opening up to the moon.

"What happened?" Sam asked as she opened the door.

"It's a sad tale."

Sam winced. "I wish you didn't say that."

The clam hung her bike helmet by the door. She had surprised herself earlier when she agreed to stop by for brunch. She was in no mood to socialize, but at the moment, she feared her own company more than she feared the company of others.

Sam's boyfriend had made shakshuka. Two other couples were already there, Sam's friends. But then, lo and behold, there was Helene, having just arrived from Paris. How does she manage to insert herself into every pivotal moment of this doomed romance?

"But I don't understand," Helene said. "It's so unsatisfying!"

The clam told the whole story again. The story was beyond her interpretative abilities. She repeated their last lines of dialogue again, verbatim, in the monotone in which they were delivered. Then she pulled out her phone and showed everyone the picture of the stone bench where they'd sat.

"This is the corner of my humiliation!" she cried. She'd gone back to the stone bench and snapped a photo of it. They passed the phone around the table.

"Now you know exactly where you stand," someone remarked.

Luckily, everyone was *on*. Perhaps they were putting on a show for her benefit. Arielle was on. Michael was on. Ashley made them go around and describe their parents' homes. Sam said her parents' house looked like everything came out of a MoMA catalog: Josef Albers prints next to Japanese silk pillows next to a giant sandstone Beethoven sculpture. Michael said his parents' house was an unfortunate mix of Asian and Mediterranean stuff, like Buddhist statuettes and terra-cotta pots. Arielle described her mom's clutter, the swan figurines, the glamour shots, and all her accumulation of "old stuff."

"Oh, antiques?" Helene asked. (Helene reported that in her bourgeois Sixteenth Arrondissement apartment, antiques were stacked up to the ceiling.)

"No. Not because they were old before, but . . ." Arielle paused. "But because they're just in the house, getting old." The clam laughed hysterically; she didn't know why. "Stuff from Big Lots. Sometimes she'll bring her receipt to show you, item to item. 'You can't beat that!' she'll say. So I'll bait her: 'You know where I can get this small thing for not very much money?' You can see her squirming in her seat; she just wants to explode. 'Big Lots! You can get it at Big Lots!' "

The clam was having a great time. Her abs hurt from laughing. Later, she would go home and write everything down in her journal, the reporting of this brunch so much more thorough and vibrant than her account of rejection. She did not know yet that this accumulation of words would one day mean more to her than her heartbreak. These words would become the official record. Having plumbed the dark nothing below, she was now recording the changes in light, the sun penetrating the inky blues, with shapes and contours reemerging in her consciousness.

The Family Unit

The clam decided she would return to Los Angeles, where she had grown up. When people can't figure out what they want to do, they usually return to what they know. She wanted to fetch the family car so she could drive it to New Mexico for the artist residency. When she'd learned of her acceptance earlier that year, she had been scattered between moving out and couples therapy and anxiety about money—she wasn't sure she would attend. Now she decided to go for it, broke or not. She would go to New Mexico in a month. One had to move on. A new beginning, a new start! When she thought about New Mexico, she thought about pink mesas and pancake moons and silent winter mornings. And, as she repeated to Sam, she wanted to be alone, alone, alone.

After she finished storing her few belongings in the closets and basements of various friends' homes, the clam went over to her younger sister Angela's for one final sleepover. Her sister lived in a tiny rented room in South Slope. The clam was lying on the lofted bed while her sister clacked away on her computer below. Angela was always working. She had a demanding full-time job as an assistant to a famous writer that required her to be on call, even late at night. The clam was so afraid to bother her. Though they lived in the same city, they rarely spent much time together. Angela could sneak in occasional lunch break walks, but her precious walking time was also needed for taking photographs—she was a photographer—so the clam had grown used to conversing in this disjointed, half-listening manner.

"At brunch, Sam's friends were talking about what their parents' houses looked like, and I couldn't remember, after Grandma died, what Mom and Dad did to the house," the clam was saying.

Angela *mm-hmmed* and clicked the mouse a few more times.

"What was it like when you went home in December?"

Angela looked up after a furious spurt of typing. "The house? Unrecognizable. They rearranged all the furniture and repainted the walls. Mom decorated it like a school. There's a world map in the living room and that waffle trim you use for classroom bulletin boards."

They both cackled at this. Their mom was such a workaholic that even in semiretirement from her job as a school principal, she still wanted to create a space that reminded you that you should be studying.

"What about Dad? Was it weird to have him at home?"

Their dad had recently returned home from Taiwan. For the past decade, he had been living in self-imposed exile there, first to write top-secret accounting software, then to complete a PhD in digital learning.

"Well, Dad doesn't leave his room. He just stays in there all day reading his wuxia novels. I was like, 'Dad, I'm never home. Don't you want to go on a walk with me or something? Don't you want to have dinner?' He ate by himself in front of the computer. He said what we were eating didn't agree with his stomach."

The clam had already heard a version of this when Angela reported it initially. During that visit home, she had begged him to please go outside, for her sake. Then, the day after she left, he wheeled the bicycle out of the garage and attempted a bike ride. He promptly crashed while navigating a curb and split his arm in half. A stranger had to call 911 for him.

"He really won't leave the house now. He says he's learned his lesson. Have you talked to them about the separation?" Angela asked.

"Not really. They still can't believe it."

"By the way, I saw him." Angela uttered the name of the husband, which the clam hadn't heard spoken aloud in a while. "He was walking in the park with a friend. He looked like he'd lost a lot of weight. I didn't say hi. I know he blames me. Last summer, he told me I had enabled you to make a bad decision."

The clam said brusquely that she didn't want to hear about how her husband was doing. His weight loss especially. She felt the panic rising.

"I get it. Rejection hurts," Angela continued. "Do you know about this guy who made it a project to get rejected a thousand times? It was like a performance art piece. To build up armor."

The clam changed the topic. "If the Camry is just sitting in the garage and Dad never goes anywhere, he won't miss it."

"But you're going to try to take it to New Mexico? Good luck," Angela said.

The clam understood. She would have to learn to reconstitute herself back into this original family unit, in which she had to ask *her parents* for things and be at *their* mercy. Marriage had temporarily sustained a mirage of self-sufficiency and aloofness; marriage had insulated her from asking for help, but she had merely traded one kind of dependence for another.

"He'll give in. He'll suffer some sleepless nights, but he'll get over it. I can wait him out," the clam said with a note of uncertainty in her voice.

Secret or Secrete

"**S**olitude is the best. Isn't solitude the best?" It was a cold December night, the last Saturday she would have in New York for the foreseeable future. The clam was standing in line outside the Guggenheim Museum, waiting to get in on free-admission Saturday. The Agnes Martin retrospective had already been on for weeks, but the clam hadn't had time to coordinate with someone to go. Then she realized she could just go by herself. Sam was right—she could learn to be alone, not rejected-alone, but alone-alone.

What she was learning: In a ticket line, alone-alone meant *feeling* rejected-alone even though you were just alone-alone. Alone in this setting was the apotheosis of entrapment. Everyone else had friends or significant others to hold their place, allowing them to wander off for a smoke or a snack. She was just clinging to her spot. She wished she had some hot beverage to keep her hands warm. But she had no money to splurge on beverages, so she buried herself into her turtleneck and resumed reading on her phone. In the last half hour, the line had expanded and contracted, forcing her to shuffle forward and back.

She was reading—trying to read—Agnes Martin's biography from various websites. She always took her museum visits too seriously, like she was trying to pass an exam. Anyway, it was a pointless review—she already knew most of these details about Agnes Martin. After all, she'd applied to the Wurlitzer Residency in New Mexico in large part because Martin had been their very first fellow.

As with all her girl-crush heroes, the clam liked to exaggerate the similarities between herself and Martin. They had both lived in Lower Manhattan, they were both teachers, and they both loved swimming. All in all, these details were minor and the likenesses stopped there. Martin was a person of extremity, and the biographies all said the same thing in the same reverential tone, emphasizing Martin's reclusiveness, renunciation, and restriction. Martin had suffered extensive emotional abuse as a child and endured long tracts of silence and solitude as a result. When she spoke, her words came out in Zen-like koans. She lived a "spartan existence" without the amenities of modern life.

Martin's first stay in New Mexico had launched her career. With the work she created there, she managed to win the approval of gallerist Betty Parsons, who sold enough of her paintings to allow Martin to relocate to New York City. But after a decade in New York, she began to suffer a series of breakdowns. Walking down Second Avenue one winter day, she overheard the first few notes of Handel's *Messiah* and fell into a trance. In another episode, she forgot who she was. Increasingly, she was suffering from symptoms associated with schizophrenia; she often heard "voices" that told her what to do. In 1967, after the death of her friend Ad Reinhardt and the end of an important romantic relationship with the sculptor Chryssa, Martin renounced art and New York completely and drove off in her pickup truck and Airstream camper. She later said, "I left New York because every day I suddenly felt I wanted to die and it was connected with painting. It took me several years to find out that the cause was an overdeveloped sense of responsibility."

She reemerged a year later in New Mexico. She took up residence on a solitary mesa, miles from any road. There, she built an adobe house by herself and cut down trees to build a log cabin studio. She lived like a desert monk, subsisting one winter solely on preserved homegrown tomatoes, walnuts, and hard cheese. Another winter, she ate only Knox gelatin mixed with orange juice and bananas. There was no electricity, no phones. Alone on her mesa, Martin began to paint again. The horizontality of the New Mexico landscape brought her back to her childhood, to the endless prairies of Saskatchewan. She drew long bands of graphite across the canvas, washed over with pale colors, like dawn breaking. Day by day, she returned to herself. "I paint with my back to the world," she said. In a later interview, she added, "My paintings are about merging, about formlessness . . . a world without objects, without interruption."

"Without objects, without interruption." The clam repeated the phrase to herself. "Without shores, without boundaries." She searched her mind, where did she read these two lines recently? There was an echo . . . somewhere. Ah. Weren't they the famous last lines of Italo Calvino's *Cosmicomics*? She did a quick search and pulled up a PDF off the internet, from the website of a Chinese blogger. She searched the phrase "Without shores, without boundaries." There it was. At the very end of the page.

"The Spiral" is the last story of Calvino's first volume of *Cosmicomics*, a collection of twelve fables that were his response against humanist realism and toward science and myth. The story is told from the point of view of the space-time traveler Qfwfq, who appears in this story as a mollusk. Qfwfq begins his tale by recounting his childhood immersed in the sea, before he realizes there is such a thing as form. A nostalgic, wonderful time when all evolution was open to him, and he could just enjoy being on a rock, "flat mollusk-pulp, damp and happy." He could simply cling to the rock and let waves bring the wonders of the sea to him; he could take it all in, all at once. "If you compare yourself with the limitations that came afterwards, if you think of how having one form excludes other forms, of the monotonous routine where you finally feel trapped, well, I don't mind saying life was beautiful in those days."

But as he grows older, he learns to discern different signals from the sea, and henceforth his suffering begins. One day he becomes aware of "others"—similar others and hostile others, but also *female* others. He hungers for the signals of one female other in particular, but he can't be sure they truly understand each other. Suffering from the pain of his unrequited desire, he begins to secrete a shell—

It was then that I began to secret calcareous matter. I wanted to make something to mark my presence in an unmistakable fashion, something that would defend this individual presence of mine from the indiscriminate instability of all the rest. Now it's no use my piling up words, trying to explain the novelty of this intention I had; the first word I said is more than enough: *make,* I wanted to *make.* . . . So I began to make the first thing that occurred to me, and it was a shell.

Secret calcareous matter, or secrete? The clam paused here. The word should probably be "secrete" there, but a typo in this online PDF read "secret," and posed a question. To *secret* is to hide away, to *secrete* is to exude—

The museum ticket line was suddenly moving rapidly forward now. It appeared they were all getting let in at once, for whatever reason. The clam was rudely shoved from behind. Everyone quickly gathered up their various tote bags from between their feet, prodded onward by the museum employees. There was again a brief pause at the entry as the security guards checked the contents of their bags.

She resumed reading—

Naturally, I had no way of controlling the form of what I was making: I just stayed there all huddled up, silent and sluggish, and I secreted. I went on even after the shell covered my whole body; I began another turn; in short, I was getting one of those shells all twisted in a spiral, which you, when you see them, think are so hard to make, but all you have to do is keep working and giving off the same matter without stopping, and they grow like that, one turn after the other.

So Qfwfq secreted in secret; he secrets away to secrete. Nobody sees him. Silent and sluggish: That's how he makes his beautiful shell. He must work in solitude; he *makes*. He *makes* and puts everything he feels about *her* in the shell, and everything he knows about himself. And with his shell, he can now *stand apart*.

It was like when somebody lets out an exclamation he could perfectly well not make, and yet he makes it, like "Ha" or "hmph!," that's how I made the shell: simply to express myself.

Qfwfq makes his shell, turn by turn, and now five hundred million years have elapsed. He looks up from where he is and observes his surroundings. From his rock along the shore, he sees a train vanish into a tunnel; he sees an ad to visit Egypt; he sees an ice-cream cart try to pass a truck on the road; he sees a hive of bees searching for a new home; he sees seagulls, anchovies, a Dutch girl listening to the radio; and even now, after five hundred million years—

It is surely she I hear singing and whose image I look for all around, seeing only gulls volplaning on the surface of the sea where a school of anchovies glistens and for a moment I am certain I recognize her in a female gull and a moment later I suspect that instead she's an anchovy.

The clam felt herself emitting saline at this mysterious section of the story, italicized and bracketed in parentheses. Five hundred million years later, Qfwfq has made his mark, and the world has changed. He has successfully secreted his shell, but for whom? He still sees her everywhere. His yearning has not subsided. That was the depth of the clam's feeling too. All week: The heart squeezed unbearably as she walked down the street, as though crushed from underwater pressure. She had lost a friend, a love, an idea of a possible future. She simply saw him, everywhere.

The clam opened up her bag to be inspected by the security guard. He paused and looked at her a moment, then waved her by. She thought she sensed a softening in his face. What was in her expression that made him look at her with such pity? She was quickly ushered inside. She stood in the middle of the ground floor as everyone milled about, looking up at the oculus spiraling above. At this vantage, the Martin paintings looked like faded little postage stamps, mounted upon envelopes of white. She felt like she was standing inside a sun-bleached shell, Qfwfq's shell, perhaps, that took him five hundred million years to secrete. She already knew that the nautilus shell had supposedly been the inspiration for the building's architect, Frank Lloyd Wright. The curvature felt organic, correct. It was one of the last buildings he designed before his death. She'd read that Eric Lloyd Wright, Frank's grandson, recalled, "Every Sunday at breakfast he'd give us a talk . . . and sometimes he would have placed before him a whole bunch of seashells. And he said, 'Look here, fellows. This is what nature produces. These shells all are based on the same basic principles, but all of them are different, and they're all created as a function of the interior use of that shell.' "

The interior use of the shell—the animal inside. The purpose of the shell was to protect and also, to say. To secret and to secrete.

Hide and exude. The shell was a technology that allowed you to do both.

Many animals must go into seclusion before they emerge, she thought as she edged up one of the smooth spiral ramps. She had tried to emerge too hastily—that was her mistake. She had leapt out into danger and desire had dealt a hurtful wound. She would go away, secret away, to secrete. Focus on her art. Self-sufficient. Untouched. Something that needs nothing.

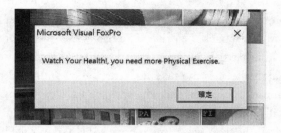

Sedimentary Behaviors

You know the best trick when you are feeling yu men, stuffy stuffy, is find some neighborhood on Google Maps, go to street view, and take a walk. This character, men 悶, shows your heart is trapped indoors, under the house. With street view, however, I can take my heart anywhere in the world while I stay inside! This morning, I already stroll for many hours, starting in Grand Army Plaza in Brooklyn and go all the way down to Sunset Park, where my younger daughter Anchi works. I look here and there, at the restaurants and stores. Make sure nothing too dangerous in her surroundings. Finally, when I see a street I like, I go to Zillow to look at the real estate prices. I study the property taxes, the area's schools, and where I can take a walk to the park. Is it a good place to make a life? I like Sunset Park. Many Asians there. I can go to grocery every day just by walking.

Each day I have my harmless little fantasy, that's it! My daughters think it is a strange waste of time. Instead of cheering my use of technology innovation, they say, *Why don't you go explore the real world with your legs! To get more physical exercise!* They say, *It is not healthy to stay in front of the computer all day!*

Why my hobby should be so offensive to them? I say, *When you are old man like me, your main principle is conserve.* I already walk to grocery store and back every day. Some days I go to the bank or the arboretum for my walk. I have a membership, so after five visits I already earn back the price. The rest is free, a gift for me!

Last month when my younger daughter Anchi come home, even though she sees me take my street view walk and then my arboretum walk on weekend, she still keep scolding me nonstop. She say, if I am *curious about Brooklyn*, why don't I visit? Me and Ma Ma don't have to work much now, so why don't we have *fun*! Go on *vacation*! Come to *New York*! *But I am already enjoying*, I say. Street view walking is cheap, easy, and safe. My favorite kind of fun: no crime risk, and I do not need to spend money or use any resource. Anyway, last time I went to Rome and Athens I got my wallet and passport stolen.

In any case, she was warning me consistently, if I neglect to use my muscle, I will become weaker, and maybe eventually I won't be able to stand up from the toilet. Well, that may be. I am not so unreasonable. After she left, I thought, *Okay, perhaps I follow her advice*. I take the bicycle out of the garage, thinking I will ride down to the new German grocery store, Aldi, where I heard sells one-dollar bread. Then, I don't know what happen, but when I was entering the parking lot, I flip over on the handlebars and broke my arm in half. That accident cost me thousands of dollars. 現在我乖乖的待在家裡. After learning my expensive lesson, I obediently stay home.

Now that I have walked several hours on street view, I am preparing to take a break. I want to stretch my legs and maybe go to the kitchen for snack, when my phone ring. I see that my big daughter Yi-an is calling. I always feel nervous every time she call me, because usually, she call her ma ma to chat, and when she call me, it is because she want something or she has some trouble.

Definitely it make my heart jump, but this is why I always have my phone nearby even though I don't like talk to anybody. For these situations when my daughters or wife need help.

"Hello?"

"Yi-an, gan ma?"

"Dad!"

(She always talk to me like I am her employee or misbehave dog.)

"Dad! I am going to ask you something but don't be stressed out, okay?"

(Why she always start every stressful question by commanding me, *Don't stress out!* Now I feel even more stress than before.)

"Could I come borrow your car to drive to New Mexico for a few months?"

"What?"

"I need to go to New Mexico for a writing residency, and I think it's better if I have a car. So I can get around more easily."

"What you saying? New Mexico? When?"

"I'm coming home in a few days."

Wah. I am so shock, I cannot even respond. But before I tell you why I respond the way I respond, I need to tell you something important. My daughter has a very bad habit. For almost her whole life, whenever she need something big, she always wait until last minute in order to force me to give it for her. Almost like, you know, hostage situation. One time when she was a little girl, I was dropping her off at orchestra, very rushed because we are late, and right before she was about to leave the car, she said suddenly, *Daddy, I need three hundred dollars to go on orchestra trip,* and right there, she push the empty check into my face for me to sign!

What? Three hundred dollars? Orchestra trip?

She really know how to torture me! Of course, I cannot even fight back because the cars behind us are honking so aggressively I don't even have time to curse her. Anyway, I sign the check. She is like hunter waiting for victim, waiting to push you into her trap! A cruel strategy that might even kill me. I told her so many times I have irregular heartbeat since I was very young, but she either forgot or she don't care.

As she grows older, she begin to revise her technique—asking me for money at a public dinner, so I must reply in front of everyone if don't want to throw my face away, or telling me her plan after she already promised something so she cannot throw her face away. One time, she even promise her school politics club she will drive them to Santa Barbara for overnight trip! What? The money amounts only getting bigger and bigger. She always had many excuses about why she needed something terribly or she will not survive in competitive America. A program at USC, then Stanford, then Georgetown, each one over $3,000. And her phone bill! When it arrived I almost heart attack again. She was talking on her cellphone carelessly not paying attention to significant roaming charges, and when I got the bill it said $550.

She knows I love the good schools and cannot say no! But everything she want, she argue was totally necessary. Not just for academical success in America, but she must also ask money for a surfboard (what?!) and even a trip to Peru! What? I argue forcefully, almost like begging, *Why a young girl need to take such risk? You cannot even speak Spanish! Why should you go into the jungle! Nothing there want you to be there, so you stay home! Do you wanna dengue fever?*

These American girls, I do not understand them. Their life already such chaos and insecurity and they still keep thinking to have fun. Why she need to go to New Mexico? Ever since she break up with her husband she must work so many different jobs and I don't know how she pay her bills. I asked her some weeks ago, *Are you sure you need to divorce?* Because when she describe their relationship issues to me, it seem so insignificant. It is not like they have any real troubles. Not like me and Ma Ma in the past.

Now however she seems to have some real problems. I overhear her complaining to her mom about no time to write, no jobs, so much stress. Why she can't settle down to find a real job instead of going all the way to New Mexico?

No, this time I will not allow such irrational behavior.

"Why you need to go to New Mexico to write? Why you don't come home and write?"

"Why would I go home if I have the opportunity to go to New Mexico?"

"If you are so desperate to pay rent, you can pay me the rent. Then, you also don't need the Camry, ha ha."

"The residency is rent-free. Lots of famous artists have gone there. It's an honor. A house of your own without any distractions so you can work."

"Work? Do they pay you? Ha ha ha. Is it really call work if nobody paying you?"

Now she is quiet. Good! I win. This daughter totally lack basic practical thinking. I don't know where she even obtain these ideas about what is good and what is bad.

"Daughter, listen to me. I will send you listing of some places that are less expensive than Brooklyn. For example, I see many listing in a place call Yonker. Do you know Yonker? Why not rent a small cheap apartment there? You mustn't have to live in that cold warehouse. Then you focus on finding a job and forget about this New Mexico idea."

"I'm going to New Mexico. I already decided. If you won't lend me your car, fine. I'll bike there. My co-worker just biked across the country no problem."

Now she sound quite mad actually. Well, I don't care. I will not surrender this time. I already open up Google to search up about this place. She will not take the car, but if she bike, isn't that more dangerous . . . ? Hm. I must think about it more. Before, she always convince me she is making the right decision about her life, she is doing the "American" thing, while I am doing the "immigrant" thing, but now her credibility is totally gone! If she was so good at making proper decisions, then her situation would not be like it is anyway.

To end the conversation, she say she will see me on Tuesday when she come home. That means I better hurry to think of my defense. Once again, she return to give me headaches, but I know her ma ma will be happy to see her.

Clam Games

When the clam was a child, she used to play a private game with herself whenever she found herself approaching the front steps of her home. The game was called Locked Out! and the objective was to guess whether she would be able to enter her home that afternoon or not. According to rules that no one understood, especially not the young clam, the clam's grandmother would occasionally refuse to open the door, so the clam would have to spend hours pounding and begging, "Hey, Ah Mah! It's me, Yi-an!" This pathetic pounding action reminded her of those Chinese melodramas her grandmother liked to watch, in which a disgraced woman would be shut out of the family compound and would have to pound, just like this, as though on the rigid chest of an unfeeling lover. The clam wondered about the cumulative effect of the daily reenactment of this small drama. She wondered what she had done to deserve this. It was easier to think this was a fun game her grandmother enjoyed playing, not out of malice but out of boredom. The clam would glimpse a flash of an eyeball at the window's peephole, then hear the sound of slippers, slip-slapping away. Their game had begun. It would be early evening; swim practice was over; she was cold and ravenous and needing to pee. She squeezed her thighs together, willing herself not to piss her pants. Although, if she allowed herself to give in to the urge, that too could be subsumed into the parameters of the game. To be locked out, not understanding the justice of it, but burning with a spectacular sense of spite that could justify any act. *I'll make my knuckles bruise today,* the clam thought with a smile. *I'll really make it hurt.* And then, without warning, the spell would be broken and her grandmother would be standing at the door. Only one constant remained: At the end of the game, it was obligatory to act as though one had not been playing the game. *I didn't hear you!* her grandmother would scold. *I waited all afternoon, worried to death!* Only later did the young clam understand that her self-doubt and guilt were all integral to the game's design.

Now the clam stood before this door to her childhood home, not yet prepared to knock. Her butt muscles clenched and unclenched. Here she was. Back in this fraught place where she had always been subjected to the unpredictable whims of her grandmother and her strange psychological games. She looked down at the cracked concrete steps covered in faded Astroturf. To the left, a sagging shoe cabinet bulged with pairs of old shoes. A withered jade plant clung to life in a planter. The wooden door that she had knocked on so many times was now patchily stained in mismatched hues of brown, its porthole window taped over in the same orange construction paper, now impressionistically sun-bleached, like tie-dye. Her dad had once cut two little peepholes into the paper so that her grandmother could scrutinize whoever was at the door without being seen.

Her grandmother had passed away years ago, but this time, she knew, she had her own parents to confront. Her parents who were home now in a way they had not been when she was growing up. Before, they were both so busy running their respective businesses: her dad doing his computer thing, her mom the principal of a buxiban afterschool, Futurelink. Hundreds of kids once passed through there, getting their homework checked every weekday afternoon, learning Chinese on the weekends. Her mom was a local celebrity whenever they went to 99 Ranch Market. Random children running up to her, tugging on her shirt: *Hi, Principal Marie!* In the hours after school got out, her mom would be occupied at her command station, either picking up kids with the big school bus or fielding panicked calls. There were a million things to do and her mom had to do all of them. That was the nature of the immigrant business. If the clam ever tried calling during this high-stakes time—times when she was locked out, for instance—her mom might pick up, hear that it was only her daughter on the line, and hang up.

Her parents came home late every night. What did the young clam and her grandmother eat for dinner? She couldn't remember. Her grandmother never prepared food for her, never spoke to her, so it was probably something microwaveable, or maybe cereal. By the time her parents and her baby sister came home, the clam would have put herself to bed. On the rare occasions when their worlds collided, the clam couldn't help but feel like a ghost who had just wandered in from another dimension, unseen, unheard. Typically, she would overhear the adults discussing money. It was always about this topic, about their survival. They cut the payroll. They cut their expenses. They had bills to pay, and the pressure of these bills pressed down on them. So the clam did her homework and didn't dare ask for help. She knew her mom scrubbed the school's toilets herself. Her movements had this flinging, last-gasp quality. With her ropy muscles of pure instrumentality, she swished the heavy mop down the empty hall.

Eventually, the young clam learned not to come home either, just like them. As she got older, she learned how to play Locked Out! on her own terms, locking herself out against her family. Why bother hoping they'll show up for this recital or that swim meet or school function? She learned to insinuate herself into other families. She always had a ride, a sandwich, a reliable place to rest. She latched on to teachers and friends and joined extracurriculars like her life depended on it. She was in fourth grade when she learned how to do this. She did this year after year.

Okay, here goes, she thought. *Let them see what's become of me.* She knocked loudly.

In an instant, she heard multiple locks unlocking. Oh yes, how could she have forgotten! There was a battery of locks, from bottom to top, four locks in all. Her body reawakened to the sound of these routine movements: swiveling the crowbar thing out of its drilled hole in the floor, unbolting the heavy-duty lock above that, sliding the golden chain out of its track, then making sure the little nub attached to the doorknob stayed depressed as you turned and pulled.

The door opened.

Dad. Dad?

They stood facing each other in the doorway. She was surprised by his odd getup: a felted, cape-like garment fastened at the neck and draped down like a tablecloth. One arm seemed to be perched on a hip, and the resulting pyramidal shape made him look like some kind of operatic limpet. He was also wearing a bulbous blue knit hat, his glasses padded around both temples with a bright, spongey material, emergency orange.

"Whoa. Why are you wearing that weird cape?"

"I can't move my arm after it's broke, so Mom made it for me." He lifted the cape to reveal a fleece cummerbund thing underneath. "It's warm."

Oh, right. His broken arm, from when he rode his bike to Aldi and flipped over the handlebars.

Now her mom appeared in the doorway, looking shockingly robust and ox-like. Red cheeks. Healthy! Were her cheekbones always so amazing? Retirement looked great on her. Her mom had a measuring tape draped across her neck, sewing scissors in one hand. Wow. She's even sewing? She has enough leisure time for *hobbies*?

They dragged her few pieces of luggage inside. "The rest is coming via Amtrak!" the clam volunteered. "Very cheap!" Her dad would want to know what everything cost to enable her arrival. The clam also felt her mom taking stock of her appearance, readying to say something about her recent weight gain.

The clam looked around the house. Somehow, in her mind, the house was cobwebbed, with dusty shafts of light and bedsheets covering the furniture. She'd half expected to see her grandmother sitting at her habitual chair in the living room, the lead monolith, the static object, repulsing the edges away. For decades, the family had hurried from room to room, nobody daring to linger in her presence. There had been an oily stain on the wall, behind the armchair, marking where her grandmother rested her head. That was gone. Her sister was right. The house was unrecognizable.

Now her mom motioned for them to sit down at the dining table, still covered in a plastic tablecloth, another taboo and uncomfortable thing the clam was not used to either. Her dad hovered uncertainly behind, his hands propped on the back of her mom's chair. "Are you hungry?" On the lazy Susan, there were various stale-looking snacks in repurposed plastic containers: roasted peanuts, chocolate-covered raisins, Ritz crackers in sleeves. It was another part of the clam's conditioning to never eat anything that was just lying around, as this was another of her grandmother's bizarre games. The grandmother used to leave snacks around as an excuse to unleash her fury. The snacks would be a test, but the rules were always changing. Sometimes to pass into safety you had to eat the snacks; other times if you ate the snacks you would be smacked in the head. *Are you hungry?* No, she wasn't falling for that. Whether she ate the snacks or she didn't, the snacks were a constant source of terror. Even after all these years, the entire house still felt like a minefield. Every atom of her body wanted to flee the premises.

"Are you hungry?" her mom asked again, pushing the snacks forward.

"No, I'm okay."

They sat in silence for a while. How were they going to begin?

NO ! DO'NT DO IT!

You cannot believe, okay? How correct I am at prediction! I tell you honestly, every year, my daughter get more and more extreme with her requests to push me beyond my limit, to my breaking point!

So, after my daughter's arrival, the first thing I notice is how unhappy she looks! Her spirit seem totally broken! Right away, I cement my determination to straighten her out. However, instead of getting down to business, her ma ma keep bringing out dishes of this and that, and the two of them are like even preparing to shoot the shits. How can they relax when there is such an urgent crisis?

I did not even sit down, because I did not want to get too comfortable.

"Dear daughter, do you still plan to go to New Mexico?" I ask her immediately. Her ma ma has brought out a plate of sliced grapefruit. They both look a little surprised by my direct question.

"Do you think it is safe for you?" I ask. "Because when I walk around the city Taos on street view it looks like it should be called No Population. I checked the crime statistics and it is worse than Brooklyn. How come you choose a fellowship somewhere like that?"

Right away when I bring up danger, daughter seems to begin to shut me out. I know this conversation about crime always make her unhappy but I don't understand why.

Her mom pushes the grapefruit forward for us. "好了好了. She's grown up, she knows what she's doing!"

They are just eating the grapefruit a little now. Quietly.

"Hey, Yi-an," I start again. "Did I ever tell you about, when I was your age, the first time I went to America?"

"Yeah."

"Yeah? I tell you again, okay? Basically, when I was thirty, I was headhunted by boss of a shoe company in America because I knew a special programming language, and they want me to set up their national networking system. At that time, Ma Ma and I wanted desperately to get one foot in America . . ."

"I know, I already heard this story . . ."

"Before I left, I was so excited! Remember, I had some fantasies about America! However, immediately at the transfer airport, I was called Chink Chink Jap Jap! Everywhere I go. Hey, Chink! Hey, Jap! Then when I arrive to the main San Francisco office with my suitcases and stuff, Robert Camel tells me I cannot stay at the company apartment, because his fiancée need to live there. Before, I imagine we are friends, but turns out he really see me like a competitor or enemy, there to take his job or become his supervisor . . .

"Anyway, thinking I must make good impression with the big boss, I started working right away with my luggage next to my desk. During break, I call Ah Mah for contact information of some 道親 at the temple. One lady say she has rental in West Oakland. Okay. I meet her in Chinatown at nine P.M. when she get off work and she drove us there.

"And do you know what happen after? In all my years in America, I never felt more betray. After I denied her dirty rental, she says, 'Fine, in that case, I will not drive you back. Take the BART back downtown by yourself!' Then she leave me all alone in West Oakland BART!

"Imagine, okay? Midnight in West Oakland! I have all my suit-cases, three thousand dollars of cash savings in my suit pocket, all the money me and Ma Ma save in our life. Everyone pass by, look at me like, Do you want to die? I see my life gone in one minute.

"Anyway, basically, after that first day, I realize America is like, so harsh. I had to live in a dangerous motel in Tenderloin for some weeks until the cleaning lady at the office rent me her family's apartment in the Mission. But nobody else helped me! Not boss, not Mom, not same-country people. Everyone is out to get some benefit. You must protect yourself all the times, prepare for the worst, or you will not survive."

After my speech, I look to her to judge her response. Will she dare to ding zui at me?

"Daughter. Your illusions and your reality are very different. You are not so young anymore. You need to start to act based on reality, not idealism. You already gave up so much time to try to pursue your dream, but reality is sacrificing your impulsive wishes to do the practical thing for the long term. The law school sugges-tion is not too late. This time, you are in the midlife crise. You have to choose the right way this time! Right now, you have no good job and nowhere to live. But you are not in such bad shape because you don't have wife, children, parents depending on you, not like me. Back in our generation, we took necessary risk for survival. What about you? You cannot keep taking risk after risk for unnecessary reasons!"

Okay, was this not a good strategy? Maybe I mess up my speech because my sleep was not continuous last night, so my brain is not working? I see she is not responding to my lesson, and apparently I say something hurtful. As I predict, tears start to come out of her eyes and run down her face silently like a dripping rock. Looking at her like this, I can feel my own face becoming very hot.

"Daughter, listen to me. You must consider, maybe you are be-ing too dramatic with your midlife crise? 這個沒有什麼大不了. You say he has a hot temper and too controlling et cetera et cetera? So what? Your husband is a good enough man and you shouldn't ask too much. At least, when you were together, you had some financial security."

Now I see her mouth seem to become very tight, almost like her mouth is sinking and disappearing into her face. Oh no. But to my shock, Marie actually jump in to support me!

"What Dad says is right. Don't make the decision too early. Marriage is not always perfect. You two need to try to adjust," her mom says.

"Yes, yes." (I was so happy to be supported!) "All we say is, you need to make more effort to become more secure, not less secure. Try to compromise with him instead of going to High Crime New Mexico, okay! Just this morning, I read story about drug addict man who smashed another guy's head with a brick!"

Now she speak up forcefully. "Those crime reports are racist! Can you not talk to me about crime?"

"Why knowing about crime should be racist? You are Asian girl in America. Do you imagine you can escape your vulnerable look?"

"This residency is an important opportunity for my career. I'm going. If you don't want to lend me your car, that's fine. But I'm not asking for your permission to go."

"What career do you think you have? Do you think your writing hobby is a career?"

At this, she mumble something so quietly I cannot even hear. "What?" She is silent. I demand again, "What?" But she doesn't want to repeat her rude comment.

Since she refuses to talk anymore, we are in a total silence like forever. Then I feel such pain in my chest I must retreat to my room. I go to my corner and close the door shut and I open my computer and open the search screen. I can hear them outside talking, probably about me. All the time, I have to play bad guy. I'm too old for this job! I cannot even click on the window to continue reading my wuxia novel.

Why trying to protect her from suffering should make me feel like a bad dad? I am not even thinking to use her for my own benefit. I am only thinking of everything for her own benefit. My own parents always use me for their benefit, and I told myself, I will not repeat this for my children.

Why must we fight every time we see each other? What did I say wrong?

Why, when I am only trying to prevent the suffering I experienced, my children say I am the one hurting them?

Shell Computing

There he goes, the clam thought. *Not even half an hour home and already a huge blowup. Didn't I expect this would happen?*

"Don't cry, girl." Her mom was rubbing her back. "You are tired. Go rest now."

The clam took her things to the "guest room" and began to unpack. Now all three of them were in their separate rooms; the house was quiet; she would fall back on years of practice. She knew how to freeze, to function, to distance, to compartmentalize, to keep going. To go to the numbing place. She could do the dishes, finish her homework, write that piece. This cold war business was what she remembered of home.

How ironic, though, that she should now be assigned to the so-called inner sanctum of the house. This "guest room," which had formerly been her grandmother's room, where the curtains were always drawn and the clam was forbidden to enter unless it was to deliver hot water bottles and medications. After her grandmother's passing, it had been like entering an enclosed tomb for the first time. The clam had looked around the room with a sense of wonder. She had never really studied the detailing of the mahogany furniture, or the closets crammed with chi paos. She helped her mom drag the armoire out into the center of the room and opened up musty drawers filled with objects of an invisible past: a collection of combs, silk scarves, makeup bags, tiny shoes, cameras, photographs, and journals, each item wrapped in layers of plastic. The plastic had seemed to act as a preservative against time, keeping these items from age. Her grandmother had been a young woman once. She had wielded her beauty like a weapon. And perhaps it was the loss of this femininity, this power, that was the source of all her grief, and from which she derived pleasure in exacting revenge. Time was ruthless; she would be too.

The clam felt a sting of regret now that she opened up the empty dresser drawers to put her own clothes into them. She and her mother had thrown away so many of her grandmother's objects. They had wanted to purge the house of any trace; they had wanted to forget her immediately. They didn't even bother to take pictures. Sorting for keeps, sorting for donation, and tossing (mostly tossing), they would try to make sense of what they were finding. Pieces of jewelry hidden in nooks and crannies, tucked in a shoe, wrapped in a handkerchief. Six thousand dollars in bills, disguised in a bag to look like trash. What were these notebooks? Written in tidy Japanese script. Her diaries. Here were Grandpa's notebooks from when he was sent to a reeducation camp. Her mom flipped through them. What were these long numbers jotted down in a ledger, these tremendous bank transactions? Oh, that was probably when Grandma was running an illegal underground bank. Her own sister ran away with the borrowed money. That's why Dad's siblings had to start making money so young, so Grandma could pay off her debts.

Their generation's lives were totally ruined overnight by war, the clam's dad once said. They developed the strategy of not feeling any connection and only caring about surviving. One minute they own everything in Shin Dian that you could see from the top of the hill, the next minute they were starving because there's no rice to eat. One minute they believe they are Japanese, the next minute they are Chinese or maybe Taiwanese. They do not know what language to think in. One minute the Nationalists are evil murderers and the next minute they are part of them. One minute they are running from American bombs and the next minute serving tea to the soldiers. One minute Taiwan is a democratic country that the West can deal with, the next minute Nixon is in China and we are orphans from the United Nations. Can you imagine? That generation had absolutely no sense of security in their lives. That's why they were like that.

The clam finished unpacking her things now and sat on her grandmother's bed. This custom-made bed was imported at great expense from Taiwan. Her grandmother always wanted her bed to be as hard as could be; she was so used to sleeping on tatami. In an attempt to make it softer for the clam, her mom had stuffed lumpy comforters underneath the fitted sheet. This gesture struck the clam as notable. In the past, coming home for a visit, the rooms would be covered in dusty bedsheets, because her mom would not have time to clean. *We are not strangers,* her mom would say, before rushing back to work.

Now the old gestures of care resurfaced. Her mom had offered her snacks and cut-up fruits. That was more than she could have afforded in the past.

The clam stretched out on the lumpy bed. She noticed the empty patch on the wall: A portrait of her grandparents as a young couple had once hung behind this mahogany dresser, she remembered. They were both wearing traditional Japanese garb, with a background of pink sakura flowers and a park bench. The portrait had been used in the funeral ceremonies of both of them, ten years apart.

The only family member who didn't attend her grandma's funeral was her dad. All the other aunties and uncles were there, plus the cousins, and former friends from the temple. The clam came home too, and spent days making preparations with her aunts. One of their jobs was to fold pastel-colored hand towels into a cheerful fan shape, with a piece of ribbon tying it together. It was customary to give attendees a fresh towel at the end of the ceremony.

The aunties sat around the table and they told her stories of their childhood. The clam noticed a common trait that they shared with her dad, which is that they giggled in between the recounting of horrific details, one-upping one another with tales of woe.

"Ah Mah didn't want me. She called me a little thief because I had a lazy eye. She starved me on purpose. She had wanted a boy! Ha ha!"

"After they lost all that money, we had to work all the time. I used to carry lunchboxes to the soldiers on the base, running back and forth up the hills. Once, I fainted, I was so hungry! He he! The soldiers would buy us food out of pity. Sometimes we just ate rice and soy sauce. Of course, we gave all the money to Ah Mah."

"Yi-an, do you know Grandpa used to force me to work day and night, to earn money for his political activities? I would come home exhausted in the evening, and he would force me to swallow a Japanese stimulant and snake gall! Gulp! Ha! That way I could do piecework all night. That's how—ha ha ha—I injured my eyes and became almost blind."

Relaying this, the clam's aunt had tears streaming down her own face but she was laughing hysterically, unable to breathe.

Whenever her dad showed up in these stories, it was often to show how sensitive and helpless he was. They remembered him as their little brother, this little boy, unwashed and unfed, shooting marbles in the dirt. He had a soft heart that got hurt too easily, they said.

"Your dad used to see Grandpa throw me under the table to kick me in the stomach. One day I couldn't take it anymore. When I reached the road, I heard a little voice calling out, 'Wait!' It was your dad running to catch up to me! He was about four years old. Stubby little legs. Snot streaming down his nose. He said, 'I am running away with you. If you run away, I will come with you!' "

With his soft heart, and his wife's soft heart, they had willingly borne the responsibility of caring for their elderly parents. Filial piety. They took their roles so seriously. None of the aunties faulted him for not showing up to the funeral. They knew what the past three decades had cost him. That he had escaped to live in exile made sense to them. They only felt sorry for his wife, left behind, who did the laundry and cooked and cleaned and served like the obedient daughter-in-law she was educated to be.

That's when the room was redecorated into a guest room, after the big purge. At some point, the clam installed the curios cabinet now hanging on the wall. In each cubbyhole, the clam placed various objects: seashells, a brain coral on a wooden pedestal, collected rocks, a pair of cheating dice, antique scissors that belonged to Grandma, an expired Taiwanese passport, the ring box she had used during the wedding ceremony. She gazed emptily at her curatorial choices, as though they were arbitrary stand-ins for future precious objects, like those pictures of generic families in store-bought picture frames.

He didn't want to go to the funeral, and he didn't want to come to my wedding, she thought now. By then, she had stopped expecting him to show up to things, but this refusal to come to her wedding, a supposedly happy affair, still managed to surprise her.

Fathers go to their daughters' weddings, she'd said tightly over the phone. *It's a normal expectation. I'm not asking you for anything crazy.*

But why you need me there? he'd fought back. *This is your choice, not my choice! If you ask me, I think this wedding party and expense is all nonsense! What you want me to do, stand there and make stupid small talk?*

Do you want me to get you some anti-anxiety medication? Her voice had turned petulant and shrill.

Withdrawing, closing, retreating, hiding. Wasn't that *classic* clam behavior? His life had become circumscribed to such an extreme degree. What were his consolations, his joys?

Certainly, if *she's* a clam, it's because *he's* a clam. A clam family. Just look at her grandmother. She was a clam too. They were all

shut tight against one another. It was the classic Chen family cop-
ing mechanism.

And what about Dad's decade of disappearance, she thought.
*When he went away to Taiwan to write his mysterious computer pro-
gram, Shell Computing . . .*

Shell Computing!

She looked at the collected seashells now in the cubbyhole—
those seashells were his. Her dad had always referred to himself as
a creature trapped in a shell. He had named his program Shell
Computing! These past months, she had obsessively amassed her
archive of others who had transformed into animal-like creatures—
she had failed to remember the example of her own dad. The most
obvious story was right in front of her.

She was tired. She lay her head on the pillow. It was like she
went in for a routine inspection and learned that the damage was
more extensive than one ever thought possible. *I'll deal with this all
tomorrow,* she thought, and fell asleep.

What If

Last night I didn't sleep very good. I recall I was having some nightmares. I was on a kind of sinking ship, maybe the *Titanic*. My mom and older sister are loudly screaming for help, but I cannot reach them. I am floating on a piece of wood and they are drowning. When I wake up, I see my mom standing at the foot of the bed. She say, "你從來沒愛過我." Then she disappear.

The room is too cold. Too hot? I am awake and I can't figure out if I am too hot or too cold. Anyway, my body is hurting. I move my fingers around under the itchy cast.

Yesterday, did I walk too much?

I walked two miles to buy cabbage and bananas from the discount market. Perhaps I was sweeping up the leaves and sticks too long. I test my toes and wiggle them around. No pain yet. When I sweat too much, I always worry I will get gout.

Do I have a fever? Yes. I feel my forehead. A little sweaty.

I go to the bathroom and take three ibuprofen and check the temperature of the house. It is fifty-five degrees outside but sixty-one inside. Not bad. I hear Marie snoring loudly in her room. Why she can always sleep like a baby?

Used to be, my mom would wake up to check the locks and the temperature setting for the heater. Now she is not here, I must take it up.

I must be cold. Pull blanket on. No. Kick blanket off. Close the eyes. Open eyes and look around. Focus deep breathing. Tapping branches on the roof. What a weird sound.

My mom never opened the windows, afraid of outside, someone looking in. So I devise to cover up the windows with some construction paper that has a small hole so she can peek through.

The construction paper was orange. After we cover up the windows, all the light in the house look orange.

My daughters say the scientific terminology for Grandmom's personality is call OCD. To explain why she must constantly check the locks and the windows and the temperature setting and get so mad if we touch her special bowl and chopsticks. Why she must boil the water many times before she can drink. Why she must stick to such a rigid routine she cannot even leave the house.

I say to my daughters, *Your generation is too obsess with mental disease label.* She is old woman, and old people always been that way. For example, look at myself. I am an old man now too.

Oh no. The tap tap tap noise begin once more. Is it someone? Sneaking around? Or raccoons again?

Last time, what a trouble! We had to spend $225 to call the pest eliminator.

The pest eliminator came and set up something call a "have a heart" trap. Next day, the trap captured a mom raccoon. You know the raccoon has hands like human. Five long skinny fingers. As her babies are still in the attic, she powerfully dig around the cage, reaching between the wire to reach the dirt. She dig and dig until all her fingers were bleeding.

Anyway, don't think about the raccoons. Not good for falling asleep. Think about nothing.

This is definitely my daughter's fault, disturbing my peace! Cannot believe Marie came into my room to scold me about not respecting and treating Yi-an as adult. Treat her as adult? She is still my daughter! Did my parents ever treat me with respect, like an adult? When we did not have control of our own bank account? If I want to buy anything, I have to get it approved by them? Okay, maybe I never learn how to be a parent! Yes, I never had good example! All of this is my fault!

Anyway, she definitely learn her bad financial planning from you, I said to Marie. *She's your daughter, I say you discipline her. I have nothing to do with it.*

Saying that made Marie mad and she went away to her room too. Finally! I am left alone! My body cannot take it.

At thirtysomething, my daughter is still trying to pull stunts. The worst consequence of my good providing is my daughter became too dreamy. I said many times to her, *You want to be a writer? What will you write about? Your generation never suffered, always enough to eat, a house to live. Never insecurity. What kind of deep literature can your life create? Also, you already miss your head start. Do you see all the most successful achieving artists? They have been practicing since tiny tots, so it's already too late for you! Look at Tiger Wood, Michael Jackson, Itzhak Perlman! They were trained by their fathers since two or three years old. How about you? You have the guts to become top cream, top brass? Better give up the illusion and make a practical decision, like getting real estate license or become a CPA.*

I remember one big fight, in middle or high school. The next morning, she had to go to the swim meet and her ma ma was crying and went to Denny's to write her a letter to say sorry. From us. Marie want me to apologize, but I refuse. What kind of system that is, when the dad must apologize to the daughter for teaching her sense?

I said to Marie, *Do I exploit her? Or beat her? Not like my mom try to exploit me my whole life, or my dad beating me for daring to disobey him. Do you know what my dad did when I played him a song I composed on the* 木琴? *He laughed in my face. I was so proud of my creations, I wanted to show him, to impress him. He slapped my head and said, "Don't waste your time."*

Money, money, money. My whole life, they only care about money. We are not children. We are like their ATM machines.

Well, maybe they were right. If I have the sense to become computer programmer and not a starving guitar player, maybe it is thanks to them.

No. I refuse to think I am so bad like my parents.

But daughter is stubborn too. It is a strong characteristic. I guess young people always want to prove they can achieve something by themselves. Endure the most challenge, the most extreme. I was the same when I was young. I had so much fire and ambition. Ziu pah biang. Back then, I had such big confidence I thought nobody would stop me.

Just consider how much risk I took when I was young! My first apartment in the Mission District, the first time I came to work in America. So dangerous! Not the Mission District like today. Back then it was like Wild West. I had three roommates, all guys. My next-door neighbor was a hooker. I remember she was always very sad. She always say, *Come on, man. I give you discount. You are nice.*

Scary males come around day and night. Sometimes she fight with her boyfriend and they use wine bottles to hit each other. I heard the shatter crashing through the wall.

How come I didn't call police? Ah, I don't know. I was stressing my own life, I don't remember irrelevant details. The day when my roommate and me are moving away from that apartment, we put the boxes in the hall, waiting for car to come. But those two are hitting each other with wine bottles again and their blood got all over our boxes.

My roommate. I remember that one day he discover something call lap dance? Wah. He was so excite. After that, he go to strip club a lots of nights. One day, I was up early in the morning, but he just came home, about four A.M. He was holding a big bottle of Sa Wei Long.

Sa Wei Long is a kind of antibiotic wash. He say, he got lap dance and now he has some problems. I say, why you need antibiotic wash after lap dance?

Ha ha. I was so stupid. Didn't know anything.

Well, not my choice. At that time, I had no time to explore, since, every day, work like death, over twelve hours, fourteen, sixteen, sometimes more.

American co-workers at the company called me "Chinese Iron Man" as I seldom eat. Drink . . . maybe.

Sunday off. I ride the BART all the way to the end, get off at all the stops.

In my spare time, I called Marie and Yi-an, who was already two years old. If Yi-an was sleeping, Marie would play the tape she recorded of her singing some songs. I knew I was missing everything. In my bed, I mound up the blanket and pillow to look like they are asleep there too.

I felt so guilty not being with them, sometimes I thought to bring them over as illegal immigrants. They were rejected at the U.S. embassy two times. She was crying on the phone when she told me.

I called once a week, at least. The international phone bill was definitely my biggest expense, over $200 a month.

Sometimes on the phone, their voice sound so far away, like they don't have enough breath to reach me all the way across the ocean.

I worked one and half years. By the end I have saved $45,000. And we use that money to move to America.

That's all I remember.

I think the details of my early work years is blurred as a protective mechanism to my current mental health because it is not joyful, ha ha.

I look at the clock again and see it's almost four o'clock. When will I ever sleep? I chant the mantra I learn recently from a show on Syfy channel. "It is always darkest before dawn!" I think the mantra means, before the light comes there is always much darkness, so just keep hope. After some time chanting the mantra, luckily I begin to feel a little sleepy.

YOLO

The clam was sitting on the floor of her room, contemplating the stack of books wedged between her feet. She had to winnow down the selection now that she had to fly to New Mexico. She picked up one title, flipped through it, then set it down on the "bring" stack.

Her dad was standing in the doorway, munching on apple slices left over from his sandwich. This sandwich he ate every day at the same hour involved apple slices, deli meat, or, when it was on sale, Spam. If no apples were available, then daikon radish was swapped in. Now that she thought of it, sandwiches were probably his favorite form of food because the contents were securely contained within two slices of bread.

He wouldn't approach so purposefully like this unless he's decided something, she thought. *He's come to tell me what he's concluded.*

"Yi-an . . ." he began slowly. "Is your residency's stove gas or electric? I would feel safer if it is electric. I don't advise you to use a gas stove, especially if the house is very small, and it's winter, and the windows are closed."

The clam was just trying to focus on her packing. *This is just insane,* she thought. *He is absolutely insane. His obsession with risk is even worse than I remembered. Are these the sorts of calculations he's weighing all day? No wonder he can't leave the house.*

"I researched a good cheap electric plate available for pickup at Sam's Club. Also, I have carbon monoxide detector."

She sensed him surveying her progress, peering anxiously over her shoulder.

"This room is not cold? Very comfortable?"

She nodded.

"The vent of this room does not work well, but I have extra space heater."

"I'm fine. Thanks though."

"Yi-an! Wah sai!"

She looked up, suddenly alarmed by his tone.

"Is that your expired Taiwan passport on the shelf?"

He pointed accusingly at the curios cabinet with the seashells and rocks. There was her old Taiwanese passport lying on top. She probably put it there years ago and forgot. He looked genuinely distressed . . . his face was getting red.

"Why don't you ever renew your passport like I say?!"

"Okay! I will . . ." (She couldn't restrain herself—) "But, why do I need to? My U.S. passport works just fine. Why should I travel with two passports when I can just use the U.S. one?"

"You never know! Wan yi!"

That old phrase again. *Wan yi,* one in ten thousand. *Wan yi what?* the clam thought. *Wan yi the world suddenly stops accepting U.S. passports and we have to flee somewhere? Wan yi I lose my citizenship or develop an untreatable disease that will require Taiwanese healthcare? Wan yi America becomes totally hostile to us and wants to put us in internment camps? He's convinced we aren't truly citizens here, so our American passports guarantee nothing. At any moment it could be stripped away.*

"Better safe than sorry!"

"Fine. I'll do it. I promise."

She got up from the floor and fetched the passport from her cubby in a demonstrative way and tucked it away in her bag.

"Good. Don't fight me! Next thing. I want us to go to Toyota dealership today to get one more key remote for the Camry. You need backup. What if you lock your keys in the car and can't get back in? Imagine. You are out in desert, no reception, very cold, the car's broke, weather bad, no one coming, only bad guys."

"Wait. You're letting me take the Camry?"

"We have to make lots of preparation before you go. After we get this extra clicker, we go to Pep Boys. I have a list. Then we take car to Dong Ming for tune-up. I want to get all new tires."

"You're letting me take your car?"

"Actually, I already have one extra clicker, but I want you to have one extra, and I can have one extra . . ."

"You already have three clickers, but you want to get a *fourth* clicker?"

He looked at her defiantly. "What's your point?"

With as much filial piety as she could muster, she kept her mouth shut and suppressed whatever she was feeling. *I am a good daughter, my father's daughter.* She nodded solemnly. She was getting what she wanted, so this was part of the bargain. She returned to her stack of books and happily placed them all in the "bring" stack. Wonderful! She knew he would come around! She smiled sweetly at him.

"However, I have one more requirement. My requirement is you must take Ma Ma with you to New Mexico. No, don't talk back! I don't mean take her to the residency, okay? Just to make sure you arrive safe and then she fly back."

"In that scenario, you'll have two precious family members in one fast-moving car. You always said it's too risky to travel together. You might lose two in one."

"What you mean fast car? No, you gonna drive *slow*. At first I was thinking to drive you *myself*, but if anything happen to me, who will manage the finances? Mom will become bankrupt and Anchi will become orphan in one minute."

The clam nodded and agreed. She would agree to any and all of his byzantine requirements until she was gone, then she could do as she wished. Satisfied, he shuffled off to get ready to go to the dealer.

Bring her mom? That was unexpected. Did he even ask before he made this pronouncement? He'd also essentially sacrificed Mom as the less-important party. Would her mom even want to go? They'd never traveled together. Mother-daughter road trip? Could be interesting.

She got dressed and went to the garage to wait for him. When she saw the Camry in the garage, it was clear he had spent all morning cleaning it—despite his broken arm. It now shone with a murderous brilliance. There was not a smudge of grease or speck of dirt in sight. It was a superstitious thing he always did. When you take care of cars, cars take care of you. That was his philosophy.

She wanted to cry. Then she saw him ambling down the garage steps. Implausibly, he was wearing a #YOLO baseball cap she had bought years ago as a joke from the 626 Night Market.

"Oh my god! Dad! Where did you find that thing? Do you know what YOLO means? It's perfect. It means, you only live once. That should be your mantra!"

She took out her phone to document it and he grinned sheepishly, not knowing how to pose for pictures.

He chuckled. "Ha ha. Good mantra. You only live once, so be careful."

At the Toyota dealership. He emerges from behind the shopping racks and presents her with a miniature pepper spray in a hot pink holster.

"Dad, no. I'm not carrying that thing around."

Without a word, he returns to the racks. He reemerges with a miniature pepper spray housed in a more subtly hued, camo-patterned holster.

At Pep Boys.

"You ever drive in snow before?"

"Yes," she lied.

"What you use? Snow chains?"

She struggled to recall details from novels she'd read about living in upstate New York.

"Yes . . . snow chains."

"Ice scraper?"

"Sure."

"Now we only need to find the emergency flares, jump kit, tire wrench, flashlight . . ."

At Sam's Club.

"Yi-an, the electric plates are over there."

"Oh, I asked the residency," she lied again. "They have electric stoves and carbon monoxide detectors too."

"That's lucky. How about new shoes? Sam's Club has good shoes. Skechers brand. I wish I could buy them but they are too big for my feet."

She looked at his shoes. He was wearing an old pair of Mom's leather loafers with panels cut out around the toe area. She could see his toes spilling over.

"Mom was about to throw this away. But I cut them to make it fit."

They went up and down the aisles. He grabbed toilet paper, a pallet of drinking water, sun umbrellas, a canister of gummy bears . . .

"Gummy bears? What's this for?"

"What if your blood sugar gets low when you're driving?"

At Dong Ming's.

"After this busy morning of chores, I will need to have some days to recover," he said while they waited for the car to get tuned up.

"But we barely did anything today!"

"I'm old. I can only do one or two things a day. Your mom always cram so many chores together, I get stressed."

"Like what?"

"She wants to return books at the library, then swing by to get grocery, then go to the bank, then go to the gym . . . That's four things in a few hours."

"You're not old. You don't qualify for AARP or Medicare. You can't even get the senior discount at Savers."

"I know. That's why I must conserve until that time."

"You're younger than Mr. Dong, and look at him crawling under the cars like that. He's so flexible."

"In Taiwan, when the young people on the bus see me, instantly they stand up and say, 'Here, uncle, sit down.' My PhD classmates all call me Uncle, Grandpa. My adviser also keep teasing me and calling me Old Man. Well, he is younger than me too."

"What's your PhD program again?"

"Using digital learning for education MBA."

"What are you planning to do with your PhD after?"

"These days, I only feel safe in Taiwan. Not like here. I am still waiting for my adviser to approve my latest paper so I can start my dissertation, then I will go back. For now, I am just waiting patiently until he approves the paper."

"Is that normal to wait so long?"

"I will keep waiting. Hey, are you hungry? You like the Taiwanese burrito at 99 Ranch Market, right?"

Inventory of items in the daughter's vehicle:

Portable jumping kit
Snow chains
Flashlights
Toolbox
Hat
Two umbrellas
Bungee cords

Emergency flares
Triangle reflector warning kit
Four gallons of drinking water
Tire wrench
Updated insurance information in envelope
New AAA sticker
Maps
Change for meters, at least $20
Rolls of toilet paper
Mason jar crammed with gummy bears

In the cup holder, tucked into a small Ziploc bag and labeled for clarity, the car keys, with a miniature-sized pepper-spray key chain. For wan yi.

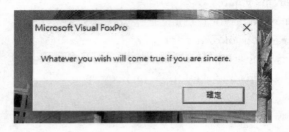

Happy as a Clam

$\mathscr{E}$ver since arriving to America, the only form of escapism available to the clam's mother, Marie, was the twenty minutes or so she spent on the toilet before going to work. Next to the toilet she kept a large stack of lifestyle magazines—*Better Homes & Gardens*, *Vogue*, *Sunset*—because her students at the afterschool were always peddling magazine subscriptions for some club or another. For her daughters, she subscribed to *The Economist*, *National Geographic*, and *Time*, but she reserved the homemaking magazines for herself. Every morning, she flipped through glossy pages of color-coordinated kitchens and luxury wristwatches. Then she would flush and "go back out into reality" to deal with her family's demands.

Her indulgences, in other words, were small. Though she'd always loved to travel, she was happy enough watching shows on PBS like *California's Gold* with Huell Howser and the one with Rick Steves traveling through Europe. She watched shows about the plum blossom festival on NHK, which was just like traveling through Japan. As for Europe, she'd seen replicas: At the Venetian in Las Vegas, she once saw the gondoliers rowing down the canal of chlorinated water in the hotel lobby, and the domed plaster ceilings and the projected sky in the Caesars Palace shopping mall.

Even cheap imitations could be transporting if you used a little imagination.

Now, Marie was finally taking a road trip through the American Southwest, all because her husband had commanded her to go. Mother and daughter were in the family Camry, driving on the 10 East heading toward Arizona. First stop, Joshua Tree. The clam looked over at Marie in the passenger seat, snacking on a bag of roasted peanuts in her lap. The papery flakes were all over the front of her sweater.

"Mom! What do you want to do once we get there? Go on a hike? Look at some art?"

Her mom thought about it. "Do you think they'll have sweet potato fries?"

"You've never been to Joshua Tree and the only thing you want to do is get sweet potato fries?"

"Didn't you ask me? That's what I want to do," she said defiantly.

They drove on in silence for a while, lost in the lull of the freeway.

"And a burger," she concluded. "Let's eat a big, drippy burger."

The clam laughed. Meat was their subversive activity, associated with untarnished freedom in America. Grandma had adhered to a militant form of Buddhist vegetarianism and any whiff of meat could send her into a paroxysm of rage. Marie often smuggled Burger King home to the girls. They would dash into the bathroom and eat in there, huddled like little animals.

"Terrible. Thirty years, we lived by the tyrant's rules! One time, I got in such a big fight with her because she accused me of secretly putting meat in her dishes! I said, 'What? Are you crazy? Why would I do that?'"

"I can't believe you put up with her for so many years."

"Ai yah, what choice did I have? Daughter-in-law must always surrender. It was my fate to suffer! We have this saying in Chinese,

逆來順受. It means, don't go against the current, just accept the difficulty."

"Remember how you had to come home every lunch break to cook different dishes for lunch and dinner because she complained there wasn't enough variety?"

"Can you imagine? Always blame, never praise. She called me a 爛好人, rotten person. How I never do anything correctly. The minute I married into Chen family, my life became like a prison. Every day, satisfying all her needs. I knew this the first time she told me I couldn't 回娘家 to see my parents for New Year holiday because I must cook for her."

"It's too bad you didn't fight back," the clam said.

"Fight back?" She snorted. "And make our family life even more miserable? No, I just bury myself and endure it. I thought, one day she will die and I will be free. Even if she lives to one hundred, then I will still be seventy-five, I can 忍耐, eat the pain."

Marie began humming an unrecognizable tune under her breath, a nervous tic, the clam knew.

"But we did many fun stuff, too, didn't we?" Marie insisted. "Remember one time we went to Solvang and got a pastry with pineapple in it? We even went apple picking."

"No, we didn't go apple picking because you guys said, 'Why should we pay to do physical labor when there are cheaper apples already picked at Sam's Club?' And Grandma and Grandpa wouldn't get out of the car so we ate our sushi rolls in the parking lot, and then we went home."

"Why do you, your sister, and dad always remember everything so negative? You guys inherited everything bad from him. Nothing from me. How about the time we went to Salton Sea?"

"You mean that ghost town that smelled like farts and fish with the condemned housing everywhere?"

"Ha ha! Oh yeah! I remember I looked out the window and thought, even living here would be better than living with Grandma!"

The clam laughed.

"Oh well. Now I'm free and I'm not even sixty-five. Lucky me!"

"If you're free, why don't you take yourself on vacation?"

"Vacation? How can I? I have to *work*!"

"What are you talking about? You're retired. You sold the business already. It's not your responsibility anymore!"

Marie ignored her and kept humming.

"Why don't you let Ms. Mary be the boss and let go? Dad said you don't even invoice her for all the hours you work. Stop getting taken advantage of! Live your own life!"

Marie snapped, "You live *your* own life and don't worry about me, okay? Don't talk about it anymore."

Marie put the peanuts away and took out her phone and began tapping furiously at it. Was she responding to work email? The clam fumed, thinking, *She is truly terrible at relaxing.*

"Mom. What are you looking up?"

"I'm just doing some research. I'm wondering, is there any Chinese food available out here? I was thinking about opening a restaurant, called Dumpling Queen. Or maybe Egg Roll Queen? Do you think I could open this kind of business? It would be so popular, right?"

The clam rolled her eyes and sighed.

How do you solve a problem like Marie-ah? Now that Marie was momentarily engrossed in her restaurant fantasy, the clam retreated into a private space of her own. Certain snapshots of her mother at work resurfaced in her mind. The memory of sitting on her mother's lap, the table at chin height, rolling eraser crumbs between her fingers. Her mother would scribble furiously then pause then erase. In Taiwan, her mother wrote television scripts for the public station, and often worked late to meet deadlines. Her co-workers teased her for the way she carried her daughter to the writer's

room, tucked under one arm like a bag. By all accounts, the clam
was extremely well-behaved. Then they moved to America. Marie
chose her English name after Julie Andrews's character in *The
Sound of Music*. In an ideal world, she would've had at least seven
children, just like in the movie, and they would've learned to sing
and dance and play guitar, wearing matching clothes made of curtains. But that was all impossible in America. She swept her dreams
aside and dropped her writing career and did what she could do in
this country—open an afterschool.

For the next decade, she didn't speak—she commanded. How
could her vocal cords take it? She shouted after children; she
stomped down the hallways. She was like an Amazon warrior. She
picked up the phone and slammed it down. She strode to the
school's kitchen and pried the microwave open and shut, open and
shut, warming up the students' lunches. She made the kids do yoga
at the start of the day. *Ten minutes of quiet time!* She was hoarse.
She lost her voice. She coughed for years. She jammed a finger
playing basketball with the boys. She shouted "Be quiet!" and
clambered into the school bus and screeched out of the parking lot.
She clutched innumerable lists, spreadsheets, and homework, with
red checkmarks noting the problems. She found solutions. The last
defense. She went on a diet. She was gaining weight. She massaged
swollen feet. She scrutinized everyone's report cards, not including her daughters'. One day she said to the clam, "Why do you
only SCREAM at me? Why can't you talk to me in a NORMAL
voice?"

"Why can't YOU talk to ME in a NORMAL voice?" the clam
screamed back. She slammed the car door so hard it fell off its
hinges. The clam's father said, "She is going through menopause."
That was the explanation. Most nights, she dozed off on the couch.
She was thinking about work. She couldn't let it go. When she
dreamed, she dreamed of roll call. When the clam called: "You go
do your work. 你去忙你的." Her standard reply. But the clam

didn't want to work, she wanted to talk. To her. She was running out of oxygen. When she wanted to breathe, she hummed a song, with its rhythmic refrains and scripted units of breath. Pause and breathe. Pause and breathe. The song required it.

Before they reached Joshua Tree, they passed a sign and detoured to a place called Pioneertown, which turned out to be a kitschy, cartoonish stage set location for Instagram selfies and concerts. It looked like a theme park, with fake bundles of hay and fake store-fronts and washing hung out to dry. Walking around, Marie immediately started humming the song the clam recognized from *Butch Cassidy and the Sundance Kid*.

Raindrops keep fallin' on my head
But that doesn't mean my eyes
Will soon be turnin' red
Cryin's not for me

They took some pictures and got back in the car. What now? Marie told her daughter to take care of the itinerary—she was happy to go anywhere, do anything, as long as sweet potato fries were involved. Fine; they went to a bookstore, got donuts and cof-fee, and went to the Noah Purifoy Outdoor Museum, a sprawling, many-acre property where the artist had worked on his sculptures for the last twenty-five years of his life. They pulled up to the com-pound, which resembled a junkyard or seemed it could've once housed a cult. They wandered around with an eerie feeling of tres-pass, as though someone might jump out from one of the wood shacks and say, "Get out of here!" In the silence, they could hear the electricity running through the wires.

Her mom enthusiastically set about photographing everything with great archival fervor.

"Doesn't this sculpture look like Dad's old DIY surveillance system?" Her mom was pointing to a pile of discarded television screens. "Remember when Dad made something like that for Futurelink?"

"To guard against kidnappers and KKK!"

Marie flapped the nonsensical idea away. "What was he so scared about? What racism? Look how Asian the Temple City is now. On Las Tunas there's only spas for cosmetic surgery and seafood restaurants. Asian invasion already happened."

Suddenly the sun was setting and they had to scurry out of there. They drove down another dirt road to the Airstream camper they'd booked, which had enticingly advertised a stargazing platform. Marie kept asking the clam to stop so she could take pictures. She got out of the car—

"Where are you going?"

"Taking a picture of a real sunset."

After checking in, they went to town in search of sweet potato fries and found them at the Joshua Tree Saloon. Marie ordered a double cheeseburger with bacon ("I want to indulge myself by eating the most unhealthy food!") plus a basket of sweet potato fries ("Savory n' Sweet"). The fries were the best ever, and they both got buzzed from their pints of beer. Then a live honky-tonk band struck its first exuberant chords and Marie shyly approached, head bobbing, daring herself to dance. "Do it!" The clam cheered her on, but pulled her back just in time to remove a fringe of lettuce from her teeth. After their full day, the clam was finally catching brief glimpses of her mom's natural constitution. She laughed with her mouth wide open.

Back at the Airstream, their hosts had laid out chairs and fire-wood. The sky was vast and gemmed with stars. "Look at the Milky Way!" Marie exclaimed, jumping up and down. "I remember when my siblings and I went camping in Alishan, we would roll out our sleeping bags and look at the stars all night." They made a fire and drank hot lemon tea in mugs. The cold seeped through the wool blankets, but they were happy. Before long, Marie was asleep, cheek jammed sideways on the pillow. The clam followed her breathing, so close she could smell the peppermint toothpaste over the sweet beer musk. Inside her mom's mouth was a cave full of patched teeth, plastered and crowned. She always said that after she had her daughters, her teeth began rotting immediately. The calcium was sucked away to fortify growing bones. How strange I was once protected in that amniotic sea, her womb.

Remembering her mom back at the saloon, wide-eyed and shuffle-dancing to the honky-tonk jam band, the clam teared up. She felt like a proud parent, a facilitator of joy. The clam reflected that her mom was still young, and her capacity for joy was undiminished. She vowed to make her mom's retirement as action-packed as possible. To recoup the lost time.

It Deepens Like a Coastal Shelf

"**B**asically, me and Dad, even though we suffered so much, it was our fate to be together," Marie said, rolling down the car window to fling a loose hair into the wind. It was the next morning. After breakfast and a short hike around Joshua Tree, the two women were continuing on into Arizona.

"In college, we had this tradition. On Sweetheart Day, it was the custom for boyfriends to bring a watermelon to the girl's dorm to show his devotion. Dad always brought me the biggest one! My roommates would eat the watermelon and tease me, joking hysterically how it was so heavy Dad almost fainted in the heat, carrying it."

The clam listened, eyes glued to the road, which was steep and winding. They were on Historic Route 66, which passed through remnants of ghost mining towns, and the moonscape geology was overly riveting. They had just stopped in Oatman to visit a haunted saloon that recalled horseback heists and gunfights. Wild burros roamed the streets. Marie was in an expansive, chatty mood. She'd already purchased an overpriced gemmy wrap crafted by a man who claimed to be ninety-five years old, and devoured a tourist-sized cone of chocolate ice cream. At a scenic pull-off spot, she'd asked a couple to take a picture of her posing in front of a giant

American flag. Now the women were on their way to Kingman, where they planned to stop at a retro diner for more burgers and milkshakes.

"Sophomore year, I tried to break up with Dad. Because I still wasn't sure. We started dating when we were so young, I thought maybe I wanted to date other people. So, I told him it was over. However, some months after we broke up, I suddenly bumped into him in our dorm courtyard again!

"I said to him, 'What are you doing here?'

"He said, 'Oh, but, why do you look so healthy?'

"Healthy? I was surprised. What else am I supposed to look like? Dead?

"Then he revealed that my roommates had secretly written him a letter, saying *rush over quickly, she is about to die*! That's why he was so confused to see me looking healthy. We both thought it was ridiculous! Why would my roommates pull such a trick? After that, we got back together."

The clam had heard this story before, usually told in the same sequence as the other recollections of her dad's early romantic gambits. Predictably, the next story was about how he had written two years' worth of love poems before heading off to military service. He'd sealed each one in an envelope, stamped and addressed to Marie, and left them in the care of his older sister, who was instructed to mail her a new poem every day. *Imagine the passion required to write all those love poems!* her mom always boasted, so proud of this detail. Even though she found him too sad and too short for her type, she was won over by his poetry.

The clam nodded.

"No matter how hard our relationship troubles were, how much pain," her mom continued, "I never had the thought, even one time, to leave Dad. Any suffering or pain, I can take, as long as it's for my family. I could never just be selfish and leave."

The clam flashed a frown, about to protest her mom's outdated notions of what counted as selfish, but Marie had already moved on—

"Hey, Yi-an, did I ever tell you about the guy I almost came to America with, the guy who was not Dad?"

"What? No!"

"The guy is a famous film critic now. I still read his articles sometimes. We had, what do you call them? Chemicals! We would sit in class together and laugh and laugh. He was tall and cheerful. Our personalities were similar. He wrote screenplays too, like me."

A new story. The clam was excited. "You never told me. When was this?"

"This was when Dad was doing military service. Of course, the film critic guy already knew I had a boyfriend! But one day, can you imagine, he asked if I would move with him to New York! He was going to study film in Tisch at NYU. I was shocked!"

"And you weren't tempted?"

"No. I never thought, *Oh, I can just break up with Dad and go to NYU with this guy.* That would be so inappropriate."

The clam had never, ever heard this story, and she felt a thrill. "He must have been in love with you! You really never thought to pursue it? Did you hold hands? Did you make out?"

Marie laughed.

"Did this guy have nice parents? Was he cute? Rich? Maybe if you went to New York, you'd be living there now, directing plays and going to Broadway shows with David Henry Hwang."

"But then you and Anchi wouldn't exist!"

"It's okay. I would be reincarnated in another form."

The clam looked over to examine her mother's face for any signs of regret. Was this a crossroad she returned to again and again in her mind, wondering whether she made the right decision all those years ago? Why was she sharing this detail now?

"So? Did you keep up with this guy?"

"No, I lost track. Actually, when we first came to America, I thought about calling him, but I didn't. Do you know why I have this cowardice streak in my personality?" her mom asked. "In my astrology chart, I have a very aggressive Seven Kill Star, a very ambitious scary one that many war generals have. But at the same time, I have another very bad star, the one that makes you doubt everything. I have this contradiction in my personality. I am brave, but I cannot take a true risk. Not like you."

This, again. What was her mom insinuating? She couldn't read if these comments about risk, selfishness, indiscretion, were meant to be an attack or an expression of admiration. Was she saying *Good for you* or *Shame on you?*

"And what about in my chart?" the clam asked. "What do the stars say about my future?"

"In your chart, it says you will have the most talented children. They will become geniuses and world leaders, so you should have a lot."

"Don't even try."

"Yi-an, I keep telling you! If you have children for your husband's family, they will love you forever. He is their only son! Your status will automatically increase overnight. Come on, don't you think so? Maybe you feel unappreciated, abused, but if you have his baby, then immediately he will be forced to spoil you, be nice to you . . ."

"Stop! Can you please stop?"

An hour later. Mother and daughter were seated at a vinyl and chrome booth at Mr. D'z Route 66 Diner, a snapshot of Americana with its checkered linoleum floors, vintage hot rods, and Coca-Cola memorabilia. A giant mural of Elvis Presley beamed down on them. It was like stepping into a time capsule. Which brought its attendant anxieties about whether they would be welcomed into this space. Whenever the clam traveled outside of large urban centers, she felt herself bracing for potential bad interactions or the offhand remark. She tried to be extra polite and avoid excessive eye contact.

The waitress, wearing flip-flops, toddled over unceremoniously and took their orders—burgers, fries, strawberry milkshake to share—seemingly indifferent to the presence of these two Asian women in her establishment. After she disappeared into the kitchen, the clam relaxed. Her mom, blissfully unaware, boldly cruised around the restaurant, taking pictures of the decor, including other customers. Her obliviousness was charming and unthreatening, and nobody seemed to mind. Still, the clam followed her with her eyes to make sure she was okay. She thought how, in contrast, whenever her dad went out to restaurants, which happened rarely enough, he wouldn't even dare to put his elbows on the table.

"Hey, can I ask you a question?" the clam said when her mom returned to the booth. "When Dad left to write his Shell Computing program, how did you feel about it? You had to take care of everything—the business, his kids, and his own parents."

"Shell Computing? Why you suddenly thinking about that now?"

"When he left, weren't you mad about it?"

"Well, what choice did I have? Your own feeling is not always so important compared to the family well-being."

"But did you think the Shell Computing made sense as something to pursue? Did you think it would be successful? I mean, he decided to write an entire accounting program *by himself*. Even when I was a kid, I knew that was unrealistic."

"After he left, we were not fighting every day, so I had much less stress."

"Didn't you ever think, this is just his excuse to run away from us?"

"What is all this questioning for?"

The clam saw an opportunity opening up. "I have an idea for something new that I'm writing. It's a story about a woman who turns into a clam after her divorce because her mom keeps texting her to clam down . . ."

"What's clam down?"

"You know. The mom character is trying to type 'calm down' but it keeps coming out in the text as 'clam down.' Like what you do all the time."

"Do I do that?"

"Yes! Look at your chat history with me!"

"How?"

"Okay, forget it, try typing it to me right now."

"Ha ha ha! Look! I wrote clam down!"

"See?"

Marie put the phrase "clam down" into Google Translate and the "community verified" translation came back as 平靜下來.

"Clam means *ham ma*, right? The little animal that closes the shell like this?"

Marie demonstrated by putting her arms together and making herself small.

"Exactly. So, in my story, the mom character tells her daughter character to clam down, and the daughter thinks, actually, this clam method is super helpful. She can close up her shell and hide away. It's safe and cozy. But then she begins to question if being a clam is a good way to be."

"Why wouldn't it be a good way? I think that's a fantastic metaphor. To me, clam is something peaceful, smiling, independent, a cute animal living in a palace with high ceilings. A clam always has imagination to retreat. A clam does not complain. A clam stays quiet."

"Right. And that's exactly why it's not good because the clam never gets to say what she wants. Instead, she closes up and lets bad things happen to her. She just takes it. She is totally submissive."

"And that is what the daughter thinks that she is like?"

"The daughter character is starting to realize that she never learned how to advocate for herself because her whole life, she was told to make herself small, to be invisible, to accommodate others, to put herself last."

"No, no. That's not what I think about 'clam down' at all."

The food arrived; they were momentarily distracted, squirting ketchup onto their plates. The clam dipped a fry into the strawberry milkshake. There was a palpable shift in her mom's mood, some uneasiness.

After a few quick bites, her mom took out her phone again; the clam heard the *click click click* sound of something being searched, the volume turned up too high for a public space.

"Mom, what are you doing? Turn it down." Her mom was playing a video. The sound of scattered applause, a woman clearing her throat.

"Do you know the Greek word for, if you think it, it will come true?"

"Oh my god. If you play that TED Talk at me, I'll scream."

"Just listen! It's only ten minutes!"

"No! I don't want to listen to your talk! Turn it off!"

"It's not long! It's good! Basically, the speaker says, if you think negative, you will become negative. But if you think positive, you will become positive! What is the phrase? Fake it until you get it!"

"We're in a restaurant!" the clam hissed. "Can you please turn it off?"

They were making a scene now—heads were turning in their direction. The clam silenced the phone and put it down next to her in the booth. Her mom was frowning now.

"The speaker says, when you force yourself to smile, you can trick your brain to be happy. When you wake up and think, *Wow, I am so happy!* and take up space confidently with a Superman power pose, like this . . ."

A napkin holder was knocked off the table, which the clam scrambled to pick up.

"Stop. Please."

"Whenever I am having any negative thinking, I tell myself, *Take a deep breath! Clam down! Smile! Power pose!* Then you do it and you feel calm. It's like a muscle. You practice, it becomes stronger. You think clam is negative, but to me clam is a role model. You don't have to think of yourself as victim, Yi-an. You don't have to stay helpless, scared . . ."

The clam looked down. It was humiliating—she felt tears welling.

"Why do you always insist our life was so bad? Just because we asked you to do chores sometimes? I always told myself I could handle anything, and look, I did."

"No. You were not happy. You were not smiling. You weren't okay. Maybe you don't remember anymore, but you were so hard. I couldn't reach you. Nobody could."

Some of that expression was returning now, brutal, brittle, lips pressed tightly into a line.

"Do you blame me? Because I didn't abandon you. My moral philosophy was, I didn't want to hurt others. When anyone hurt me, I let it go, because what is the benefit of fighting? If I could take it, I take it. To make the peace."

"What was the price of that, though? You had to swallow everything. And you wanted me and Anchi to do the same thing as you. You told us to see whoever was hurting us as people who couldn't control their emotions. But we were the children. And you never defended us."

To her horror, the clam was crying now, blowing her nose and failing to compose herself. *Don't make a scene,* she'd thought when she first walked in here. *Don't call attention to yourself.*

"I always think, if you try to consider what the other person is suffering, you will understand why they are like that, and you will stop being mad at them. Aren't you a writer? Isn't it your job to get into someone's suffering to understand them? I think, if I can help someone, if it is in my ability, then I will help them."

The clam was shaking her head but no words were coming out. Her mom continued.

"Okay, I was not going to tell you originally. But I will say it now. I talked to your husband last week on the phone. Yes, I called him. I wanted to make sure he was okay."

"What? Why? Why did you do that?"

"I bought him a Valentine's Day gift, and I wanted to make sure he got it. I wanted to say to him, we can still be friends. But on the phone, he was crying . . ."

"Oh my god."

"Don't you know how bad he is doing?"

"Why do you care more if he's okay than if I'm okay?"

"Because I can see you are okay! But I don't know about him. I feel bad for him."

The clam could hardly modulate the volume of her speech, which was coming out in shouts. "Yes, I feel bad for him too, Mom! But what do you want me to do? Sacrifice my whole life like you did for the Chen family? Resign my own happiness and put on an act for the rest of my life just because it would be better for him? Why do my feelings disgust you so much? Whenever I feel anything, it's 'Clam down! No big deal!' You can't even listen to it. It disgusts you. You think it's because I'm weak, because I'm whining. But someone else's suffering, that's your first priority. The minute someone else needs something, you jump up. Okay, fine, tell me to clam down. But why don't you ever tell him to? I know you don't mean to be hurtful, but you frame things in this way that is so invalidating. It's like you want me to be totally weak. Don't make trouble. Just let others have their way. Give in. Why? Why

did you raise me to be this kind of person? No. I don't want it anymore."

"I never told you to be weak and have no self-confidence. I said,
have *more* confidence. You can build yourself up. You don't need
anyone or anything. You can be strong. What's so bad about just
living your life? You live yours, and he lives his. That's a marriage.
Look at me and Ba Ba. We endured all this time . . ."

"No, I do want more. I don't look at your relationship with Dad
and think, that's what I want. No. I look at your relationship and I
think, that is so, so, so fucking sad."

At this, the clam leapt up from the booth, gathering up her wallet, keys. She marched to the register to demand the bill. She could
really use a cigarette right now. This whole thing was such a farce.
This is my legacy, my inheritance, she thought. She dinged for the
waitress and nobody came, but when she glanced back at the table,
she saw her mom hunched over her phone again, absently eating
the plate of fries. The clam instantly recalled seeing this exact silhouette, countless times throughout her childhood, Mom eating
alone at her desk, shoving food in her mouth distractedly just to
get it over with. This was what her upbringing had conditioned her
for. How to be a woman, a wife. Her own feelings might be inaccessible, but pity and guilt could be acute. The clam saw this
hunched posture and she wanted to throw herself at her mom's feet
and apologize, apologize! Anything to keep from feeling this, this
feeling of having hurt someone you love.

Love was suffering. Love was tamping it down, gritting your
teeth through it. Yes, she remembered this silhouette. All the times
it was her dad on the speakerphone, her mom barely listening,
doing something absently on an Excel spreadsheet, going "mm-
hmm, mm-hmm," her dad speaking as though into a machine, ut-
terly indifferent about the listener, trapped in his litany of woe.
Tuned out. This would be her dad's only human interaction for the

day, and her mom knew this, so she stuck around because it was her duty, and as painful as it was for her, she bore this burden alone, her daughters never once attempting to chime in, to say, "Hello. Hi, Dad." The clam walked out of the room every time because she could. This was how she learned to equate feelings of pity with romantic love; forbearance and disappointment as the glue that bound a couple together.

The day Marie's own mother died, the clam had called and gravely asked, "Hey . . . are you okay?" Marie had not washed her own mother's laundry, had not cooked or cleaned for her, had not stayed up late playing mah-jongg, or watched TV, or rubbed the sore back of the woman who had once loved her so deeply. She had not been there for Ouai Puo's passing, or Ouai Gong's for that matter. Instead, she had decided to sacrifice her prime years to live with a mother-in-law who hated her, because that was just what daughters-in-law did. Marie didn't want to talk about it, and replied curtly, "I'm okay. You go be busy with your own business, 你 去忙你的." As though one should never forget that life was toil, and the toil never ended. She thought love was like that. Make a commitment. Clam down. Carry on.

Mother and daughter eventually met back at the car, a cold rift between them. They drove on. Way out here, there was no reception, no Wikipedia to read, no TED Talks about positive thinking to be summoned. They sped past escarpments of pink and yellow rock, past ancient asteroid craters, past solemn, cathedral-like stretches between reservation territory. Beyond the windshield were twisted formations of sandstone that looked like storybook characters immobilized in flight. Mountains cragged up into the white sky. Valleys, peaks. It reminded the clam of footage shot by submarines navigating the Mariana Trench.

How would she write out this scene, the clam wondered, clam girl, clam mother—

"They fuck you up, your mum and dad . . ." The first line of

Philip Larkin's poem abruptly came to mind. It made sense now. The rest of the poem, in singsong, lullaby verse. This passing on of fucked-up stuff was a tale as old as time.

> *Man hands on misery to man.*
> *It deepens like a coastal shelf.*

The mind reaches for a geologic metaphor when thinking of generations. Misery was sedimentary matter, layer upon layer of accumulation. Uplift, erosion, compression. Each generation, minutely altered, living, dying, and drifting down to build upon the faults of the old. After a lifetime of shoring up these genealogical influences against the tide, one nevertheless succumbs. Blink hard; suppress a shudder of recognition. It's useless to try to escape fate— isn't that what all the ancient myths say? The more you struggle, the deeper you go.

They drove on in silence, the sun setting behind them. In the late afternoon, perilously drowsy, the clam broke the spell by putting on a CD audiobook to stay awake. The only disc she had was about America's inadequate healthcare system and its racist origins. Marie, despite herself, listened carefully, being the good student that she was. First an interjection, pause and rewind, then a scoff. Was this history true? Her eyes seemed inflamed. All the anger that was absent from her own life, that she had not allowed herself to feel, she now poured into this topic of healthcare. She was scandalized by what she was hearing. She grew more animated with outrage. So they talked about this third thing, the intermediary topic.

The impulse to forgive, forget, move on, clam down, was so ingrained, they absorbed it into their bodies and there it went. Soon, they were talking again, these two tourists, mother and daughter, driving through the desert. They pulled into Flagstaff just before a snowstorm was about to hit. The motel owner asked,

"Are you ready for this?" with a cocked eyebrow. "We're expecting two feet." Mother and daughter squealed in terror, having never driven through such volume of snow before. No, they couldn't stay! They bought two gigantic gas station coffees and a share-sized bag of M&M's and sped ahead to the next city. They arrived in Gallup at two in the morning. Out of the highlands and into another weather system.

"Why's everyone's car covered in mud?" her mom asked, making a video with her phone. The clam laughed. They checked into a business hotel, the only place still open at this hour. The lobby lights were blinding after all that velvet darkness.

They could only manage to brush their teeth before collapsing into bed.

Lying there, the clam tried to organize some thoughts about how, in her previous survey of fairy tales, it's usually the father who decides what's what but the mother who drives the plot with her spells and subterfuge. Fathers may be bumbling and misguided, but they are rarely malicious. They've got too much to deal with, ruling the kingdom. Mothers, lacking power, rely on other means to get what they want. They employ magic, spin webs, manipulate emotions. They are jealous, spiteful, wicked. Or, mothers are beautiful, passive, blameless, idealized—often dead. The good mother and the bad mother can never coexist; they must be split in two. The bad mother punishes the child by inflicting upon them their animal form while the good mother protects the child by disguising them in the same form.

But the clam didn't believe in good and bad mothers anymore. There was only one mother, this mother, her good enough mother, her mother who was always there.

The fact of their family's collective clamhood was indisputable, but whether it would turn out to be punishment or protection was still to be determined. And that was okay.

"Hey. Are you awake?" Marie was shaking her daughter.

"Hmm?" The clam had fallen asleep.

"Hello?"

"I'm listening!"

"Yi-an. I was thinking more about the mom character in your clam story. Do you think your mom character will have any development in the book?"

"I'm not sure yet. Why?"

"I think . . . you should have the mom character realize something. She didn't know until her daughter told her that her clam behavior was hurtful. But now that she knows, she is sorry she wasn't able to make her daughter feel more supported and protected. She did not realize how this has contributed to her daughter's self-esteem issues right now."

"It's okay, Mom. It's past now." The clam kept her eyes shut, glad they were both in the dark. "It doesn't matter anymore. The daughter will tell the mom that she understands already. That it took a lot of courage and strength for the mom to do what she did. That they all got through it. That's what matters."

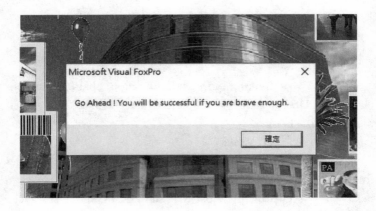

The Low Road to Taos

The next day. From Gallup, they drove east toward Santa Fe. In Cochiti, they attempted a short hike at the Tent Rocks. Marie said gleefully, "These rocks look like penis!" They were lightheaded from the altitude and laughed all the way to the bed-and-breakfast. After roaming their spacious suite, taking photos, and eating complimentary chocolate chip cookies, they FaceTimed Dad. By the time they set out for dinner, a Southwest BBQ joint, it had begun to snow.

Snow! Snow! In all her years, Marie had never seen snow. Except for that one time in Boston when flurries had leaked from the sky. This snow was wet and voluminous. Large floppy flakes dropped weightily like petals, landing on lashes, dissolving on contact. Marie shuffled around with an umbrella—Did one use an umbrella in the snow?—gazing up, mouth agape. She stood underneath a streetlight. It cast a warm triangle where visible snow drifted down as in a snow globe. The clam followed behind. It was like watching a child. Her mother swept one tentative finger along a window's ledge, then popped it into her mouth. "Mom!" the clam shrieked. "Is that even clean?!"

A transformation had occurred. For the first time, the clam

could link this person to the stories she'd heard from her mom's childhood friends in Taiwan. Her dad always said that she'd been the most vivacious, bursting with life. That was what he fell in love with. Now every day they were experiencing something entirely new. "I've never done this before!" Marie would say. The clam felt like she was falling in love with her mom too.

And then, before they knew it, it was time to say goodbye.

To save the clam the additional two-hour loop to Albuquerque and back, Marie arranged an airport shuttle from Santa Fe to catch her flight. That way the clam would only need to drive two hours north to get to Taos. "Do you know how to drive in the snow?" Marie asked suspiciously.

"No," the clam admitted. She did not. They were Los Angeles mollusks, after all! Well, better wait it out in Santa Fe until the snow goes away, they both decided.

So the clam linked up with a colleague's father who owned a second home nearby. After her mom left, she could stay overnight until the snow passed. He greeted them at his door with a yapping dog at his heels; he was an easygoing retired track coach who seemed unconcerned about whether the clam could be trusted to lock up properly, or use the stove without burning the house down. The clam found his lackadaisical attitude alarming. As he showed them around his house, the clam looked around with affected ease. I've done this itinerant thing a million times, she hoped her body language would suggest! Before handing over the keys, he said passingly, "Oh, don't turn off the heat when you leave because otherwise the pipes will freeze. That will cause me a lot of trouble!"

With that, he relinquished his home into her hands and drove away with a friendly wave.

"Okay. Now my turn to go," her mom said when the shuttle arrived. The clam thought she would thrill when her own solo journey could finally begin, but the instant she waved goodbye, watching the shuttle van descend the hill, she was stricken with that queasy summer camp feeling.

That night, the temperature dipped below zero, something she had never encountered before in her life. The caliber of silence up here was unbelievable. She could hear her own heart pounding, so she put on a podcast, but in that large house, the reverberant voices sounded tinny and demented. For the first time since leaving New York, she was truly alone. The empty space pressed against her skin. How could she be thirtysomething and still so afraid of being alone? After a mug of tea and some dry cereal for dinner, she took a bath, which seemed to help, then sat on the couch and looked out the picture window—a million-dollar view into the canyon. Other houses in the distance had their lights on. That was somewhat reassuring, to see evidence of life.

Next morning, after the snow stopped, the clam dug the car out and stuck a key into the ignition. She had fallen asleep to the thought that if homes had pipes that could freeze, did cars? If the heat in homes was supposed to stay on, what about in vehicles? A frantic hour of googling had revealed a surprising lack of information about car pipes freezing, suggesting that perhaps this was something so obvious that it did not need explaining. As a *wife*, she had never concerned herself with topics of car safety. All these years, she'd imagined herself as a co-pilot, learning through observation. Turns out, she was only a passenger.

The engine jerked awake with what she thought was a straining, huffing sound. She leapt out of the vehicle and studied it from a distance. She imagined tubes cracking, liquid bursting out, gas or some other combustible fluid. Flames. Explosion. Smoke pouring from the hood. She entreated various higher powers, blessed herself, got back in, and eased the car down the hill, foot steady on the brake. She went slow enough in case she needed to eject and roll to safety.

"Hi—" She had gone to the closest autobody shop. "Can you tell me if my car's okay to drive in this weather?"

"Are you out of antifreeze?"

"I don't know."

She crossed and uncrossed her arms as the mechanic inserted various gauges and meters. He seemed to be doing all of these things perfunctorily. Checking the tire pressure, checking fluid levels. After a few minutes, he said she was all set, cleared to go.

"I'm sorry, could you clarify? I don't need to do anything more?"

The mechanic faltered.

"I know, it's so stupid," she said. "I don't know anything about cold weather. I have to drive to Taos soon and I . . ."

He laughed. "Oh, that all? You'll be fine. They plow the highway pretty frequent. Are you taking the high road to Taos?"

She balked. "Why? Is there a *low* road?"

The low road to Taos turned out to be so unequal to these hours of worry that she would have hated herself intensely had the mountains not stunned her into submission. Every curve in the road, every dramatic incline that dipped into a decline, gave way to a yawning vista of pink and purple clouds that she thought only existed in desktop backgrounds. It felt incredible, in a sweaty palms kind of way. A new feeling bubbled up. Terror? Elation? Taking responsibility for yourself, trusting yourself in your own hands. *You're going to be okay; you're not going to die! Here we go.* Her stomach dropped as she passed over another hill. *Work, work, it's time to work*, she repeated to herself. *Work the hardest.* She was blasting her music at top volume and singing along to Prince in her insufferable falsetto. The road kept unfurling, and the sky seemed infinite. Here was the big, beautiful world. She was in it. Could she get a witness? She was doing this.

Freedom to Nap!

The clam arrived at the residency's administrative office in the afterglow of her bravado. Together with the director, she drove to the small compound that contained her assigned casita. "Where are the other fellows? Will there be any programming?" she asked a little desperately.

"No, no," the director said. "From this moment on, nothing will be expected of you. If you wanted to take a nap the entire residency, that would be your prerogative."

Freedom, freedom to nap!

These were words he probably thought she'd like to hear, but they landed like a death sentence.

There was so much yard. So much open, uninhabited space. In the bedroom: a chaste narrow twin bed, outdated flowery linens that looked as though procured from a grandmother's attic. Faded blue armchair, threadbare at the seat. A massive radiator chuffing affably in the corner. Then there was the huge wooden desk, looking out toward the cottonwoods. It was perfect. Only, it was horrible, the solitude, the quiet, the darkness coming on. Shadows danced on the walls as she tiptoed from room to room, imagining the configuration of bare branches as a gnarled hand, a contorted limb. She imagined someone barging in, subduing her from behind. Her brains splashed upon the wall.

After everything had been unpacked, she took down the guest book from the shelf and flipped through it. Entries from past residents were filled with exclamations of gratitude. These prior residents unanimously felt *wonderful, restored, transformed!* Nobody wrote about experiencing home invasions. Reading the testimonies was soothing in the same way as reading online product reviews: They promised a reliable, predictable future, because others before her had already dealt with the unknowing. Maybe she would be fine, just like all these others had been fine.

She sat at the desk and drew up a schedule for herself, to account for her four months of solitude. She would swim in the morning, write until she got tired, then hike or walk in the afternoon. Before bed, she could review her writing with a drink or something else relaxing.

Before bed that night she called her parents.

"Hi, I arrived, and everything's great."

"Did you put your pepper spray on the key chain?" her dad asked.

"Yes . . . yes."

"Yi-an, I want you to be careful. Make sure all the doors, and your car doors, are locked before sleeping. I read report about someone hiding in back seat and murdering the driver when he was driving to work in the morning."

"Um. Okay."

"Do you have enough money?"

"Yes," she lied.

"Be safe," he said before he passed the phone back to her mom.

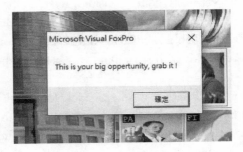

Feel the Fear and Do It Anyway!

"I read in a popular science blog that people high on the neurotic spectrum are much more likely to see faces in inanimate objects," the clam wrote in a new document, titled "Notes on My Genealogy." Earlier, an article had showed up in her feed, accompanied by an image of a standard electrical outlet. It looked, to the clam, like a face with a shocked, dismayed expression. Neurotic people, this article said, were prone to see faces because they were constantly scanning their environment for threats so that they could be prepared, at the least provocation, to flee. The article linked to a "pareidolia test," which showed a series of fire hydrants, cars, mugs, stereos, icebergs, and knots of wood. *Do you see faces in these objects?* Even as the clam took the quiz, clicking away pop-up ads every other slide, she already knew the result she would get. Truth be told, not only did she see faces, she also saw *expressions*. How could anyone not see the circumspect side-eye of the fire hydrant, or the scandalized pout of the old-school boom box, or the smug coffee mug with its patrician nose? No wonder she saw herself so readily in a bivalve's pinched profile.

The kettle whistled; the clam got up from the desk to make more tea. When she came back, she turned the radio up a few more decibels. Alone, without her usual soundtrack of buses and jack-hammers, she tried to keep herself company with the radio, which was on all day at a murmuring white-noise level.

God, what the hell was she writing? She reread the lines and hated the cadence of them. The morning had ticked by as she re-worked minutely different versions of these sentence fragments, making changes and unmaking them. She'd had a disastrously un-productive week. Her plan had been so simple: swim, write, hike, repeat. But she couldn't write, that was clear. And when she tried to swim, she lasted only thirty minutes. She thought that the life-guard, who was helping her sign up for the adult swim team, had asked one too many questions during registration, questions that later made her wonder if he was watching her too intently. In the pool, she sensed herself swimming in an assertive, masculine man-ner, whatever that meant. Then her body did it without consulting her; she jumped out and escaped.

Later that night, working late, she thought she heard footsteps, a scrape of brushed vegetation, a snapped twig. A long exhale, fol-lowed by the smell of marijuana. She froze. Someone was at the door. She eyed her pepper spray on the table and stood up slowly. Who could it be? At least, she reasoned, this person, undoubtedly the lifeguard, based on their drug of choice, would be mellow and nonaggressive. She swung the door open bravely (pepper spray in hand). "Hello?" Nobody was there. Instead, she saw two bright eyes blinking up at her in the dark: a skunk.

She had to laugh after that episode. *I am my father's daughter,* she thought. Then she pushed the thought away. *No, I'm different.* A lifetime of indoctrination and rejection. Twin desires to obey and destroy. All her life, her father has filled her with his edicts and opinions, some insalubrious, others sound. When everything was stripped away, this was what was left, these neuronal tributaries. *But all he's ever done is teach me to fear,* she thought. *Why inflict this outlook on me? I don't want to be paralyzed by fear. I don't want to second-guess everything and everyone. He's afraid of people. He's afraid of driving. Afraid of spontaneous combustion, housing collapse, identity theft, skin rashes, exorbitant water usage, the electricity bill, taxes, dogs, neighbors, flu season, white supremacists, gangsters of any race or nationality, middle-aged women of any race or nationality, chlorine, acid reflux, cholesterol, high blood pressure, having a stroke, thick slices of pork belly that will undoubtedly cause said stroke, dust, dirt, windows, chores of any kind, pickup trucks, leisure activities, swimming, emotional movies, complicated foods, earthquake, forest fire, home invasion, debts, siblings, siblings asking for money and favors . . .*

Everything but solitude. *He's* not afraid of solitude.

You know what, she thought. *That's it.* Slam laptop shut. Coat, boots, keys, out. Rush to the door. Where was she going? Hiking, apparently. Yes! Why not? She could hike!

The entire drive to the trailhead, she tried not to interrogate what she was doing. She had never gone hiking before alone, especially not in a wild place like this. She wondered whether she should look up instructions on how to defend herself from mountain lions. There was no reception though. She had her pepper spray. Maybe that was enough. This pepper spray her dad had irritatingly foisted upon her turned out to be the most practical tool one could possess in the wild. Then she remembered how some zoo animals, when released, instead of roaming free, returned eagerly to their pens. After years of being fed and cared for, these animals preferred their entrapment. Think of it: The alternative was sleeping with one eye open.

Idling in the lot, she waited until she spotted another couple, skipping up the trailhead with their dogs. Look at them, so unburdened by fear! How did they do it? Well, they were a couple! Couples did things without thinking; they passed the fear back and forth so the weight wasn't so heavy. She tried to follow the couple, but they were too fast. Soon she was gasping. This trail was steep and relentless. It was the Devisadero Loop, the markers said, with white arrows pointing up. Switchbacks zigzagged back and forth. The mud had iced over in places, and she imagined slipping and sliding off the mountain. Oops. Bye-bye, world. Her calves felt like tenderized meat. Blood thrummed in her temples.

It would be so easy to turn around, she thought, give up. Just give up! That's the thing with fear. Once it creeps in, you can't go on. But to survive, to accomplish anything, you have to reject fear. Right? Some fathers teach their children to fight to the death. Charge ahead and never admit weakness. Dominate others or be dominated by them. Her father had taught her many, many things, but not this. No. He was the man who had once purchased a book titled *Feel the Fear and Do It Anyway* sometime during his writing of Shell Computing. She remembered the exact day in elementary school when she noticed the book on his shelf. Seeing it there, she had instantly averted her eyes as though it were something private, like seeing someone in their underwear.

Feel the fear and do it anyway. But why? Fear was a gamble. Monkeys that were afraid stayed put and probably survived longer, whereas monkeys that acted fearlessly were more likely to get killed. On the other hand, a brave monkey's willingness to venture farther made them more fit and able to spread their genetics around. High risk equaled high reward.

Now, as she stood on the side of the trail, looking down into the valley, she was trying to remember the basic facts about evolution. Survival of the fittest. Modification with descent. Evolution had something to do with being adapted to the environment. What was the thing about Darwin's finches? Animals evolved, and advantageous traits that survived into offspring tended to endure. Some traits were more adaptable than others, it just depended on the situation.

Thinking of all this, the clam lit up. She turned around to head back down to town. She knew where she had to go.

Consider the Clam

The clam went straight to the library. What was Darwin's story again? How did Darwin land on his theory of evolution? She marched to the shelves, pulled off a dozen or so books, and went to the reading tables.

Before Charles Darwin became Charles Darwin, theorist of evolution, he was a floundering student trying to find a direction in life. His interests were many—too many—and this worried his father. Robert Darwin wanted his son to *settle down* and pursue medicine, or become a clergyman, but Charles was more interested in geology and natural history. Why couldn't Charles ever stick to one thing? "You care for nothing but shooting, dogs, and rat-catching, and you will be a disgrace to yourself and all your family!" Robert told Charles once. Now, at twenty-two, Charles had another outrageous proposal: He wanted to sail around the world with the HMS *Beagle* as its resident naturalist. He had to go! But Robert objected. A useless undertaking, Robert said. A wild scheme. Most uncomfortable. The ship must have invited Charles because they couldn't find anyone else, so there must have been some serious objection to the vessel or the expedition.

Oh well. Charles was young and ready to risk it all. Robert eventually relented and granted his permission. So now Charles and the rest of the ship's crew were waiting it out in Plymouth, for the foul weather to subside so the *Beagle* could sail. At night, unable to sleep, Charles paced about, trying to quiet the "palpitation and pain about his heart." This was the "most miserable" he had ever been. He wondered whether he had made a grave mistake. This expedition would certainly last two years or more; how could he endure? Charles was thus far proving to be a hopeless sailor, as seasick as anyone could be. And he had been hired to keep the captain, FitzRoy, company. The previous captain had committed suicide from the loneliness and hardship, so in a sense, Charles was placed onboard as a kind of emotional support animal. If someone like the previous captain couldn't survive, how could he? It wouldn't be too late to withdraw, go home, decide this had been an episode of youthful indiscretion . . .

Perhaps he should have listened to his father?

Day by day, Charles stuck it out. He got by with various distractions. He wrote letters. He went on short trips to boost his spirits. He dined with an expert on electricity. He visited quarries. He packed and repacked his "frightfully bulky" belongings. Among his personal effects were pistols for fending off robbers, rebels, and revolutionaries. Books: the Bible, *Paradise Lost*, and Charles Lyell's *Principles of Geology*, which Captain FitzRoy had just given him.

Like many historians and philosophers of centuries past, from Aristotle to Strabo to Avicenna, the geologist Charles Lyell had come to his ideas about geology by studying the traces of shelled creatures. The frontispiece of his 1830 edition of *Principles of Geology* showed an illustration of the Temple of Serapis in Pozzuoli. In the illustration, three marble columns sit on land that is shallowly submerged in water. Halfway up the columns are black bands of discoloration, the borings of a local clam that Lyell knew as *Lithodomus,* and that Linnaeus had named *Lithophaga,* or "rock eater." These familiar bivalves—actually a kind of mussel—ate into the rock and left distinctive markings. Recognizing them, Lyell made the following hypothesis: These columns were obviously erected in antiquity, above water. At some point, this area flooded and submerged for long enough to allow *Lithodomus* to leave its mark. Then, the water subsided once more. This process of uplift and depression, largely due to the volcanic activity in the area, was still taking place. Perhaps, Lyell concluded, the form of the Earth, or how rocks, landforms, rivers, and coastlines appeared today, was the result of these same geologic forces of rain, wind, volcanic action, clam borings, and time. Lots and lots of time. This was the principle of geology.

Darwin turned the book over in his hands. He could not know at that moment, but the geologic principle contained within Lyell's book would permanently alter the way he formed connections in his mind. Small change over long periods could result in dramatic physical changes. Indeed, in the first place where he disembarked from the *Beagle*, St. Jago, Darwin noted that the same seashells that littered the beach could also be found, fossilized, in a seam of limestone on a cliff high above. He was seeing firsthand what Lyell described. For the next five years, as Darwin scrambled up the volcanoes of the Galápagos, unearthed fossils from mountaintops, and witnessed ocean beds uplifted and collapsed in dramatic earthquakes, he began to see the world through Lyell's geologic lens. If mountains could form after millennia of shifts and upheavals, then perhaps the same principle could be applied to animals. Darwin tracked his observations in his notebooks. Finches from the isolated Galápagos Islands, lacking predators, exhibited a lack of defensive behavior, and he was able to get close enough to throw a hat over them. On the Falkland Islands, the equally naïve upland geese could easily be pummeled with sticks, whereas their counterparts on the mainland, who had been hunted for generations, fled. Whether an animal was afraid or not depended on their environment, and the types of risks they faced.

After Darwin returned from the *Beagle* expedition, he began to jot down his ideas in an attempt to synthesize all he had seen. There were three main principles:

Plants and animals are not fixed and unchanging.
They are all related through common ancestry.
They change through time.

In 1837, he drew his very first evolutionary tree. The oldest forms were at the bottom and their diverging generations branched off along the trunk. On the top, he wrote "I think." In the following year, inspired by Malthus, he considered the factor of scarcity. All organisms were constantly struggling for survival, for food, shelter, and mating partners, so any plant or animal with a competitive edge would live longer and produce more offspring. These offspring would also have a better chance of surviving. Useful traits would pass on and be preserved in what he would later call the process of natural selection.

This! This! the clam thought happily, packing up her stack of library books and heading to checkout. *Even Darwin was totally freaked out! Even he struggled with heart palpitations!* Okay, circumnavigation wasn't quite the same thing as a residency in New Mexico, but everything by degrees. It was reassuring to know that someone like him could feel the fear and do it anyway, with such radical results. Whenever she needed an answer, she went to the shelves. That was her modus operandi. In books, you got to see how the story turned out. She could seek companionship with these previous others, piecing together bits of biography and experience to provide a passable road map for her own journey.

Here was proof that risks were necessary: If Darwin hadn't taken the risk of going on the *Beagle* expedition, against his father's wishes, he never would have formulated his evolutionary theory. Darwin had to keep pushing through his fear by writing and theorizing. By 1844, when he was finally ready to confide to his friend, the botanist Joseph Dalton Hooker, he knew with a fair degree of certainty that species were not immutable, as scripture stated. Darwin hesitantly proffered this theory, but carefully added in parentheses, "It is like confessing a murder." If true, this belief would have serious ramifications for Christian thought. If species evolved on their own, then God did not create all creatures simultaneously, and the doctrine of creationism would be toppled.

Incidentally, another book was published anonymously around the same time, tracing the origins of life from marine invertebrates to modern man. Darwin followed its progress with high suspense. Titled *Vestiges of the Natural History of Creation*, the controversial book sold out within a few days and thrust the topic of transmutation into public debate. It scandalized and titillated all strata of Victorian society, from high to low. But it must have mattered to Darwin that some of his respected mentors discredited the book. Darwin's then-friend, the geologist Adam Sedgwick, said the book was so crazed and childlike that it must have been written by a woman.

So Darwin locked his own secret theory into a drawer, all 231 pages of it carefully copied out, with special instructions to his wife about how to deal with it should he die prematurely. He wasn't ready to reveal his ideas in public—not yet. Darwin knew he had stumbled across a new grammar for biology, a new system of organizing the natural world, and nothing would ever be the same again. But he had to be absolutely sure before he spoke. Shelled creatures had provided an early spark of inspiration, daring him to link the present with deep time; soon they would teach him valuable lessons on caution and circumspection, to weather the challenges to come.

My Cirripedal Task

The clam excitedly checked out a dozen or so books, and she took these back to the casita for further perusal. One of the books she checked out—*Darwin and the Barnacle* by Rebecca Stott—was about Darwin's yearslong obsessive relationship with a mollusk-like creature. *No way,* she'd yipped, when she scanned the preface. Here was another example of someone like her (and her father) who had fallen under the spell of a shelled creature! A not-so-well-known story about Darwin: Apparently, in that pivotal, frightening period after completing a draft of his species theory and before the publication of *On the Origin of Species,* Darwin, casting about for a new topic to occupy him until he could figure out what to do, latched on to a strange barnacle he named Mr. Arthrobalanus. This creature had confounded him since the *Beagle* days. Barnacles were supposed to build their own shells, but this one was discovered drilled into another conch. Could it be classified as a barnacle, even if it behaved so divergently? Darwin thought he might spend a month, two at most, answering this barnacle question. Little did he know, he would spend the next *eight years* in a feverish fugue state, furiously collecting, dissecting, and categorizing every known barnacle on earth.

The clam continued reading. By this time, Darwin had married and settled permanently in Down House, a remote countryside property on the outskirts of London, where he would remain for the rest of his life. There, he received boxes of barnacles from around the world, hundreds of specimens, which piled up in his study. He struggled to keep up with the disarray. "Literally not one species is properly defined . . . the subject is heartbreaking," he lamented. Darwin felt he had to dissect and describe as many barnacles as he could in order to show—and this was critical to his theory—how one species within a genus might branch into another species.

In one sense, it was unsurprising that Darwin would throw himself into the study of such a humble animal. Lamarck, the early evolutionist, believed that invertebrates would be key to understanding how higher forms evolved. Zoologists, such as Darwin's teacher Robert Grant, were also looking closely at the creatures of the sea, pursuing research on sea sponges, starfish, jellyfish, and mollusks. And now that Charles thought of it, even his own grandfather, Erasmus Darwin, had once argued, well before Lamarck, that all of life descended from a single aquatic filament. But all of these predecessors had lacked conclusive evidence, and that was what Darwin set out to provide.

The barnacle research was not a lighthearted pastime. Darwin felt he had yet to prove himself as a scientist. He was known as the author of the *Beagle* books, as a swashbuckling young sailor, but not as a *systematist*. He had to get it exactly right. To do so, he turned into a barnacle: "My life goes on like Clockwork, and I am fixed on the spot where I shall end it," he wrote to his old captain and friend FitzRoy in 1846. Four years later, he wrote to Lyell, who had now become a friend, "My cirripedal task is an eternal one; I make no perceptible progress—I am sure that they belong to the Hour-hand,—& I groan under my task." Two years later, Darwin was still at it. "I hate a barnacle as no man ever did before . . . not even a Sailor in a slow-sailing ship," he wrote to W. D. Fox in 1852. "I hope by next summer to have done with my tedious work."

Darwin eventually wrote and published hundreds of pages on barnacles, amounting to four volumes. With each volume, he built up his reputation and his inner network, amassing a body of evidence that would "overwhelm opposition by its sheer vastness."

The intense scrupulousness and exactitude, however, took a toll. During this time, Darwin suffered from a host of ailments that some historians speculate to be psychosomatic, anxiety-related disorders. Per doctor's orders, he doused himself with ice water even in the coldest weather. Any social stimulation threatened to derail his research, so he had a mirror installed to spot any unwanted visitors coming up the drive.

The hour hand passed; he toiled, cautious to a point beyond what was normal. By all accounts, he possessed an "extraordinary diffidence" and "passion for completeness" and "a reluctance, so extreme as to appear almost pathological." Close friends urged him to move on already, drop the barnacles, and publish the species theory! At this rate, Lyell argued, others, like the naturalist Alfred Russel Wallace, would surely preempt him. Like a barnacle, Darwin grabbed at evidence with fine feathered feet, to filter, process, and digest, sheltering himself behind his growing volumes of unimpeachable science.

The clam paused here. Darwin's barnacle work was such a monumental undertaking, it must have been driven by some powerful inner fuel. What was it? Perhaps Darwin couldn't let go because he was hiding from or postponing work on his more important, but dangerous, species theory, so fear was that force fueling his production. He was *escaping* into barnacles, the safe topic that would cause no controversy. Or perhaps he was doing this grueling, backbreaking work *because* he was in it for the long game and knew this would be required, foundational, and without it, the species theory would crumble. In his dismissal of *Vestiges*, Darwin's friend Hooker had said, and Darwin agreed, "no one has the right to examine the question of species who has not minutely described many." Minutely describing: That's what Darwin was bravely doing, despite his ailments and anxieties.

And the clam's own father? What were his motivations? She

had never tried to figure it out, but what happened to her father during his years writing Shell Computing? Was he running from something or postponing? From what she had been told, he wrote Shell Computing alone because of the perceived risk that competitors would steal his idea. Which was preposterous, because small business accounting wasn't exactly top-secret stuff. The story she told herself in less generous moments was that he was hiding something more nefarious—an addiction, an affair. She never dared to interrogate further. The decade he spent cloistered writing this program was a void in her memory. So much so that in 2014, when she clicked on a news article announcing the true identity of "Satoshi Nakamoto," inventor of Bitcoin, a middle-aged Asian man discovered in Temple City, California, she almost expected to see her father's face splashed across the first page.

What was Shell Computing for her father? An expression of hope and ambition or an excuse to escape from problems he couldn't face? He always said his ultra-secure accounting software would change their lives. Did he believe what he said? When he didn't return home, year after year, because he was not yet done with the program, did it pain him? She never wondered whether it hurt him to make that compromise.

The clam read on.

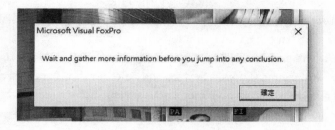

All from Shells

Fear of failure, fear of judgment, fear of speaking out and getting it wrong. *Or:* courage to fail, courage to speculate, courage to act on an inner conviction. Why did Darwin take so long to publish *Origin*? Rebecca Stott proposes a theory: Darwin was anxious about what he had inherited from his family.

Among the early theorizers of transmutation—those who, like Lamarck, believed that life emerged from the sea—was one Erasmus Darwin, Charles Darwin's own paternal grandfather. Erasmus had been an eccentric freethinker, radical for his time. A medical doctor by profession, he was also an inventor, botanist, and poet. He staunchly opposed slavery, advocated free love, believed women ought to learn professional skills, and had tremendous, insatiable appetites, requiring a special hole to be cut out from the dining table in order to accommodate his girth.

Of Erasmus's many unconventional beliefs, however, it was his belief that life emerged from the sea that proved to be too outrageous. Captivated by the fossils that his dearest friend Josiah Wedgwood had sent him, Erasmus maintained, ever after, that all life descended from a single aquatic filament. He was so convinced of this that he changed the Darwin family motto to *E Conchis Omnia*, or "All from Shells," which he had painted on the family's carriage doors. The new motto adorned the family's crest, which featured three scallop shells. The crest was printed on bookplates to be glued into the family library books.

Darwin's new family motto immediately drew harsh criticism. The local canon, Thomas Seward, ridiculed Erasmus and warned that if he didn't recant his blasphemous statement, his patients would soon leave his medical practice. Reluctantly, Erasmus painted over the motto where it could be seen publicly, but in private, he maintained his views. Toward the end of his life, in 1794, he published a massive two-volume book titled *Zoonomia; or, The Laws of Organic Life*, in which he stated that animals change through the three driving forces of lust, hunger, and desire for security, and that

> all animals undergo perpetual transformations; which are in part produced by their own exertions in consequence of their desires and aversions, of their pleasures and their pains, or of irritations, or of associations; and many of these acquired forms or propensities are transmitted to their posterity.

In 1803, a year after Erasmus's death, his poetry book, *The Temple of Nature; or, The Origin of Society*, was published posthumously. The book not only elaborated on the ideas in *Zoonomia*, it did so in a pioneering new form: speculative eco-poetry.

> *Organic Life beneath the shoreless waves*
> *Was born and nurs'd in Ocean's pearly caves;*
> *First forms minute, unseen by spheric glass,*
> *Move on the mud, or pierce the watery mass;*
> *These, as successive generations bloom,*
> *New powers acquire, and larger limbs assume;*
> *Whence countless groups of vegetation spring,*
> *And breathing realms of fin, and feet, and wing.*

Erasmus had anticipated Lamarck. And although Erasmus's science was shoddy, lacking in evidence, his ideas were a definite precursor to his grandson's. Too far ahead of his time, Erasmus was summarily dismissed. Samuel Taylor Coleridge began to use the word *Darwinize* as a verb to mean to speculate wildly, to be "all surface and no content, all shell and no nut."

Did the weight and shame of being a "Darwin" who "Darwinized" affect Charles and his unwillingness to publish *his* ideas? Darwin *was* afraid to be associated with his grandfather. Though he had written "Zoonomia" across the opening page of his first transmutation notebook to indicate that he had read the book, he maintained for years that it had no effect on him. "[It] does not include so many facts as mine." He tried to distance himself whenever he could. But he had already linked himself with his grandfather. In 1838, around the time he drew his evolutionary tree, he returned home to spend sixteen days with his father and sister, collecting information on inheritable traits. During that visit, his father, Robert, may have shown Charles some of Erasmus's letters, after which Charles wrote in his notebook that he had the same handwriting as his grandfather and had taken after his father in the "heraldic principle."

Charles did not elaborate on what inheriting the heraldic principle meant to him, whether he was acknowledging, with trepidation or horror or pride, that he was more similar to his grandfather than he previously knew. Perhaps inheriting the heraldic principle meant that Charles would have to remain vigilant against the urge to speculate wildly, as his grandfather had done. Or, the clam thought, perhaps the heraldic principle meant that as a Darwin, he possessed the courage to think independently, against prevailing trends, to say aloud what others did not even dare to think.

At the start of the *Beagle* expedition, when he had been seasick and afraid, Charles concluded that life had to be about more than careful preservation. "If one lived merely to see how long one could spin out life.—I should repent of my choice.—As it is, I do not.—" Courage and risk were just as important as caution and safety, and the good life was a negotiation between the two. In 1839, a year after he had gone home to research his genealogy, Charles wrote to a cousin to ask after their family motto because he meant to have it "solemnly engraved." Indeed, there is at least one letter in the Darwin archives that bears the family seal that young Charles made purely for himself. Interestingly, the motto on this seal is not *E Conchis Omnia* but *Cave et Aude*, or "Beware and Dare." Whether young Charles had forgotten the motto "All from Shells" or simply wanted to try something new, the clam didn't have time to find out. But it was oddly fitting, the clam thought, that these were the two Darwin family mandates: "All from Shells" and "Beware and Dare." Another way of putting it: Exercise caution until it is time to leap out courageously. Or, as the clam might have paraphrased it: Feel the fear and do it anyway.

Stott believes that the barnacle, rather than being a cul-de-sac in Darwin's journey toward *Origin*, was actually a necessary stage of maturation. Darwin himself judged that he had "gained much by my delay in publishing from about 1839, when the theory was clearly conceived, to 1859; and I lost nothing by it." After eight years of learning from barnacles, Darwin perfected the art of evasion, finally able to write the following sentence, which channels both open-ended doubt and unequivocal certainty, the art of saying without saying. From the opening of *Origin* comes this masterful rhetorical example that would make any barnacle proud:

> Although much remains obscure, and will long remain obscure, I can entertain no doubt, after the most deliberate study and dispassionate judgment of which I am capable, that the view which most naturalists entertain, and which I formerly

entertained—namely, that each species has been independently created—is erroneous.

The clam closed the book and turned out her light. It was dark outside, beyond her yard, a dark so potent the rods in her eyes definitely got the message. Time to sleep! Time to become oblivious! As she prepared for bed, she wondered how she would answer the question of what she had inherited from her father. There was his ever-present fear, yes, but there was yet another thing: He had the blind determination of the artist. He charged fearlessly ahead, encouraging himself when nobody believed in him. Retreating into solitude to actualize your own vision, even if it meant hurting people, even if it meant effectively leaving your family . . . putting up walls between yourself and the people who love you the most . . . was that a virtue to emulate?

I have been accused of running away, the clam remembered saying to the therapist, who then pantomimed the motion of putting an oxygen mask over her face.

The plane is losing altitude in a life-threatening emergency. You must save yourself before you can save others, she'd said.

Seashell Sounds

The clam woke this morning with a vague desire to call someone. She looked at the list of "Favorites" on her phone. Swipe. Delete the husband, top of the list. She then arranged the list in order: Anchi, Mom, Dad, Sam, Mike, and three other friends. One person on this list she rarely called. She hovered a finger over the screen.

Once, when the clam was a child, her father gave her a seashell to press to her ear. *Do you hear that? Doesn't it sound like ocean waves?* There was, as promised, the sound of the sea. She wasn't old enough to comprehend the playful cadence in her father's voice, so she smiled and accepted the minor miracle the way she had learned to accept the other mysteries in her life. The appearance and disappearance of family members was a constant feature of her days.

Faces came and went. Disembodied voices crackled through the receiver. She knew her father was on the other side of a big ocean, 太平洋! So far away, he sounded as though he were shouting down a long, thin tube.

She didn't know it yet, but for the next three decades she would sustain a relationship with him through this acoustic object. She talked to him with earbuds in as she hurried to and from errands and appointments, out of breath while cupping one hand to block out the wind. She put him on speakerphone as she paced around the room, doing stretches. They were rarely in the same room together, and even when they were, he was not really there either.

The spiral cavity in the inner ear is called the cochlea, for "spiral," *kohlias* in ancient Greek. The seashell-like chamber in our inner ear is one part of a "bony labyrinth" filled with watery fluid; the ducts and paths are called "canals." When sound "waves" enter the ear, they vibrate a tympanic membrane connected to mallet-like ossicles, which strike an oval window. Vibrations travel through the cochlea and activate tiny hairs, which move back and forth to generate electrical impulses that are transmitted to the brain. In anatomical illustrations, the inner ear resembles a kind of miniature sea. Anemone-like hairs undulate in currents of sound.

A pupil of Galileo's was on vacation at the beach when he thought to drill a hole into a shell he identified as an "aurita." When he held this contraption to his ear, he could hear sounds from far away that he could not hear otherwise. A few decades later, another seashell enthusiast, an English scientist named Robert Hooke, developed the first cup-and-string phone, guessing correctly that sound waves could travel down a string or wire. In 1956, the world's first transatlantic telephone cable for transmitting speech was laid beneath the sea.

Within the first twenty-four hours of service, hundreds of calls were made. There was such a hunger to close the distance.

The clam imagined a montage of all the times she'd ever called him, all the times he was away—

Hey, Dad! she shouted.

It was always this voice that came out; she couldn't help it.

Single User Mode

Like a kind of nightmare, my daughter now calls me from New Mexico all the time to squeeze out some information about my life history. Luckily, Marie had already updated me about the daughter's clam project, because I often hear them talking on the phone about it. To me, that is fine if Yi-an wants to write her strange ideas, but I do not appreciate how she is forcing me to participate too.

"Dad!"

"What?"

"Dad! I only have a few small questions, okay?"

(Always a few small questions before the big request!)

"When you were writing your Shell Computing program, do you remember what you were thinking or feeling?"

When I hear this question, I almost fall out of my chair. What? She wants to know about my *program*? Indeed it is called Shell! I am so stupid I did not make this connection before. Of course! She intend to drag me into her story as well. But why she need my *thinking and feeling*? Sometimes I scratch my head: Why my American daughters care so much about emotions? They tend to frame things as Happy, Not Happy. (When I pick up the phone and say, "Yi-an, gan ma?" in a cheery voice, then I can trick her into thinking I am happy, then she gets off my case.) Personally, I never think, when I am in some sticky pickle, how I feel.

"What do you want to know?"

She explains that she is putting together a story relating to shell lovers and I am one example. But to write her story, she needs to understand better my emotional situation and have a lots of personal details. Will I cooperate? If I care about her academical success, she said, then I should try to give her as many personal details as possible.

Well, okay, I can be obedient employee and answer her question. I explain diligently: The shell symbol in Shell Computing means to shield, to protect. It means something strong. Originally, I thought to name the program Shield, but it was too close to Blue Shield health insurance.

I can hear her typing in the background.

"Could you send me a copy of your program so I can look at it? I need it for the story."

"Daughter, I tell you honestly, your idea sounds very boring to me. I am not sure it has any unique selling point. Will your story have any scene of betrayal or murder? Spy mission or some romantic affairs? Kung fu or fighting?"

(I can almost *hear* her annoyed expression.)

"Also, if I send you the program, your computer cannot run it. Only my computer can. It is the only one left that has the 2001 Windows XP operating system."

I can hear her typing again. Then she asks if I can send her some "screenshots."

"I can't, I'm busy," I said.

"What are you busy doing?" she said.

"I'm waiting for my PhD adviser to respond to my latest paper so I can revise it."

She sigh loudly. "Are you still doing that same research paper? It's been months. I think your adviser is ignoring you."

"If he is ignoring me, that is according to my plan. I don't want him to remember that I should be working. I will drag it out, then, he will be so tired to deal with me he will surrender and give me permission to do the work in a quick and dirty way, and then I can pass more effortlessly."

She sigh again loudly.

"Daughter, if I can understand the purpose of your story, then I can fulfill your request, but right now, you don't explain very well the thesis, so to me it seems like a waste of time."

After that, she got very annoyed and said bye-bye. I am happy she received my message that I don't want to participate. However, the whole day after I had no peace because I was wondering what she intends to say about my computer program. She never had any interest in it before! In the past, when I ask her to help me, to write the program's user manual for instance, she always refuse. What changed? Is she writing about flagpole figures of small business in Southern California? Not knowing what kind of story she is trying to tell makes me nervous.

So today, when Yi-an calls, my skin seem to 發毛, grow hairs. I say to her, "I can't talk now because I am sick with a fever. I think I walk too much yesterday."

"Really? How much did you walk? You can't get a fever from walking."

"I walked more than three miles to get the discount cabbage from Guang Hua."

"Oh, that's not a lot of miles," she says. "Maybe your face got sunburned because you're not used to the sun."

So strange. Whenever I am sick, seems like she barely care. She say, "Are you *sure* you are sick?" Compare this to merely a few days ago, when she called her mom, and they were talking and talking like parrots, and I shout in the background, "Hey, Ma Ma has been sick with fever for some days now, and she has a painful rash all over her body!"

When I say that, my daughter becomes very angry and talk so fast I cannot understand. Something about, "How come you didn't tell me? What are the symptoms? Is it shingles?"

I said, "No, definitely it's not shingles because I have much experience with that one."

"Don't go to Yeh Hsih Ren," she commanded to me. "He doesn't know anything. He's a quack."

What is quack? A phony, a cheater. (I looked it up in dictionary.) Daughter has been mad at him ever since she came home from college and he dared to scold her for piercing her lip.

"No, that's not why!" she argued back. "It's because every time we go, he pushes some designer drugs for health issues we don't even have!"

Apparently for these two reasons, she hates our doctor. But what can we do? He has been treating us so long already without killing us.

She forced us to wait on the phone until she can google some other doctors with good "Yelp" reviews. I see Marie seems mad at me for revealing her rash. She is pretending to write down the phone numbers Yi-an is giving her, but I know Marie will just go see Yeh Hsih Ren, who will give her some penicillin.

After the phone call, Marie gave me a stinky face for the rest of the day.

What? At least I am honest reporter.

Anyway, back to today—since my daughter won't accept *my* excuse of fever, even though I have this cold sweat, I quickly try to find her mom to pass off the phone. But I cannot find Marie anywhere—she is not in her sewing room or in the backyard.

Too late! Big daughter is zooming in—

"Hey, Dad, I have an idea. After the residency, I'll be home for a few weeks. Why don't you walk me through your program then?"

"Why?"

"For my clam story. I want to see your program."

"I work hard not to have any emotions in my daily life, so I don't want to revisit the past. Anyway, I am going back to Taiwan."

"You are? Did you hear back from your adviser already?"

"No, but I think it's best for me to go there to wait for his email."

"Why do you have to go to another country to wait for an email?"

"Ah, you don't know anything."

To appease her, I tell her I kept some journals in Taiwan during the time I was working on Shell. I can look for them when I go back.

"You're sure your journals are still in Taiwan?"

"Yes . . . I believe so."

"Please find them for me if you can! It'll help me write this story . . . It'll be *so* good. I need it . . ."

"Sure, boss!" I say, very enthusiastically. "But since I don't have it now, I can't help you."

"Okay, Dad, one more thing?" (She is never satisfied!) "Did you consider more about sending me some screenshots?"

As she is talking, I am looking on the shelf right next to my computer desk, where I keep all my backup disks of Shell Business System. Back then, whenever I needed to back up my work, I would burn the program on a CD, write the date on, note some quirks or flaws of the newest edition, then add the CD to the ring. Look at the big stacks of CDs! So many hours of work! So many years . . . I could insert one of these disks into my computer and give her what she wants right now.

Under those stacks, I see there are the rows of journals I kept.

Ah. So they are here, not in Taiwan.

Well, I am positive I don't have the energy to look through them, so my harmless lie to my daughter is not so dishonest! Even though they are right here, I will not open them.

She says she just wants some screenshots of the program. Can I obey? That is simple . . .

"Okay, boss. I send it to you after my nap. Is that enough?"

"Thank you, thank you, Daddy!"

Daddy! She never calls me Daddy anymore unless she is very pleased. Ah. What can I do? When my children are happy, that's all that matters.

HENRY080203-03.JPG   HENRY080203-04.JPG   HENRY080203-05.JPG   HENRY080203-06.JPG

Henry Old Stuffs

A few days later, the clam's father sent the screen-shots via a Google folder, which he also shared with Marie and Angela. The folder was titled Henry Old Stuffs. The clam immediately called her sister.

"Check your email!" (For a second it seemed Angela was about to say she was busy, thinking it was another draft of a story the clam needed comments on.)

"I asked Dad to send me some screenshots of Shell Computing and, oh my god, it's even *better* than I remembered."

"Right now?"

"Get ready for another installment of Chen Sisters Looking at Things! I'm ready to type. Tell me everything you see."

"Fine. But we need to do it quickly . . . I'm supposed to finish fact-checking this piece by the end of today . . ."

The clam listened to the sounds of her sister opening up the shared Google Docs.

"How's Brooklyn?"

"Oh, the same. The tub is still clogged and my roommate still refuses to use a hair catcher. This morning . . ."

"I get it! I'm still mentally scarred from the last time I had to shower at your place . . ."

Her sister's icon popped up in the folder.

"Oh my god."

"I know, right!? Isn't it incredible?"

The clam was delighted. She readied herself to type.

**CHEN SISTERS LOOKING AT SCREENSHOTS OF THEIR
DAD'S ACCOUNTING PROGRAM, SHELL COMPUTING**

TIME: 12PM EST in BROOKLYN; 10AM in TAOS

Angela: Whoa. This is a clip art masterpiece!

Anelise: Totally. I can't believe I never looked at it carefully.

Angela: Can you imagine something like this in a folk art museum? You could set up a desktop with the program installed and people could click through. Should I start describing what I see?

Anelise: Yes.

Angela: The home screen of the program looks like . . . a collage. Like copy and paste with scissors, or stickers in a sticker book. There's a glass-fronted corporate-looking office park in the center, reflecting blue sky. Going counterclockwise from top right, a graphic of young people in business attire striding across the lobby, slender female

hands typing at a PC keyboard, a freight truck with some boxes waiting to be loaded, a giant barcode scanner . . .

Anelise: Do you think that woman on the right is Jennifer Aniston?

Angela: Looks like!

Anelise: Remember Dad used to hate for us to watch *Friends*? He thought
it was going to brainwash us into moving to New York and becoming
stupid Americans.

Angela: Ha ha. Which happened. I remember going to Borders with
him to buy these folders of clip art.

Anelise: What do you think the woman holding an apple is supposed
to represent?

Angela: Maybe this landing page tableau represents some kind of
fantasy. In his corporate park, sexy white female employees do his
bidding. They are constantly working, they never stop, not even to
eat. This one is holding out the apple in refusal.

Anelise: "No, thank you, I don't *want* this apple."

Angela: I mean, if you ignore the weirder stuff, it looks like the prompt
was "tell a middle-aged Asian man to depict Western corporate
hegemony circa the early 1990s."

Anelise: It looks like clearly this program was not vetted by any kind of
sales team or even *one* other person.

Angela: It looks like only one person, Henry Chen, had a hand in this.

Anelise: Ha ha ha. Okay, tell me all the other details you see.

Angela: I see that the words "Shell Computing" and "Shell Business
System" and "Shell" and "SBS" are everywhere, accompanied by
pictures of shells and other marine creatures.

Anelise: I count at least five different shells.

Angela: There are also colorful balloons that float up vertically on the
screen, even though you can't see that they're moving in the screenshot. Remember how, when you clicked on them, they'd burst and a
fortune cookie message would appear?

Anelise: Ha ha. How did he come up with this stuff?

Angela: Wait, is that a crab . . . ? That's one of the icons that crawls around the page, too, right?

And what's that figure under the Shell Computing logo? Is it . . . ? Can you zoom in?

Anelise: It's a saluting soldier.

Angela: Weird.

Anelise: And why do you think all the inanimate objects have arms and legs? The globe, the cellphone, the clocks. They're all like cute cartoon characters.

Angela: They're little friends that are keeping him company. In his fantasy world, the machines, clocks, and cellphones are friendly and animate . . .

Anelise: Wow. He must have been so lonely.

Angela: This makes me think how when I was a kid, I used to draw princesses in big poufy gowns, and castles and jewels and wands that were all kind of floating around in the space of the paper. I feel like this is the same kind of drawing, but the adult version.

Anelise: I never fully appreciated the genius of this home screen. It's *truly* one of a kind.

Angela: Yeah. I guess it's harder to appreciate when you're just a kid and you want to hang out with your dad but instead of hanging out with you, he's doing this.

Anelise: Do you see how the two "L"s in Shell are like . . . spooning each other?

Angela: What are those lines inside the letters? A globe? Networking lines?

Anelise: They're clamshells!

Angela: That's so perfect! Are you succeeding in asking him about the program for your project? Is he responding?

Anelise: I'm trying. I don't know how he feels about the whole thing yet. I can push but I don't know how much.

Angela: Just don't make any kind of critical comment. Don't say anything about his typos. When I tried to correct them before, he was like, "You're a child, what do you know!" Anyway. Good luck! I really have to go now, but can we talk later?

Anelise: I miss you . . . !

With Practice

A few days after her initial failure to swim, the clam forced herself to return to the pool. As with the Devisadero Trail, which she could now hike without any difficulty, she marveled how she was once so afraid. Now it was all easy. She enjoyed the predictable structure of the swim practices and the strength returning to her body. This morning, per usual, she snoozed until the last possible moment, wiped crud from her eyes, and groped her way to the door. Snow had fallen overnight. She schlepped through the mud to her car, her shoes squelching and pulling like suction cups. The drive to the pool took fifteen minutes; she watched the sky lighten imperceptibly behind the ridge.

For two hours, she moved her limbs in concert with others. It made her happy in a basic, elemental way, boring and not worth commenting on. Today, the coach had her working on her breathing again. Two weeks ago, he told her there was a problem with her breathing pattern; namely, she breathed too much. This made her stroke choppy and inefficient. "It's the altitude," she demurred. She imagined herself bursting out from each wall like a desperate whale breaching for air, looking completely undignified. For the exercise, she was to swim very calmly with flippers on and kick eight times off each wall. "Count in your head," he said. "Take it easy, very easy."

She performed this exercise diligently each morning, kicking and holding her breath, calmly blowing a steady stream of bubbles from her nose. The need for breath is an illusion, she told herself. Free divers can hold their breath for four whole minutes. The exercise had its merits. Soon she was able to pass the flags off each flip turn more easily. With the right kind of training, she thought, anything was possible.

But then, she revised, now driving back to the casita, practice over, limbs heavy: What was the point of all our efforts if decay and deterioration were equally swift? Once she stopped attending practice, her muscles would soften, her lungs would shrink. Everything falls apart. Gardens weed over; memory peels away. You blink and it's gone. The minute you neglect your project, it abandons you. She was listening to Patsy Cline, the morning sun already high overhead, thinking about yesterday's conversation with her father.

NegativeQtyOK?

Daughter called again yesterday, complaining.

"There's too much I don't understand from the screenshots! Can you just explain some of the features to me?" she said.

"Didn't you read the user manual I sent? Everything is explained. Look at the FAQ section."

"The user manual is almost six hundred pages! And the questions I have are not answered in the FAQ."

"You young people always want everything right away! Fine, quick version? It's very simple. Basically, the main feature of Shell Computing is the security hierarchy."

"The hierarchy?"

"Of course, the hierarchy! That is the special feature of Shell Computing! Don't you know? It's my main innovation! Everyone who uses the program must have a special security clearance that allows them to do a specific job. The manager sets up passwords and privileges for each employee with yes or no checkpoints. Like allowing them to create a new invoice but not allowing them to edit or void invoices, or allowing viewing of sales cost but not viewing of inventory cost, and so on. Do you want to block certain employees from big money accounts? Do you want to prevent right to extend credit limit? Or override the record? Can employee oversell unavailable stock? The managers and higher-ups can decide who is trustworthy enough to have these privileges."

Again daughter is whining about how she doesn't understand, it is all so abstract and she can't tell any of that just by looking at my home screen. Can I show her the program in action?

Fine, fine! I surrender. Actually, after all of these questions I am even quite curious to revisit the program myself—it has been so many years!

"You want to do screenshare?" I ask daughter.

"Huh? You know how to do that?"

"Do I *know*? I networked international company's computers around the world. I am getting a PhD on computer teaching in higher education. You think I don't know how to do screenshare?"

She sounds impressed that I know some basic things. My god. I sign on to Skype and I tell her to open her Skype but she is like taking forever to guess her username and password. Doesn't she have the information recorded in a notebook? When I ask her this, she actually started to laugh. "Who does that, Dad?"

I said, "I do!"

"Oh, of course you do."

She finally logs in after many guesses and I see her online. I remember how I used to call them on Skype when I was in Taiwan. I had bought many credits to do that. It was the cheapest way to make international calls. She said she always knew I was calling because the caller ID would say 0123456789.

"Okay, you are here? Can you see? I will start with the system manager's opening screen, okay?" She says she is ready.

The program is unfortunately taking a long time to load. We are waiting and waiting, and I think maybe this was the normal loading speed of 1999, but in 2017, we cannot tolerate it. To distract, I open one of the picture folders in my files.

"Do you want to see the first office in Taiwan that I rented?"

"Yes, yes! I'd love to see!"

I click through the photos and give her a little tour. She reports she never saw it before, and keeps asking me things I don't remember. I told her I mostly remember the cost of the rent—too high.

Ding ding ding! Good. That is the sound I know means the program is done loading. I feel suddenly a little nervous. What if it does not work? What if I catch some unsatisfying quirk that I will not have energy to fix?

Ah ha. Relief. Here it is! So far, it looks exactly like I remember. Cheerful!

I quickly type into the manager's broadcast, *How is everybody doing?*

"Wait, why did you type that? What is the broadcast?"

"Imagine you are working in a very big warehouse and there are lots of salespersons and employees at their desk in different places. If I am the manager and I want to send them all a message right away, I send it to them in this broadcast.

"Remember, this is the manager side. Only one manager can have the authority to see this screen."

I type in the broadcast, *Everyone out of the system, time to close period!*

She laughs, I don't know why. Why is that funny?

"Imagine the manager need to communicate something very fast. This message will show up on everyone's home screen. For example—"

Leave the building!!!

She laughs again.

"Why does everyone have to leave the building?"

"Because there is a fire."

"Wow, you've thought of everything."

I click into the home screen, eager to revisit how the program can control the user hierarchy.

"Another important feature of Shell is how it prevents other users from interfering when the manager is in the program. If the manager, like me, wants to work peacefully in single user mode, they can broadcast to everyone to log out and quit the system. And if the users don't get out, manager can manually evict them."

She types her notes. I ask if she is ready to go into the main program's home screen. She is. On this screen, oh wow! I am amazed I managed to make it so lively! I had a vision and I accomplished it. Look at all the colors, the palm tree, the shells, the balloons . . .

I wait for her to slow down typing.

"Is that a picture of Jennifer Aniston answering the phone?"

"Who is Jennifer Aniston?"

"Why did you pick this picture of a woman in a business suit holding an apple?"

I do not have a response for this question.

"And why do the clip art objects, the globe, the clock, the cellphone, all have legs and arms?"

Basically irrelevant questions, in my opinion. I want to show her everything my program can do, instead of focusing on these tiny unimportant details.

"All these buttons represent a different module with a lots of capabilities. Mainly, my clients requested one program that could do everything, like keep track of inventory, print invoices, calculate and send shipping orders, accounting, all that stuff. They were tired of using many different programs for different jobs. For example, we can go into the accounts receivable module here . . ."

I show her the sales order module, shipping and packing, sales management and invoicing, order entry. Wah. I can't believe how much the program can do! So incredible! Almost every kind of job a small business needs, it is here. Did I really make all of this? How did I get so much energy?

"Wait—" Daughter makes me stop while we are demonstrating the sales manager customization module. She asks about one of the privileges. "What does this button mean? NegativeQtyOk? Does that mean you're giving an employee permission to interact with a client with negative qualities?"

"No, this means negative *quantity* okay, which is like, this privilege allows the user to input negative IOUs. There is *another* place in the program to keep track if they are trustworthy or not. The program knows how to deal with naughty customers too!"

"Comprehensive."

"Yes. I would feel honored to use this program myself! It's a shame I did not try harder to sell it. Ah well. Past is past! Sometimes you reach your limit and you cannot push further."

I click on a few buttons to implement some command, but unexpectedly, I got the blocking command:

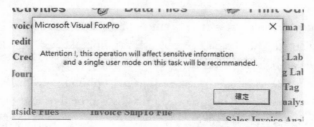

Attention!, this operation will affect sensitive information and a single user mode on this task will be recommended.

Hmm. Why did I get that message? This is supposed to be a standard task, but I must be forgetting to follow the appropriate workflow and now the system is alert to some suspicious behavior.

I clicked *OK*. Another command showed up.

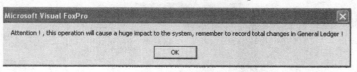

Attention!, this operation will cause a huge impact to the system, remember to record total changes in General Ledger!

I clicked on more *OK* but the system was totally blocking me. What was I doing wrong? When I designed this, I made sure everyone would follow a very exact path to input the accounting data, because messing up can have big consequences. The system does not wish you to keep opening new windows and doing something here and there. It wishes you to finish one job before starting another one, and it must think I am being too exploring right now. The program doesn't understand my behavior.

Warning!!! Before use this Function, make sure you are the only one doing this. Because two Administrator editing User privileges will cause a BIG BIG TROUBLE!

I click *OK* and *OK* and *OK* and finally I cannot go forward. I am totally stuck. The cold sweat comes back. How can it be? Has it been so many years I cannot remember how to use my own program? The creator cannot enter his creation? I have to force quit the whole thing and start over.

"You see, daughter? This is a very secure program! If anything fishy is happening, the program will put a stop to it right away. It seems even I don't remember how to jump through the security hoops! Ha ha. Maybe I need to review the user manual myself . . ."

So, I think the interview is done and anyway she must get the idea. I dare not attempt to trial another module before I get the data flow straight. Back on the home screen, we are doing nothing, just watching the screen for a while, watching the balloons drifting up the screen. I click one. It presented us with some dice numbers.

"What is that?"

"This is a gimmick. This is for the user to kill time. It is like rolling a dice."

"Can you click on the shell that is going left to right? What does that one do?"

"What! What is that?!"

I clicked again.

Again.

Stupid.

"Don't pay attention to this stuff. It's because, you know, sales-persons, they are so bored. They look at this screen all day long. I had to build something to make them entertained. This feature is call bua bui, for decision making. When you go to the temple, you throw up these two wood half-moon shapes, you see how they fall on the floor. How you say? Heads and tails. That will tell you what fortune you receive. If it gives you the smiling face, when both moons are facing up, that is the 'laughing' response. It means you should decide yourself. Who cares. This is all nonsense that is just for fun."

"Can you click on the soldier?"

Go Ahead ! You will be successful if you are brave enough.

"Why did you pick a soldier as the graphic?"

"Sometimes you need to hear something cheering. Get some en-couragements and advice. Imagine someone, like me, is having a bad day, and they need to hear some positive phrase. To help them keep going. I want to give the user some motivational messages."

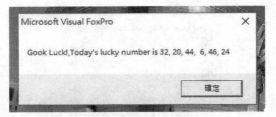

Gook Luck!, Today's lucky number is 32, 20, 44, 6, 46, 24

"Ha ha. I even thought to put in lottery numbers!"

"Do the numbers change every time you click on it?"

"Yes. It's according to the algorithm. But, daughter, this stuff is so stupid. Don't pay attention to it, okay? It is not the important part of Shell Computing. Fine, last one?"

Whatever you wish will come true if you are sincere.

I suddenly feel so sad, I don't know why. What a lie these messages are. They are cliché and meaningless words. They are just like drugs to make people feel good. I end the screenshare. Demonstration is over. At least daughter seems to be satisfied with the interview. I could hear her typing many notes on her computer.

"What is your next plan, daughter? When are you coming home? Please take car to mechanic to get checked up before you take any long trip. Let me rest and don't force me to worry."

"Thanks, Dad. I really appreciate you showing me this whole thing. I really do. I . . ."

She keeps saying thank you and thank you and thank you, but what did I do? And why should I feel so empty? Isn't this why I always insist I don't want to do anything that will make me feel any emotion? My family pushes me, they don't respect this boundary, but when I give in, they always seem happy.

In Sun Tzu's *The Art of War*, there is one chapter that says, You know the enemy is weak when the enemy's soldiers are drinking from the well themselves before taking the water back to camp. That means they are thirsty, they are tired. The soldier cannot perform his role because he must first sustain himself.

I am always trying to bring the water back to the camp, to my family. I always have this intention, but I know first I must keep myself alive. That is the most important thing.

To Shield and Protect

What the clam's dad told her: In 1994, he had been a salesman for a small business accounting software called SBT. His clients were mostly small wholesalers of fish, toys, school supplies, and tiles, but one of his largest clients was a national fingerprint recognition company. The work was profitable, and the company rewarded him with regular bonuses and recognition plaques. But suddenly and without warning, SBT merged with a larger company. His clients panicked. What would happen to their existing databases? There was no Windows version of their accounting software, only an outdated DOS version that crashed often.

So he devised a solution. He could build another program and migrate the SBT data into a new operating system. In the process, he would fix all the problems and irritations he had ever encountered as the result of human error. When he pitched his idea to loyal clients, many agreed to wait. He thought he had a maximum of five years to write the conversion, so he began immediately. He moved into the warehouse and vowed to let nothing distract him. He couldn't afford the extra overhead costs of hiring another programmer, so he did the work alone. He would work "to death" for five years, and push himself beyond his limits. Once the program was complete, he would obtain the patents and copyrights, turn it into a franchise, and wait for the profits to roll in. It was an enormous job, and he knew it, but he was forty-three years old, in the prime of his life. He would complete this job if it killed him.

. . .

Anyway, that was the current iteration of his story, which sounded rational enough. The clam realized, as she listened to her father, that she wasn't convinced, though she wanted to be. In this simple account, he had a goal, and he pursued it. Why should it matter whether he *believed* in it? She realized now that the program's plausibility could justify the price it exacted. Each day, he had to wake up and make the decision to go to his office, to protect his mind against intrusion, to excise himself completely. To miss out on their growing up, on everything that seemed (to the clam) worthwhile. If his faith was real, then he could be forgiven for choosing it. If not, then what would that mean? That his absence was no sacrifice at all, that he simply loved his solitude more.

(And so what? Why couldn't someone choose solitude because they preferred it?)

As the clam watched him struggle to outwit his own security features, she couldn't help but think: This program is a lost world, a lost language. He constructed it and now he is forgetting how to use it himself. It's so private even he can't enter it. She imagined all those lines of code, all those backdoors and if/then statements, falling away, flattening into an indecipherable hieroglyph. *NegativeQtyOk.* One day, all that will remain of these ruins will be the home screen—with its floating balloons and scampering crabs and saluting soldiers, piping staid messages that seem directed at the only other entity in this space: his subconscious. With these messages, he was talking to himself. *Follow your heart. Truth will reveal itself.*

Now the clam sat in the big armchair with her notebook open on her lap, thinking. How would she have narrativized his retreat, from one office to the next, year after year, each one farther and farther away? She writes—

1992. The office is in a plaza on Rosemead Avenue, a plaza shared with a dentist's office, a travel agency, and a restaurant. The rent is $500 a month. This is where he runs his computer repair business, where he retreats after a full day of working at his other day job. Recently, he has discovered the magic efficiency of uttering the words "tired to death." Whenever his mother approaches him with her incessant demands, he only needs to recite these words to repel her away. With a disappointed shrug, she shuffles off, muttering: *You must be making so much money. Why don't I see any of it?* Now he can watch TV in peace, with his feet up on the coffee table. His performance is convincing, but soon the guilt catches up to him, and he makes sure he is always exhausted and overworked, so it will not have to be a performance.

1994. This office is now attached to his wife's afterschool, and the business has become their home away from home. Often, working late, he gazes upon the sleeping face of his young daughter, five years old, curled up in the child-sized armchair that Robert Camel sold him at a discount. The tiny armchair is upholstered in blue velvet. She has fallen asleep under his workbench like a cat, a picture book flung open at her feet. After she eats her dinner— usually scallion pancakes from Dumpling House downstairs— she comes in here to read quietly. He doesn't talk to her and she doesn't bother him except to ask when they're going home. What a good girl, he thinks. I have such good children. Both daughters are mature and obedient and they get such good grades except this one barely talks. The teacher wrote in her progress report: "I don't know what your daughter's voice sounds like because I've never heard it." When his wife asked his daughter why she never speaks, she reported brightly: "It's because Pang Mei had a bloody nose." They don't know what this means exactly, but they are nevertheless satisfied by her answer, and he remembers that he will have to tell Marie how pleased he is that his girls never trouble him. Then he thinks, *These children have nothing to do with me. They are genetically more similar to their mother. Thank god, they inherited nothing from me.*

1995. This same rented office now contains a foldable sleeping cot, and a plastic tub in the bathroom, for bathing. He is proud of this contraption. It's a storage tote, the kind for winter blankets, with high sides and two sturdy handles. He figures he can stand inside this tub and pour water on himself from the office sink, or perhaps he can attach a hose to the faucet for an improvised shower. He doesn't need much. He lays out his toiletries on the narrow sink. In the mirror, he catches himself smiling and wonders why this whole thing feels so delightful. He has just been pushed out of his own home by his own mother. He pays the bills and holds the title, yet she implies that he does not belong there.

For dinner, he buys a Whopper combo from Burger King. Living alone is so simple, it's a wonder people suffer by creating families. People have too many petty requirements. Here he is able to get by with nothing. The first night that he attempts to use his bathing tub, he realizes that, counter to his expectations, the bin isn't actually large enough to catch all the water. He can't figure out how to shampoo his hair and turn the faucet on at the same time, and the shampoo stings when it gets into his eyes. The brand he uses is Pert Plus. It's green, it's soothing. He wonders why shampoos and soaps always come in shimmering blue and green. It is meant to evoke water, which feels clean. His favorite soap is Irish Spring soap. It is also green and marbled. He loves all things Irish, their sad songs especially. His mother nags him to use Head & Shoulders because she can't stand the drift of dander on his shoulders. She is so ashamed of his appearance, always has been. Shape up! Don't wear dark colors! He is wearing a wine-colored "DNKY" sweater he bought in downtown L.A. (Nobody can tell the difference.) When he's home with her, all she does is criticize his eczema, his way of sitting, standing, walking, existing. The soap gets everywhere, this first night, and he feels sorry for himself. How has it come to this? He imagines the rest of his family taking showers normally. They don't even have to think about it. Only he has to suffer. He is always the one who has to suffer.

The next day, a Sunday, his wife and daughters come to "visit" him. It is like they are coming over to his new house for the first time. He shows them his setup cheerfully. *I'm living in the office!* he announces. *It's so comfortable! Here is where I take a shower!* He points to his tub. *This is where I sleep!* His younger daughter bounces up and down on the wire sleeping cot and giggles when the springs squeak. To her, this whole thing is like make-believe or summer camp. She wishes she could come play this game too. Play sleep, play shower, play home.

His older daughter picks up his electric razor and frowns. *You brought this too?* The fact that he hasn't purchased a new razor and has brought his old things suggests to her that he is not returning home. He does not wish to be in two places—sometimes here, sometimes there—with two sets of toiletries, but only in one place—here—away from them. She doesn't understand why he seems so proud of himself. Does he enjoy living apart from them? She doesn't know if it's normal for dads to escape from home to live in their office. Everyone is smiling, joking, but why? Should she be joking and laughing about this too?

1999. As their business expands, they make a brazen purchase: a whole United Way building, thousands of square feet, requiring a tremendous loan. Here, Marie will continue to run her afterschool, and Henry will run his computer business. The new building is so large it has its own warehouse attached to a loading dock. Inside is all concrete and exposed wiring. There is a windowless back room in the innermost recess of the warehouse, a former janitor's closet. It has one of those industrial sinks, caked with rust and paint and years of gunk, and an open drain in the corner. He claims this airless back room as his new living space. Unfortunately, there is no toilet, so he buys one of those bedside commodes for infirm people.

Why don't you just use the bathroom in the hall?

Now his wife is nagging.

I don't want to see people when I just need to use the bathroom, is that so wrong?

They never stop harassing him!

So he has the sleeping cot, the plastic tub, the shower hose, the miscellaneous toiletries, these items follow him to this next office too.

2001. The next office is in another city, a twenty-minute drive away. He no longer wants to work and live in the same building as his wife, her business, and their children. Not that he doesn't want to; he can't. He needs true solitude to focus. This next office more resembles a windowless closet, it's so small. He has rented the cheapest one. He goes in there and loses all his senses, so he brings in a small aquarium and a rock fountain, so there is always the sound of running water. He can't see the sun, the sky, the trees, so he must import a bit of nature to soothe him.

Soon he decides that this office is too expensive. He must look elsewhere, to Taiwan, where rents are more affordable, where he can spread out. There, thousands of miles away, he will finally have the solitude he needs to finish his program. There, in that office in Taiwan, he will finally find peace.

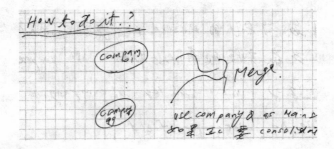

2/26/03

Today came to work. Yesterday stomach so painful. This morning, heart and body not tied together well. 身心還拉不太緊. *Diarrhea many days.*

How to do it?

Foggy and rainy. Look out the window. Streets are empty. Not many people in the office this morning. The walls feel damp and the cold tile floors seem to echo more.

It is so boring, the hours passing. Sometimes after a whole day working, I don't remember who I am. How did I end up doing something so boring, so lonely?

Is this my escape or my torture?

Look here, the copy machine and reception area. The brand-new microwave and fridge in the kitchen.

I set up the camera tripod and try to figure out the self-portrait function.

After some tries, it still comes out blurry. Very frustrated!

Oh! The camera beeps already! The red light count down the seconds. One, two, three, flash! I try again and move the camera back because I want to fit my teapots in the frame. Success!

Perhaps it is more convenient to ask someone to take my picture. But then, I have to knock on someone's door, say hello, am I bothering you, this and that, just to ask for some small thing. When you ask for a favor, the other think it is permission to ask for ten favors.

I hate middle-aged women. They are just trying to see how to feel superior to me by asking me nosy questions. Why I am here? Where is my family? America? So far away?

This will take longer, but it's easier. I can do everything like this, slow and steady.
See. I don't need others. Yay. I feel happy.

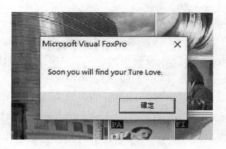

The Clam's Emancipation

Two years ago, on her thirtieth birthday, the clam deactivated all of her social media accounts and headed to the sea, not wanting anyone to wish her well. She was unable to explain this urge to hide on what most considered a momentous transition—thirty!—a day that's usually reserved for last-hurrah debauchery. Instead, she googled cabin rentals in Sag Harbor, where she and her husband would be unlikely to run into anyone they knew. On the drive out, a misty rain cloaked the empty highway. The rain continued all night, so they stayed in, drank bourbon, and watched *The Shining* in bed. The next morning, when she went for a jog along the shore, the liminal space between sea and sky looked fuzzy, indistinct. In the city, she tended to look up, searching for scalloped edges and glimpses of figures in lit windows. But by the sea, she looked at the sand. Whatever she picked up she put back down, knowing from experience that these objects would never be as beautiful as they were at first glance, half submerged and luminous in the frayed light.

Wandering through the Parrish Art Museum on that same trip, the clam came across a painting that she found so amusing she took a picture of it and sent it to her friends. Titled *Portrait of Shellfish*, it featured an array of clams, mussels, oysters, and a conch, plus two crustaceans—a crab and a lobster—perched on a lighthouse window ledge. The arrangement recalled an awkwardly posed family photo. An opened oyster quivered, fleshy and beige, like a well-fed aristocrat. The closed-lipped shells looked like pouty, uncooperative children. The placard informed the viewer that "in the 1860s, Sag Harbor portrait painter Hubbard Latham Fordham became the keeper of the old wooden lighthouse at Cedar Island." When he made this portrait, he had been "looking for a new direction" in his art.

At the time, the clam didn't know why she found this painting so funny. Perhaps it was the unsettling expressiveness of the shellfish, or simply that phrase "looking for a new direction"—a flippant way to describe an existential crisis. She imagined that Fordham had an extremely limited range of possible subjects, ensconced as he was in the solitude of his lighthouse, but now, writing this, she recalled that even artists with a wide range of possible subjects tended to gravitate toward shelled creatures in times of crisis.

The clam was now spending most of her afternoons at the library, digging into old books and studying artworks featuring shells. There was the example of Rembrandt, who made his well-known etching of *The Shell (Conus Marmoreus)* the same year he committed his second wife to the Gouda House of Correction (1650). Six years later, he would file for bankruptcy and liquidate all his assets. Among his personal effects were enormous quantities of shells and coral branches, including a rare conch, imported from the Far East, for which he paid eleven guilders, more expensive than any other item he possessed except for a print by Raphael. His determination to acquire this shell against all good sense can only suggest temporary insanity—perhaps the seventeenth-century equivalent of buying a sports car.

Yet Rembrandt's collector's mania made sense on some level. Shells are beautiful, morbid objects, much like skulls. Both are the calcified remains of some long-dead animal. They straddle a boundary between nature and art, necessity and excess, form and function—the coveted ideal for any artist. Perhaps they also represent the possibility of immortality, of living beyond the flesh. Both were used as motifs in Dutch vanitas paintings of the sixteenth and seventeenth centuries, popular still-life compositions of hourglasses, flowers, skulls, and overripe fruit, meant to remind the viewer of the transience of life. The word *vanity* comes from the Latin *vanus* or "empty," which may very well apply to the bereft shell.

This year, for her thirty-second birthday, the clam decided to drive to Abiquiú to visit the retreat of yet another artist who had briefly succumbed to shellfish: Georgia O'Keeffe. Everyone had instructed the clam, with the hushed reverence reserved for saints, "Oh, but you *must* visit Ghost Ranch in Abiquiú," as though it were a pilgrimage site. M, a filmmaker who lived in the casita near hers and who sometimes asked to hitch a ride to the grocery store, had mentioned her willingness to take other excursions. The clam walked over and knocked on the door; M said she was happy to accompany the clam to Abiquiú. Now they were edging the car up the hill and coasting down into the wide valley. The landscape that spread out before them was like nothing the clam had ever seen, striated in pastel pinks and yellows and grays. M, sitting in the passenger seat, audibly gasped. To their left, Abiquiú Lake shone brightly in the sun.

Admittedly, the clam had never been especially interested in O'Keeffe, a dentists' waiting-room favorite, but now that the clam was in New Mexico, she found the painter impossible to avoid. Everywhere she went, she was confronted with Georgia anecdotes and Georgia rooms, even Georgia ghosts that lurked in otherwise unremarkable buildings. The entire local economy seemed to be powered by the Georgia nostalgia machine: flower and skull images on gift store knickknacks, horseback riding tours to stirring Georgia plein air locales with sack lunch included. After some initial cynicism, the clam admitted there was something singular about Georgia's vision. Certain moments began to transform themselves into animate Georgia paintings: the stark late-afternoon shadows, the cow skulls hanging over low casita doorways, the herds of clouds stampeding across New Mexico's preternaturally blue sky.

The clam gave in and got Georgia's biography at the library.

O'Keeffe began her first clam series in 1926, during a difficult transitional period in her life. Her career was taking off just as the health of her husband and mentor, the photographer Alfred Stieglitz, was in decline. By this time, they had grown disillusioned with each other and possibly with the whole endeavor of marriage: After more than a decade together, she was no longer the naïve "woman-child" (or the "little plant" he had "watered and weeded and dug around") and he was no longer her sole authority. O'Keeffe became increasingly indignant as muse and wife, requiring more and more time alone. That summer, at their country estate in Lake George, she stopped socializing with others, stopped eating, and lost fifteen pounds in two weeks. Then she fled to York Beach, Maine, where she began, once more, to paint.

O'Keeffe's first clam series is solemn, quiet, and bleached of the ecstatic hues that characterize her earlier flower paintings. While the flowers represent an explosion of fertility and abundance, the clams are cold, austere, painted in white, tan, blue-black, and gray. In *Slightly Open Clam Shell* (1926), the interior of a clean white shell is exposed to the viewer, revealing an ominous black hinge. The composition of *Closed Clam Shell* (1926) is even more forbidding: The hunched dorsal edge of the clam cuts vertically down the center of the painting, reminiscent of a shrouded figure in prayer. O'Keeffe's biographer Hunter Drohojowska-Philp comments, "If, as suggested, O'Keeffe's paintings are self-portraits, these offer evidence of a woman who had shut down."

O'Keeffe knew these paintings were a departure for her, but she couldn't quite articulate why. She only knew she was attracted to these forms—shells, shingles—which were calling out from her subconscious. She confessed distractedly,

> I do not seem to be crystallizing anything this winter. . . . Much is happening—but it doesn't take shape. . . . I am not clear—am not steady on my feet. . . . I have come to the end of something—and until I am clear there is no reason why I should talk to anyone.

Despite her own reservations, the clam paintings were well received. The paintings sold—one woman offered the price of a Rolls-Royce for the entire *Shell and Old Shingle* series—and garnered a new kind of cultural cachet for O'Keeffe: This was "high" art now, and "French." Critics praised her mature palette and restrained subject matter—one male critic noted that it operated on an "intellectual" rather than "emotional" register, since "emotion would not permit such plodding precision." Glad for once that the reviewers weren't belaboring the sexual nature of her paintings, O'Keeffe responded that she was "pleased to have the emotional faucet turned off." The exhibition also turned out to be a watershed moment, marking a new period of financial security in which she would be able to support herself through painting alone.

However, as O'Keeffe's career took off, her marriage worsened. Dorothy Norman, a young woman forty years Stieglitz's junior, appeared at one of O'Keeffe's exhibitions, insinuating herself as Stieglitz's new lover and muse. O'Keeffe had no control over this affair (she was instructed not to "intrude" on the nude photo sessions Stieglitz conducted with Norman on the bed he shared with O'Keeffe), so she continued on with her shells, returning to York Beach to paint *Shell No. 1* (1928), her first nautilus-shaped shell, and another clam, *Shell No. 2* (1928), draped with sinister-looking seaweed. For Drohojowska-Philp, this painting symbolizes what

O'Keeffe called her "black-hearted" disposition; strikingly, O'Keeffe constantly chastised herself for not attending to Stieglitz's needs more thoroughly, describing herself as a "heartless wretch." She remained a dutiful wife, caring for him even after they stopped speaking to each other. Later at Lake George, she painted *Yellow Hickory Leaves with Daisy* (1928), a painting easily symbolic of a fading May-December relationship.

In the spring of 1929, O'Keeffe agreed to visit New Mexico with the painter Rebecca Strand, a trip that would change the course of her life. The two women went out West at the invitation of Mabel Dodge Luhan, an art critic and socialite who was trying to set up an artist community in Taos. For the first time in their lives, the two women were free from their controlling husbands, and while they had always regarded each other with suspicion, in the absence of men, their friendship blossomed. They sunbathed nude, went out dancing, drank liquor, learned to drive, and even smoked a cigarette once in a while. The open landscape reminded O'Keeffe of the way she used to be, before she met Stieglitz, when she was still living in West Texas and supporting herself through teaching.

When she returned from New Mexico, O'Keeffe began painting *Inside Clam Shell* (1930). It had a different kind of composition from the previous clam paintings: Rather than showing the half-opened seam, it depicted a zoomed-in view of the clam's interior, a landscape so vast it couldn't be contained—it spilled off the edges of the canvas, stretched beyond the frame. It was a declaration of her own immense subjectivity. Confident that she contained an entire world, she was eager to show its contours. She might be a clam, but she was an expansive one.

"So I was like, isn't it crazy that Georgia O'Keeffe *also* became obsessed with clams during her separation from Alfred Stieglitz?" The clam was recounting all of this to M in the passenger seat.

"That's too much of a coincidence!" M said.

"Look, we're here!"

After their hike up Chimney Rock and an obligatory stroll through the archaeology museum ("Oh my god, they even named a dinosaur after Georgia!" M said), the two women were sunburned and ravenous, but happy. They got lunch from Bodes General Store and Kitchen, which had been highly recommended by the Ghost Ranch employees, then sat on the benches outside smoking cigarettes and eating ice cream. "Is this a strange combination?" The clam laughed.

"No, we did this all the time in Iran," M said. "Women can't smoke or eat ice cream outside, so we did it all the time to rebel."

The clam, meanwhile, wrapped up her O'Keeffe story: Many more hardships would transpire in the decade after her clam paintings, but in 1938, Georgia painted *Red Hill and White Shell*, depicting a monolithic white nautilus shell securely nestled in the center of a vivid blood-red landscape. The progression from clam to nautilus: Perhaps she was ready to become a mollusk with propulsion. A nautilus had agency, could ascend and descend into the water column as it wished, or move to New Mexico. In 1940, she purchased her first parcel of land here at Ghost Ranch.

"Do you think you'll leave New York too?" M asked. "Be like Georgia and move out West by yourself?"

The clam said that was probably a good idea.

"Okay." M wiped ice cream from her face. "Let's go do something impulsive."

The women headed to Abiquiú Lake to see if they could swim. Because they were told it would be far too cold this time of year. The sun was already low in the sky, no longer radiating much warmth. At the beach, they encountered another group of women grilling burgers on a mini cooker, shaded beneath colorful umbrellas. "Is this the best way to get in?" the clam asked, and the women nodded.

"Good luck," they said sympathetically—they had braved the frigid water earlier.

By the time the clam looked over, M was already standing shin-deep in the lake, shrieking about the pain. "You just have to go for it!" the women called out from the rocks, laughing. There was no way they could not swim after they had come all this way, and now they had an audience, so the two of them launched pathetically into the water, dog paddling for several minutes before the merciful onset of numb skin. The barbecuing women shouted, "How is it?" and M shouted back, "Like torture, but so good!" They got out and got in and got out and got in and got out, dripping and goose-pimpled, scrambling for towels.

"I'm glad we did that," M said, out of breath. "I feel like a powerful woman." Then they lay out on the rocks awhile, their limbs outstretched, absorbing as much of the waning sun as possible before it finally set.

Do Not Be Fooled by Someone's Good-Looking!

few days later. M and the clam were in the common lounge working across the table from each
other. M was typing something with great intensity. Then she
turned to the clam with a pleading puppy dog look.

"So . . ."

"Yes?"

"Remember how I told you I met this cute filmmaker at a film
festival? He just invited me to a party."

The clam laughed. She was impressed. While she was busy hiding in her room, avoiding people, M had been *networking*.

"Can I read you the guy's text? This is verbatim. Ahem. The
party will be held in a, quote, intimate VIP setting. Other industry
professionals will be there. Feel free to bring friends. I'd like to see
you shake your Persian hot stuff."

The clam groaned and made a face. "You're making that up."

"Can you come with me? It's tonight."

"Nope. No way."

"Please?" M was shaking her forearm. "I need a wing person. Plus, you have the car . . ."

The clam shook her head, smiling, privately annoyed. But then again, why shouldn't she go to a party? Why did she fight so hard for freedom if she didn't even want to use it? She thought briefly of the last time she went to a party—*the corner of my humiliation*—which was enough to make her follow through on her vow of celibacy.

"Okay, just this time," the clam finally agreed. "As a chaperone. I'm chaperoning."

When M and the clam arrived at the party, the filmmaker greeted them at the door with two cocktails. "You made it!" Beside him stood another man, with a pinched smirk. He was—and the clam couldn't help thinking these adjectives—tall, dark, and handsome: brown hair tied into a low bun, turquoise studs in his ears. He was fingering a packet of American Spirits in his shirt pocket, which the clam recognized immediately as the fellow smoker's promise of escape.

"This is my chaperone." The filmmaker pointed at A. "He's visiting from Utah." M was enormously delighted by this.

"And this is *my* chaperone," M said, pointing at the clam.

At that, M and the filmmaker peeled off. He was already directing her by the waist to meet this or that "industry professional." The clam saw M nodding and hugging everyone graciously: the endless adaptability of outgoing people who could make do anywhere.

The clam swigged down her drink, then pointed to A's chest. "Could I bum a smoke?"

He led her through sliding doors outside, where a fire smoldered in the damp courtyard. The clam rubbed her arms, which A noticed. After scrounging up a few pieces of wood, he bent down and blew into the embers with assured confidence, and the whole thing roared dramatically to life. *This is such a stereotype,* she thought. Primal. She was getting turned on by the sight of an attractive man building a fire.

"Are you an industry person?" the clam asked sarcastically. "How'd you get looped into this?"

"I'm just the chaperone, remember?" He laughed. "He's a buddy of mine. We used to work together as photography instructors at Ghost Ranch."

"Ghost Ranch! I was just there!" she exclaimed, then realized how stupid this sounded, like a tourist marveling that someone worked in the Empire State Building.

He handed her a smoke and lit it for her. All of his mannerisms were careful and unhurried, unlike the dodgy movements the clam made. He asked what they were doing in New Mexico, then what she did back in New York: the same generic questions the lifeguard had asked her back at the pool, which seemed more charming when extended by A.

After she answered, she turned the questions back on him. Where was he before this? He said he had just returned from Standing Rock, one of the last protestors of the winter. "If you think this is cold," he teased, "imagine twenty below, with windchill, while living in a tent."

"Your jacket," she pointed out, and he turned around to show her. A fist holding a feather, with the words "Peaceful Protector" emblazoned.

"Could I ask? What was it like?" She had followed the protests the way most of her friends had, through social media. He willingly described everything in great detail, from the cannons to the helicopters to the militarized police response. The idea was to keep them awake and stressed, to wear them down. He didn't sleep for months. The cold got into his bones, was still lodged deep inside. He was still working through the experience. A friend had returned home and committed suicide. It wasn't an uncommon story.

So now he was just seeing where life took him. That's how he ended up at the party. He wanted to mend his relationship with his father, but that got sidelined. He got in a bad motorcycle accident recently, and his head was still groggy from the concussion. His cousin . . . He choked up attempting to explain, and decided not to. His stories folded effortlessly, one into the next, each one equally dire, fascinating, urgent, heartbreaking. She was just nodding and nodding.

Eventually he asked her, "Are you in love with someone?" which was startling.

"Why?"

"I can sense it," he said. "Especially now that we're sitting next to each other."

"Okay, super empath," she joked. What else had he picked up about her? She was nervously tearing up a piece of dry leaf until it was practically powder in her lap. She always fidgeted with her hands, while A, by contrast, sat very still with his hands gently clasped together. He wore several bands of braided silver, jewelry that he had smithed himself.

She looked up at the sky again, wondering whether the moon was out.

"I'm not in love," she said. "Well, I was, but it was a stupid in-fatuation, and I learned my lesson. How about you?"

He shook his head and said he wasn't in love with anyone.

"Tell me about what happened," he said.

It all felt trite and insignificant compared to everything he had gone through, but the clam attempted to explain anyway.

This was around when time began to melt and the clam was less able to string the individual moments together. There was talk of this movie, then that one; a book by N. Scott Momaday. The clam hadn't noticed that he had already put his jacket over her shoulders.

"We're best friends now," he said with a laugh when she asked if he felt okay sitting so close. "I feel you are a safe presence."

"Oh, I'm the most benign," she said. "My friends would say I'm spineless *and* toothless."

At that moment, M emerged from the sliding doors. "Girl talk!" she cried, yanking the clam's arm and pulling her inside.

"Do you want to stay?" M asked, gesturing toward A, eyes bright. They were the last ones left aside from the catering crew, cleaning up.

"Do *I*? Why? Do *you*?"

M smiled.

The clam went back out to find A.

"Hey! Do you want to go kill time somewhere until the sun rises?"

Paradox Formation

*A*pril already. After recovering from the three days she spent with A, the clam looked over her notes and wrote something with them. She couldn't believe the time had passed so quickly. A small seedling had begun to sprout from the window frame. Its roots found damp adobe, its head found the light, and it decided to grow. She watched the young plant unfurl its tender green solar panels and tilt toward the sun. Outside, leaves burst out from their buds and creatures woke from dormancy. Birds swooped into the yard to gather nesting material; a pair of mourning doves built theirs in the crook of the cottonwood tree. One morning, she came home from swim practice and saw what she thought were large black trash bags caught in the tree's branches. Glasses on. The tree was covered with vultures, their massive wings spread in full heraldic pose. A few days later, a kind of red beetle descended, smashing against the window screen, marching around with their asses attached. Monochromatic winter had been a convenient season for monkhood, but now desire lurked in the air.

She couldn't concentrate. Desire was so distracting. It made the clam want to go outside, do things, meet people. It didn't help that A had sent her a text to say he was glad they'd met. Now he was back in Utah. How was she doing? She texted back and he texted back and soon they were actively conversing, sending jokes back and forth. Instead of writing, she sometimes wasted her morning scouring the internet for traces of him, with her researcher's focus. She found a story on a popular news outlet that featured artists and activists at the front lines of Standing Rock. Another story featured his line of ceramics and jewelry. He'd written a few articles too, with a sensitivity that sounded like a transcription of his talking. Everything he wrote or uttered sounded wise and weighty, the clam thought, untouched by shallow quotidian matters. His photograph was always prominently displayed in all the stories of him, and the clam spent an embarrassing amount of time studying his face.

It was actually unbelievable he was talking to her, she decided. Why her? She had internet stalked him enough to know that his ex was formerly a beauty queen with a public, and extremely active, Instagram account. The clam felt amused, and oddly proud, scrolling into his ex's extensive feed and seeing photo after photo of them together, not so much with jealousy as with pure awe at their existence.

One day, she casually mentioned that maybe, after the residency was over, she would come up and visit him? "That would be great!" he said, with a happy face emoji. She perceived this response to be insufficiently enthusiastic, and felt grazed with hurt. She ignored him for the rest of the day, then cried herself to sleep. She woke the next morning thinking about simple meals and monastic life, how clean and easy that would be.

"I decided to stop talking to him because I went from okay to panic in 25 min," she texted Sam. "He seemed indifferent about my visiting. Why would I drive all the way to see him if he's going to be so lukewarm about it?"

"I get it," Sam texted back. "But you have to tell yourself you're the real deal."

"What do you think it means that he keeps hounding me for a picture?" the clam asked. "Does it sound like a red flag to you?"

"Nude photos??" Sam texted back.

"What if he's trying to see if he's remembering me correctly?"

"It's hard, actually hard, to find someone you connect with," Sam said. "Try to remember that. There's no reason to dismiss all of it."

Uneventfully, the end of the residency approached. Four months prior, she had felt queasy with dread while unpacking; now she felt the same queasy dread while packing. Why did she have to go? Clams hated to go. Once a clam got settled, she preferred to stick around. She procrastinated until the very last morning to gather her belongings. The final thing she did was record her own message in the casita guest book. She wanted to cry. She *had* transformed. She was no longer afraid of her solitude.

She loaded up the Camry and drove off in a daze.

To visit A or not to visit A was a question that began as a harmless test, but as each day passed, it appeared that the clam was going to go for it. M had been amused about this spontaneous detour to visit an attractive man she knew not-so-well to learn about quote unquote "time." The clam insisted that with A, time had passed differently. It was almost spatial: The moments cohered, gained mass, glommed together. One of A's favorite things to say was that "time was an illusion." He said this whenever she complained via text that she hadn't "done anything all day." As a timeless person, everything he uttered seemed to have universal import. She wanted to be his receptive student.

"I'll only stay two days," she had reassured A over text, or perhaps it was more to reassure herself. A didn't seem to care either way how long she was staying. She remembered the last time some man had suggested to her, as an invitation to live with him, *Why not stay forever?* But she already knew how that story turned out.

. . .

Back on the road, a heady feeling pervaded. She drove the scenic route, northwest along 550, past Jemez, Counselor, and Nageezi. She was entering the Colorado Plateau. In the rain, the slick, iron-rich hillsides looked bloody and alive. Even at eighty miles per hour, the landscape spooled out before her in one tremendous vista after another. It was relentless. She tried to take photos through the windshield—all blurry and worthless—but she wanted to remember.

Only someone who had grown up in the Colorado Plateau would be capable of earnestly saying things like "time is an illusion" in semi-half-joking tones, she thought now, driving through the terrain. After A left, she got a library book that compiled excerpts and commentary from nineteenth-century Euro-American explorers. They regarded the Colorado Plateau with apprehension and horror. In the 1860s, an expedition sent out by Brigham Young to survey the Uinta Basin declared the entire territory a "waste." Clarence Dutton, one of the first geologists to survey the plateaus of Utah, was more measured, saying that someone trained to appreciate nature in the Alps or the Appalachians or New England might find these rock forms "grotesque." She preferred the naturalist writer Joseph Wood Krutch's passage about the erasure of human time:

Wherever the earth is clothed with vegetation . . . it makes man feel to some extent at home because things which, like him, change and grow and die have asserted their importance. But wherever, as in this region of wind-eroded stone, living things are no longer common enough or conspicuous enough to seem more than trivial accidents, he feels something like terror.

The rocky formations were a confrontation with time. Staring down into the Grand Canyon was like staring down two billion years of history—with no foliage to hide behind, Earth made its age known. One was forced to acknowledge the sheer amount of time that had transpired to uplift the plateau, while slow erosional forces cut that rock into chasms, mesas, laccoliths, and hoodoos. Human history was nothing but an "accident" in the face of geologic history. Yet the clam found some comfort in their collective insignificance. Nothing was permanent. This, too, would pass.

Around Farmington, the clam got sleepy and turned on the radio, and stumbled on a Christian station advertising audiotapes that promised to prove the historicity of Noah's Flood. Of course, of course! In this seemingly indifferent landscape, man *would* need extra assurances that there's some bigger picture that centers him. She was quite familiar with these Flood arguments from her mollusk research. The blog posts she encountered often had suggestive, rhetorical titles like "Seashells in the Desert?" or "Marine Fossils Found in Limestone of Egyptian Pyramids?" that attempted to account for whale skeletons in the Atacama Desert or clam fossils high in the Andes.

Most cultures have some sort of flood myth. According to Hindu legend, Vishnu incarnates into a fish to warn Manu of a coming flood, advising him to collect all the grains of the earth and board an ark. The *Epic of Gilgamesh* tells a similar story: The gods conspire to flood the world, but one of them, Ea, reveals the secret to Utnapishtim, also resulting in a lifesaving boat. Cultures in Siberia and the Caucasus have their own versions. In China, the goddess Nüwa saves the world from water after one of the pillars of heaven comes crashing down; in Yoruban myth the goddess Olokun floods nearly everyone in a fit of rage; the Inuit, too, believe the presence of shells high in the mountains is evidence of an ancient flood. Later, A would tell her that the Navajo emergence myth also involves a flood: After Coyote steals Water Monster's baby, she floods the third world in her grief. Begochiddy, the creator god, summons a tall reed through which everyone climbs into the fourth, glittering world.

Encountering seashells in the desert sent the mind into contortions. How did these shells get here? Shells activated the imagination, linking disparate things, calling forth water—the sea. They were catalysts for storytelling, linking bygone worlds with the present world. Perhaps this was why shells were found so often in burial sites and places of worship—they served as portals into other realms.

If shells were objects that testified to a time long past, inferentially, they also ensured continuation and reincarnation into the future. The Aztec creator god Quetzalcoatl is said to have created the world by blowing on a conch, and is depicted wearing the cross-section of the same shell. The temple dedicated to Quetzalcoatl in Teotihuacán featured wavelike motifs and rows of univalve and bivalve shells, illustrating the creation of the universe from the sea.

And then there was the example of Vishnu again, the Hindu god of preservation, always holding a conch shell, the *shankha,* in one of his left hands. According to some versions of the myth, a demon crowned with a conch-like jewel stole the Vedas and took it down to the bottom of the sea. Vishnu, turning himself into a fish, dove deep underwater to vanquish the demon and recapture the sacred texts.

There were several ways to interpret this, the clam thought. If myths were like dreams, revealing through the subconscious what we already knew, then one might consider reframing the myth in this way: A mollusk, by some accident, ends up possessing all the wisdom of the world. Humans, desirous of this knowledge, bring the mollusk back up to the surface in hopes of retaining its secrets and repossessing some long-forgotten wisdom. As she continued her drive—past Farmington and Shiprock, past the Four Corners Power Plant chuffing toxic fumes into the haze, past pipelines, oil drums, and refineries, past the uranium processing mill a few miles south of Blanding—the clam wondered how humans could benefit once again from contemplating the mollusk. It was clear that another flood was in the making.

The clam arrived at the address he gave her, pulling into the empty parking lot of what appeared to be a museum housing dinosaur vertebrae. Meanwhile, she knew that A was at the chiropractor's, a plaza over, getting his own vertebrae adjusted. The museum wasn't open, as she later learned was often the case in these small towns. She stared at the ridiculous T. rex sculpture out front. Clams could never anchor a museum or star in their own IMAX experience. They were so banal and recognizable as forms that John McPhee once described a reef of 350-million-year-old Devonian clam fossils as having a "Fulton Market look." So what was it about these shells that filled her with such longing? The thought ended abruptly there. A was knocking on the car window, subsuming her back into the present.

"I can't believe you're here!" he said, shaking her shoulder.

"Did you think I wouldn't show up?"

"It wasn't impossible," he said. He looked thinner than she remembered. How did she seem? They hugged—and the clam suddenly realized that she did not know this man at all.

Did she want to go on a hike first? They could leave her car in the lot and go together in his truck, he said. It was the vintage one there that she initially mistook for a fixture of the museum. It looked like a prop for a movie about the Southwest.

"This is the coolest vehicle I've ever ridden around in," she said. He patted the middle of the leather bench seat. This car was so retro there were no seatbelts.

"Why don't you sit here?"

"I'm too nervous!"

"I can tell!" She stayed on her side of the passenger seat, trying not to sweat.

"We're here," he said a few minutes later, pulling off onto the gravel.

"What? Where?" There was no parking lot, no trail markers. He just pointed up at a rock face.

"We're going up. We make our own way."

She followed him up. The climbing was steep; he said he was impressed that she was not out of breath, as most newcomers were.

"It's because I lead hikes at Ghost Ranch, with tourists, it's kind of my job," he said. "What were *you* thinking?"

"I didn't even say anything!"

"I felt your suspicion!"

She laughed.

"Watch for those cryptogams," he said, pointing to these fuzzy black patches, which he said were delicate organisms that took hundreds of years to grow.

It turned out that A had lots of stories to tell during their hike up Comb Ridge. Here was the spot where——, and that was the spot when——. The clam had never seen this kind of sandstone before, swirled in pink white gray. Navajo Sandstone, he answered. He named the sage-green succulent growing in patches, but his points of reference were not botanical or geological, but emotional. After years of returning to the same place, every fold of rock summoned a memory.

From the top, they looked down toward Cedar Mesa and the road swooping through it. A quote came to her unbidden. Oliver La Farge——

" 'Unexpectedly, I saw the sea.' "

"How is it decided where roads go?" she asked. He told her that ancient roads often began as animal paths, which then became game trails. Over time, these well-trodden routes were widened into roads.

"So the animal decides?"

He clarified: "The animals followed water. So it's the water that decides."

On the way down, everything looked transformed with the light. Then they got back in the truck so he could drive her to another beautiful location. Even the roadcuts were breathtaking. Soon they were parked next to the aqueduct, to watch the sunset. Golden hour. He was telling her stories about high school, about his friends who once tried fishing with dynamite and cracked the old dam.

"Honestly, this *feels* like high school," she joked as she continued to cower in her corner of the passenger seat. She was just staring straight ahead, out the window, but the tension was real. Someone had to make a first move. Mercifully, he scooted in, and their faces met.

Etymologists disagree on the origins of the verb *to long*, which may derive from the Old English *langian*, which means both "to extend, to grow long" and also "to desire." Anatoly Liberman suggests the word may also derive from the Old English *lengan*, which means "to prolong" or "to put off." Then there are similar German verbs: *lungern*, "to loaf"; *erlangen*, "to attain"; or *langen*, "to reach for something." All these are possible roots for longing, since lengthening and desiring instinctively correspond. "If German *lungern* once meant 'to long,' then from desiring something the path may have led to being always near the coveted object and from there to lingering," he writes.

What the clam was doing: putting things off, lengthening. Despite her best intentions, her two-day detour lengthened into two more days, which lengthened into two more. One day was spent sifting through A's collection of Ni'ihau shells from the Forbidden Island of Hawaii, each sacred shell the size of a pinhead. They lived exclusively off the shores of the island, and the only way to see them was to be invited by one of the gatekeeping families who lived there. Gathering enough of these shells to make a traditional Ni'ihau lei could take years. A said it took him more than a month to collect three small vials. An exercise in patience.

Another day was spent at the ceramics studio, where A was busy making his marbleized clay. She was sitting next to him trying to read a geology book. The swirled patterns of the clay reminded her of the Vishnu Basement Rocks she was reading about; the kneading actions he was performing seemed exactly the same. She read to him:

"The oldest rocks here, found deep in Grand Canyon's Inner Gorge, are gneiss and schist nearly two billion years old. Crushed and partly melted, distorted, folded by collision between crustal plates, they were the foot of ancient mountains."

Yet another day was spent looking for seashell fossils in the hillsides. "Ask and you shall receive," he said, picking up an unassuming piece of white rock. There was a brachiopod shape indented in the stone, encrusted with a sparkling mineral that looked like salt. "We used to find shell fossils in Jeddito," he said. "We thought they were magical, these seashells in the desert." The adults thought it was cute that the kids cared. The adults had gotten so used to seeing these shells, they no longer held any magic.

In quantum physics, time isn't linear, the clam read. A month before his own death, Einstein wrote in a condolence letter to a friend's grieving family that "for those of us who believe in physics, the distinction between past, present, and future is only a stubbornly persistent illusion." Rather than describing time as a scroll or a flow, physicists will describe time as a block, a loaf of bread, a room, a sea. Fay Dowker invites us to think of atoms of space-time accreting as though they were layers of sediment laid down on the seafloor.

But our lived experience of time is still very much Newtonian: Time feels as though it is unidirectional, thus irreversible. Time is going on all the time, whether we want it to or not. To say "time is an illusion" is to ignore obvious empirical evidence that people age and die, that when you miss an exit on the highway, there are no shortcuts, no rewinding of time. You still have to take the long way around. And when you linger longer in a place than you meant to, time does not stand still.

Some physicists will go on to say that what we experience as time is merely change or the relation between things. Matter changes or entropy increases. A unit of time is simply a convenient but arbitrary placeholder that helps us to describe these relations, and to allow trains to arrive on time. It's the same idea with money, which is an arbitrary placeholder that helps us to simplify economic transactions.

So why not measure time in units of shell, just as shells were once widely accepted units of currency? It's not too much of a stretch: We already do it. In 1833, Charles Lyell subdivided the Cenozoic era into epochs based on the percentage of mollusk fossils found in different rock strata that were still living into the present. The Eocene contained about 3 percent of living species, while the "newer Pliocene" contained nearly 90 percent of surviving species. Mollusks, in their constancy, served as a kind of clock, just as rock strata tell stories for those who know how to look.

The day before her last day of lingering, the clam joked she would stay "forever." Her real life could be put on hold indefinitely, she argued. This life could become her real life. Think of desert snails— some species sheltered in deep rock crevices for up to 95 percent of the year, just waiting for rain. When conditions were right, they came out to feed and mate. Were snails capable of saying, *I am putting my life on hold*? Did snails ever differentiate between waking and resting, or grow impatient, or wish that time passed differently?

"Why don't you stay?" A kept asking. "You could stay here and write."

"I really don't want to impose," she insisted.

"Oh, because you've been such an imposition," he said.

Some unnamed worry gnawed at her. They were sitting in the ceramic studio and she was weeping silently. He apologized if he had accidentally said something hurtful. "You know I do want you to stay." He was rubbing her back. "You know me. I was joking."

"But I don't know you," she returned. "I actually don't know anything about you." He drove her to the pharmacy then, after he saw her wheezing through another bout of stomach pain. Too much pizza? It's true, they had consumed nothing but pizza, popcorn, coffee, and beer, most of it while in bed.

In the morning, out on his deck, she looked out and saw rain clouds. You could see for hundreds of miles from his deck, in all directions. When she'd arrived, she was still in the habit of checking her phone's weather app. He had teased her about this by pointing at the blue sky. Today was the first day she had simply looked out to see what was coming toward them. Why did she always need to know what was coming? She needed assurances. She needed to know that she could anticipate and then control the next thing that happened. But after more than a week with A, she understood that he was always going to go wherever the water went, following the path.

Shells were instruments to alleviate longing; they closed the distance between time and space. When the clam looked at the objects on her desk—a brachiopod fossil, a ceramic pot carved with shell motifs, a clamshell, a hair tie A left in her car—instantaneously, the memories returned.

On her last day, A recommended that she should at least try to take one more detour to Goosenecks State Park, one of the best places to observe an "incised meander." He didn't say much as she packed, but after the car was loaded up again, he handed her a gift—the ceramic pot he had been working on all week. Since they didn't believe in time, they said goodbye unceremoniously, as though she were going down to the store. She tried not to think too much about it, and listened numbly to a random Spotify playlist without once fast-forwarding.

When she got to Goosenecks, she pulled into the lot and looked down. (Another woman next to her did the same, and vomited into the void.) More than a thousand feet down, the San Juan River wound through the rock in a tight, serpentine coil. She read from the plaque that the bottom layer was composed of limestone, part of a stratum of rock called the Paradox Formation.

Some detours cut deep. It was necessary to let things take their own course, and to do things at the right pace. Time was brutal enough without rushing. The stretch of Los Angeles River near where she grew up had been cut and diverted so many times it was no longer afforded this luxury. The water shot straight down its concrete banks, with no time to tarry or carry fresh sediment to the shore.

She got in the car and programmed directions to her next destination. She would go south to Arcosanti then, as she had written in her original plan. Earlier, when she'd tried to explain to A why she needed to go there, he couldn't understand, and to be honest, neither could she. She just needed to go. *I have things to do,* was all she could manage to say. He didn't argue with her. She drove on into the desert, into the dry golden heat, and each tumbleweed that blew into her path made her think of him. She listened to the lyrics of the Mitski song, calmly, rhythmically—

> *One morning, this sadness will fossilize*
> *And I will forget how to cry*
> *I'll keep going to work*
> *And you won't see a change*

Freedom

What is freedom? Daughter asks me the question in her newest email. What was my concept of freedom before, and what is it now? How does someone know if they have achieved freedom?

This morning I was doing my shoulder exercise in the living room while Marie is on the couch teaching herself to swim by watching YouTube. She is scared to swim, but I used to swim a lot, in the little stream behind our Shin Dian house. She said she almost drowned once, that is why she has the fear. "You know how many times I almost drown?" I say to her. Since my parents never bother to instruct us anything, my older sister used to throw me and little sister in the stream with a washtub, and we must hold on to the sides, kicking for life. That is how we learned.

Some years ago, I went to check up on our old swimming places again in Shin Dian. Around Bitan, they built high-rises around the lake and make it look like a dirty pond. City planning is so bad. You don't recognize anything. Before, the water was so crisp and clean, we often filch the 篩子 for filtering vegetables to catch little shrimp to duel each other. 鬥小蝦. Ha ha! We also capture little fish inside glass jars to observe them. We climb a tree branch and jump—splash! My parents always forbid us to swim, especially the girls, who must not be wild, as the whole town will happily report the naughty doings of the Chen daughters. Public Advocate Chen Shui Gui must not lose face. When we come home, my parents strip our socks to see if the toes are white and wrinkly. If yes? *Pah*

pah pah! Whip us everywhere. Little sister always got whip the worst. Usually they don't punish older brother.

Anyway, the beating was terrible, but we had to escape to make ourselves happy, so we were willing to take any risk. What is life worth if we cannot have some fleeting little fun? By that time, my schooling was already a failure. For my rebellious attitude and low grades, I was typically filed into the second class, the bad class sitting in the back. Each day, we boys move our table closer to the door slowly, so we can be the first to jump up and run outside. Ha ha, we were very determined to play! The old man teacher or substitute was often too lazy to take attendance, so we quietly sneak out to local college to play ping-pong, or just roam around. Really. We were country kids. Run everywhere. Kick tin can. 彈珠 marbles. Our toys all DIY. Kites, paper boats, bamboo lantern with fire inside, like a torch. We shoot each other with rubber band gun. Throw rocks. Run on the roof like gangsters, *chiu chiu chiu!* Gong lai gong kee. Since our street was narrow with tall buildings on both sides, sometimes we shoot fire rockets from one roof to other, or make little bombs by stuffing explosive into bottle, then throw from higher floor down to the street. *Bang! Pah!* Duck down fast! Car swerve. Someone cursing and screaming. How dangerous! Sometimes the boys mess up, explode themselves and lost their fingers.

That childhood time was a kind of true freedom, you know? Being so reckless and not caring about the future. I hated everything. School with corrupt teachers who force us to pay for afterschool tutoring to pass any test. If you don't go, and remember, my parents never gave me money, you don't pass the test. The teachers cram the test with tricky questions only their afterschool students can answer. School was the most oppressing environment and took away all my natural curiosity. Or maybe it is my dad's cruelty? I was born loser in his opinion. Even when I won the school poetry award, he laughed at my amateur effort.

The history textbooks by KMT government were totally fake. Actually, that is why my older sister, the first of us who goes to America as exchange student, quit her graduate history degree. When she went to Alabama, she had to spend all her time in the library reading and relearning all the history we were taught. *Why you're so slow?* The teacher scolded her about why she can't finish simple assignments. Second sister told her adviser she can't study history anymore, it's too painful. So that was the kind of trauma I experienced by myself, about the lie that I was told by authority. Near my high school, there was one alley call Guling Street. Famous for cheap secondhand books. Whenever I ditched school, I spend much time there flipping through old texts about history, literature, everything. Lots of used book from China or from before the war. I try to figure out what's going on. That is how I learn that, in school and everywhere, we are fed propaganda. I couldn't believe anything from authority.

I wonder how come we couldn't run away when we were children. Instead, we bury ourselves and become even more dedicated to supporting the family. At home, I do the chores and serve my mom's every command. Wash all the windows. Take care of the bird cages in the backyard. My dad somehow imported many rare birds from Japan and force me, a little boy, to take care of them. It was fashionable at that time, and maybe he believe we might make some money. Every day my job is to change the water, feed, clean the shits. Even though I try my best, I believe they died because nobody instructed me to do it the proper way.

Every day we were brainwash to serve others. Make money, take care of family, restrict yourself and kill your dreams. For making sure all the family can survive. After you accomplish that goal you must serve your country. In Taiwan, everyone knows that to grow up means sacrifice freedom for survival. That is natural. I don't recall we ever use some word like *freedom,* or have any concept. I never hear the word until I come to America.

Is that why I have desire to escape to America, to learn what is freedom? So now, when I hear my daughter use this word, *freedom*, I don't know how she define it as, or why she feels she don't have it yet. All her life, I never ask her to do much for us, not like my parents, who force me to give them my paycheck and control every aspect of my life. I never gave her same pressure. She always do whatever she wish. How much more freedom can she have?

In Chinese, the word for *freedom* is 自由. The first character means "self" and the second character means "however one wish to go." Now, I can take the bus to the Gold Line, and take Gold Line to Downtown L.A., anytime I want. I can look at Google Map whenever I wish.

I am free, right? So how come she thinks I am not?

Invasive Asian Clams

The clam had booked a night in Arcosanti.

"For one?"

"Yep, just me," she told the receptionist.

The guest lodges were simple, glass-fronted prefab boxes at the foot of the property, looking out onto the desert. The white sky vibrated with heat. After a quick swim in the pool, which cooled her down considerably, she hiked out on one of the trails and looked back at the scene. Arcosanti, a once-thriving utopia, now looked like an archaeological site, with its vaulted domes and brutalist cement. When the project broke ground in the seventies, "arcology" had seemed like an exciting solution to segregated suburban sprawl. Paolo Soleri, the lead architect, had envisaged a self-contained, high-density metropolis that would grow its own food and provide its own power and water. In this communal hive, conflict and crime would disappear. But the commune soon fell into stagnation. Closed systems can only sustain themselves for so long, she thought.

After the hike, she showered, fixed herself a cheese sandwich, and ate it on the terrace. She strained to hear what others were saying. What brought them here? Everyone had the same drowsy vibe. Nobody seemed to be in any hurry. That night, she fell asleep without difficulty.

The next morning, she quickly toured the terraced gardens, the library, gym, and ceramic bell workshop. Now she was working in a shaded alcove, when she noticed an older man hovering in the entryway, studying her. It was the kind of overlong, unabashed staring that made her check her shirt buttons, to see that nothing was untoward. She took her earbuds out.

"Hi. Is there a problem?"

"Here for the Wi-Fi?" He went first.

Oh, this. She sighed. *Here goes.*

"What are you working on, there? Are you a student?"

Sure. She smiled and nodded, learning from past experiences to keep things simple. Offer vague answers, appear compliant but excuse yourself quickly without inflaming any man's hurt ego.

"Shells?" He gestured toward her books. A delighted twinkle ignited in his eye. He jerked his head toward the parking lot. "Wait 'til you see what I have out back!"

He had a boat, and he wanted to invite her on an expedition. Because he knew this spot along the river where you could reach down into the water to harvest whole bucketfuls of clams!

"They're invasive, but *tasty,*" he said. "In fact, they're *Asian*—" He drawled this word out meaningfully. "I bet you'd like them *Ay-si-an clams*!" he repeated, booming with laughter.

Later, in a motel room far away in another city, the clam took out her laptop and did a search. Asian clam (*Corbicula fluminea*) appeared to be an unremarkable bivalve, about the size of a coin. The shell was yellow-brown, dull, and grooved with growth rings. The only luxurious feature was a paunchy swell at the hinge. For unknown reasons, this clam was also known as the "good luck clam" or the "prosperity clam."

The clam scrolled down and clicked on the next results, from aquarium hobbyists describing the clams' suitability as pets. Asian clams were "peaceful in disposition, content to find a spot to feed, and remain there for days on end," they wrote. On selecting the right tank mates: "Asian Gold Clams are non-aggressive by nature. They have no ability to defend themselves except to close up their shells." These descriptions made the clam chuckle.

Next, she clicked on a .gov website that described the clam's invasiveness in North America and how awful they were. As invasives are wont to do, Asian clams appeared to be outcompeting native species and contributing to biodiversity loss. Due to their high filtration rates and robust reproductive abilities, they quickly established themselves in rivers, lakes, and channels. Although they were shown to improve natural habitat by filtering water and providing food to other species, they had undoubtedly caused major problems for human infrastructure. Asian clams were a serious bio-fouler, interfering with power and water treatment plants. The clams shut down a nuclear power plant in Arkansas. They slowed and blocked irrigation canals by encouraging sedimentation, requiring frequent draining and dredging. They burrowed into the gravel used to make cement and spoiled its integrity. All told, they caused millions of dollars of damage.

The literature also stated that although the first documented population on the West Coast was discovered in the 1920s, the clams were most likely introduced earlier, brought over as food items for Chinese immigrants.

A shaft of light in murky water.

So Asian clams may have been food for the Chinese during the Gold Rush? Imagine that!

The clam stretched, rolled a cigarette, and wandered out into the motel parking lot. It was quiet here, unlike the other roadside motel where she almost stayed, with the vrooming cavalcades of motorcycle gangs. After all this reading about invasive Asians, she saw herself as though lit by a flashing red arrow: *Alert! Asian invader!* Earlier, she had approached the front desk with her usual apprehension; her face was her face, her eyes her eyes, there was no hiding what she was. But so far, she mostly registered the childish curiosity of attendants and waitresses, who cooed and smothered her in cloying endearments. *Sweetie pie, what can I do for you today?* She and the hotel clerk had traded pleasantries, and that was that. There would be no underhanded remark, no rib of hostility.

She unlocked the door to the room, and everything was perfectly fine.

Why would these early Chinese immigrants go through the trouble of bringing seafood all the way from home, she continued wondering, pacing the lot. These would be the miners, shrimpers, agricultural laborers, and railroad workers who came during the Gold Rush. Didn't the oversea journey take months? The imported clams couldn't have been very fresh, but mostly, it seemed unnecessary. She remembered from her years of California schooling that the San Francisco Bay was once known for its bounty, with dinner-plate-sized oysters and abalone and fish. Why did the Chinese go through the trouble of importing their own clams when so much shellfish was available nearby? Well, she corrected herself, even today, live crabs occasionally spilled out of suitcases at JFK because *someone* badly needed to eat them. Not just any old kind of crab—*those* exact crabs. Homesickness made one do crazy things.

The clam returned to her room, readying for a long night of reading. She pulled up several articles from historical databases, eager to know what life would have been like in the nineteenth century. What could the Asian clams tell her about their journey, how they arrived, and what they saw? She wanted to know if there was some historical context for her family's Asian clam tendencies, if only as an imaginative exercise.

TRANSCRIPTION OF INTERVIEW WITH ASIAN CLAM 32
(*Corbicula fluminea*), TAPE #1

The journey across the Pacific was long and arduous, so maybe that's why the details are hazy. Were we carried in the ship's ballast, or held in crates filled with water and sediment? You suggest that perhaps we were imported to serve as food for the ship's passengers? If there is some truth to this, the memory resists. Please grant us some laxity. All we know is that, however we arrived, it was against our wishes.

There had certainly been seagulls overhead, screeching, *Gold Mountain! All aboard!* Because it was from them that we learned of the human activity called *mining*. Similar to what we clams do, miners spent most of their lives squatting, half-submerged in muddy water, filtering, sifting, and letting most

of it go. Gold was what they sought. For us bivalves, the buildup of heavy metals is never a good
thing, so we found this impulse exceedingly curious.

We also made acquaintance with the ship's spiders, who plucked musically at their webs, *twang
twang twang*, and knew everything. They were the
progeny of generations of worldly travelers, who had
flown onboard using their famous technique: standing
on tiptoes in the direction of the wind, then sailing off on a piece of silk. They did this whenever
they wanted to seek a better life.

High in the sky, the spiders saw everything with
their many eyes. They saw the British East India
Company attack the Chinese junks in the bay, saw the
plumes of smoke and ash. The British were fighting
to force China to open up her ports for trade, they
said. To gain unfettered access to China's silk and
porcelain. Then they got the Chinese hooked on
opium. Here, the spiders hissed vengefully. "You
can't imagine the unacknowledged labor our silkworm
cousins perform day and night, munching mulberry
leaves, spinning cocoons, only to be boiled alive
for their silk! It's to our credit that we spiders
make silk that humans despise."

"Do you know about opium?" the spiders asked. "It
numbs the senses and makes you feel happy, the way
our toxins paralyze our prey to make them lie still
as we suck their juices."

"You do what?" we stammered, shivering in our
crates.

"Oh, don't be afraid of what we do; be afraid of
what the humans will do to you," the spiders said
contemptuously.

The days went on. Waves pummeled against the
hold. To escape the wind, the spiders retreated into
their corners. Soon our own breath fouled up the

crate's water. Unable to speak, we listened. We listened to the humans nearby, who smoked their love-
lorn grass, played cards, and ate sunflower seeds
with their tea. They talked about the humiliation
of losing Hong Kong to the Brits. Forced to pay in-
demnities, taxes spiked. Farmers lost their lands.
Famine. Crop failures. Floods. Sick mothers, young
wives, tilling hopeless fields with their babies
strapped on their backs. Then Jesus's self-
proclaimed brother, a Hakka farmer's son, arrived
to inaugurate the Kingdom of Heavenly Peace. Foreign
ideas had invaded his mind. Brothers too young and
uncles too old were out fighting the corrupt Manchu
government. The floods had starved them for years,
merging land and river and sea into one shining
sheet. Now it was war.

Oh, the floods, the floods! Mention of the floods
made us think of our own families back home. Our
kind lived along freshwater riverbanks, so we were
familiar with floods. But in recent generations, more
and more mud and silt seemed to be streaming down
the mountainsides. After each rain, the waterways
packed with mud, burying us and smothering out the
light. Our food, too, became scarce. In the water,
we scouted for news, but everyone moved downstream
in such a rush, we caught only snippets. "Change is
coming," the small fish said. "Prepare, prepare," as
their voices disappeared into the murk.

One day, a strange man came down to the river to
wash. He looked like a scholar or official, not a
common farmer. "Everyone sees that the mountains are
melting away, revealing their stone skeletons. And
still the government does nothing," he mumbled. He
sat upon the water's edge. In flints and flecks, we
learned that the erosion upstream had something to
do with the new crops that farmers were planting.

Instead of rice, they planted maize, potato, and tobacco, lucrative crops from far away. Maize and potato grew well in poor soil and had temporarily provided nutritious food to a growing population. But because the area of cultivated land stayed the same, the pressure increased to maximize profits on each plot. Poor farmers planted tobacco until the soil was depleted, then they moved on to the next plot. When that was done, they went to the hills, cutting down trees that had held the soil in place. Without trees, the soil buckled and slid down to the lowlands.

As we listened, we understood what the human trouble was. Closing distances was something humans had done their entire history, but they kept getting better at it. What happened on the local level was increasingly determined by what happened far away. This increased contact altered the ecology in ways they could not anticipate, and they could not stop themselves. Why couldn't the humans see what we simple animals saw? We reasoned it was because humans were helplessly forward-looking animals, with eyes in front of their heads, like most predators. These men may have cast a few wistful glances back toward shore, but as a default, they set their eyes to the horizon.

Sometimes, our crates would be opened and we would be swirled around with a wooden spoon. Ooh. Oxygen. Sunlight poured in and we saw their faces trembling over the water for a moment. We studied them and they studied us. What did they see in us? The future entwinement of our fates? They called us the golden clam or the good luck clam. Maybe our swollen bellies looked like those gold ingots they were so hungry for. We looked to them like full bellies, like gold, like luck, like hope.

TRANSCRIPTION OF INTERVIEW WITH ASIAN CLAM 561, TAPE #2

After we arrived in San Francisco Harbor, there was a great commotion as the humans rushed to the gangplank, so eager were they to disembowel the mountains. We all tumbled off the ship freely. No customs or immigration tests like you have today. To our surprise, within half an hour, most of the humans were gone, leaving us stacked alongside the other unclaimed cargo: dried cuttlefish, vermicelli, sweet rice crackers.

The crate we were in was left pitched at an angle, and we were smashed to one side. But the clam on the top of the heap whispered that they had a decent view of the environs. A foggy type of sky. We were all eager for the report. "Please describe

what you see! Is everything gold? Are there many
birds or large fish predators?"

"Push me higher," the clam said. "Higher!" We all
strained to lift him another fraction of an inch.

"Ooooh, ooh," the clam wailed.

"What are you seeing, dear clam?"

"It's a waste, a waste!"

Initially we refused to believe we had arrived in
a wasteland! But we had to agree, after the clam
described what they saw, that we were doomed. Hastily excavated holes for shoddy foundations. Hungry-
looking men lurking around half-constructed shacks.
Mountains of oysters at the water's edge, routed
from their beds and tossed into decomposing heaps.

Just then, we were interrupted by the voices of
two men, speaking the language from home:

"Those fools. Let them learn. It's useless to go
to the mines now."

"They tolerated us when we picked through their
leftovers, but not anymore."

"Look what they did to my face! When the gold
runs out, they will come after us again. Where can
we hide, then?"

These men were heaving us onto a creaking wagon.
Rich smells traveled through our water, the taste of
horse manure, woodsmoke, and some kind of ammonia.
They were complaining about a foreign miners tax, en-
forced only with Chinese and Latino miners. This tax
was less than the original twenty-dollar tax, which
was so burdensome it almost deterred them from mining
altogether. But this new tax seemed calculated to extract a maximum of misery along with a maximum of
profit for the California government, they said.

The two men affirmed to each other: No, they would
not return to the mines, where they had been chased
out. They would learn to cook, or they would learn

to sew. They would go down to the fields and dig ditches, farmwork they were familiar with from Guangdong. They could endure the mosquitoes, fevers, and cutting reeds. They would spend all day waist-high in putrid water if that's what it took to send money home. Their families didn't need to know of their suffering. Working for Ah-Sing was temporary. That crazy old man was already facing competition from the societies back home and he wouldn't be in business much longer.

So this was the fabled Gold Mountain we had heard about aboard the ship? How awful; what a deception! That's when we clams learned that the stories digested by humans were often false. Those words printed on pieces of paper—newspapers, permits, promissory notes, letters back home—they spread information that was no longer true, or entirely invented.

"The poisonous gold fever has possessed every human," the clam wailed to the rest of us below. Indeed, there was nothing in the cove but abandoned ships. Dark masts bobbing up and down. A ship graveyard. Like the remains of a charred forest. Those ships had been abandoned just like ours. We finally understood the scope of the phenomenon. This entire city was built on madness.

As we predicted, many of those abandoned ships sank under neglect, after harsh weather, and would not resurface again for centuries. You say you still occasionally find these sunken ships in the foundations of high-rise buildings? That does not surprise us, because we know the shore used to begin around Montgomery Street. The left-behind ghost ships comprised the first layer of landfill, cast off with the other detritus of human activity. Layer after layer. Until it became solid ground.

TRANSCRIPTION OF INTERVIEW WITH ASIAN CLAM 592, TAPE #3

"Will chef cook these clams right away? If I can get one last taste of home, I'll die happy."

"Why didn't you bring a packet of homegrown soil? Stir it in some water and drink it before bed."

"I don't believe in that superstitious stuff."

"Well, you're the one who's homesick, not me."

These were the first words our ancestors heard, which lodged indelibly in their mantle ever after. We clams acknowledge with great humility our place in the food web, but that does not mean we don't feel scared when we hear we are about to be tossed into a sizzling wok. In their shock, some of our ancestors released larva into the water. The logic being: If not us, then the second generation will live. Then they recalled trembling for hours, dreading their delivery to the kitchen.

The proprietor of the restaurant, Norman Asing, was held up in his office that morning. Asing was busy writing an impassioned letter to the governor of California, to be printed in the *Daily Alta California,* the most prominent San Francisco newspaper. Governor Bigler had just argued before the state's legislature for the exclusion of Chinese miners. He argued that the state *must* prevent Asiatics from coming in their swarming hordes to dig up the state's limited store of precious metals. The Asiatics did not intend to become useful citizens, Bigler argued. They were sojourners and aliens who had no morals to speak of.

Our ancestors, awaiting their destiny in the crate, were distracted by Asing's rantings and ramblings. His blood was boiling! *Asiatics weren't citizens?* he bellowed. What about him? He had become a citizen in South Carolina, converted to Christianity, and learned English. Now in San Francisco, he wasn't there to chase a fortune in the hills, but to settle and provide services! He opened one of the first eateries, the Macao and Woosung Restaurant, right here on Kearny and Commercial Street! He served as a *critical* liaison between the Chinese and the whites, translating, advocating cross-cultural exchange, tolerance, and assimilation (to a degree)—

He sat down, dipped his pen again, and struggled to restrain his emotions with cool, measured prose.

"I am sure . . . your Excellency . . . cannot . . . prevent your being called . . . the descendant of an immigrant . . . for I am sure . . . you do not boast of being . . . a descendant of the red man." He wrote extremely slowly, scratching away at the paper.

"But . . . your further logic is more reprehensible." Asing then paused at this word for a long time, as though to think if he ought to choose another. He went on: "You argue that this . . . is a republic of a particular race . . . that the Constitution of the United States . . . admits of no asylum to any other . . . than the pale face."

Our ancestors now strained to hear, for he was mumbling, picking up speed—

"This proposition is false . . . in the extreme . . . and you know it. The declaration of your independence and all the acts of your government, your people, and your history are all against you."

Asing shuffled a few papers, groaned with weariness, and then dipped his pen.

"You say that . . . gold . . . with its talismanic power . . . has overcome those natural . . . habits of non-intercourse we have exhibited. . . . I ask you . . . has not gold had the same effect upon your people, and the people of other countries . . . who have migrated hither?"

In other words, Asing was trying to say that the Chinese were immigrants, too, just like Bigler's ancestors and everyone else who had arrived to this country. There was no attack on the Chinese that could not also be applied to the white newcomer. He tried his best to point out the blatant hypocrisy.

Our ancestors were entranced by these remarks, but then they heard a younger voice calling out: "The chef wants to know where his clams are!"

The next thing our ancestors remember is the chef, reaching into the crate, laughing deliriously, scooping them up close and nearly inhaling them. Some of our ancestors fell into the sizzling wok, never to be heard from again. But some of them survived by playing dead, and their larvae, our genetic line, survived, drifting about in the mucky water they traveled in, when they were dumped carelessly, or fortuitously, out into the culvert.

TRANSCRIPTION OF INTERVIEW WITH ASIAN CLAM 988, TAPE #4

There used to be a road that went west from Portsmouth Square to the Presidio, to a place called Washerwoman's Lagoon. You see it shining there in the middle of the photograph? Sweet water flowed from springs and streams and the sand dunes blocked the water from going to the bay. The lagoon was beautiful back then, clean and inviting. Men used to do their laundry here. Can you believe it? Back in those days, California was filled with bachelors who didn't know how to do their own washing, so some of them shipped their laundry back to China. But by the 1850s, there was quite a washing industry on the lagoon. The majority of the laundrymen were Chinese.

Our forebears landed in this lagoon after they arrived. Whenever they tell us the story of their immigration, they always tell us about that first day. Like it's an action-adventure movie they've played over and over in their heads. But after that, their life story becomes like a featureless block of drudgery, with nothing worth noting. Whenever we ask a question, they might smile, squirt some sand, then say, "Oh, you know. Life was hard." A kind of stupor sets in, a bafflement. We wonder if arrival was the pinnacle of their immigration experience, because it only went downhill from there. We will never fully understand, because we have been many generations in America now. We no longer remember what it feels like to be transplanted in that way.

After they arrived, they remember they waited at the wharf for some time before they heard some kind of human scuffle. An altercation between two groups, either Sam Yup or Sze Yup. Then a gunshot rang out. Oh, they were horrified! A robbery! They were violently jostled around in their crates. They felt themselves lifted up. Before long, their kidnappers were huffing up a hill, hurrying along a sandy path. After about half an hour, they put the crate down, breath heaving. "Are they gone?" They took a sip of some astringent beverage and quieted down. In this resting spot, our ancestors reported hearing sounds of flitting birds and faraway surf. The men sat down and suddenly a wonderful smell wafted through the air. It made our ancestors tingle all over. It was a kind of minty herb. Then they heard a bright voice calling out.

"Why, hello there, stranger. We are being smothered."

They were being addressed by the minty herb! "Yerba Buena is our name," the voice said. "Welcome to our territory."

Our ancestors recalled that Yerba Buena spoke in a delightful American accent. This herb, once so

plentiful that the region was named after them, said
they had lived alongside the Native Americans before
the Spanish, who later became the Mexicans, arrived.
Our ancestors said they hailed from across the Pacific Ocean, from China. This astonished Yerba Buena.
How was that even possible? As quickly as mint
spreads, they could not imagine such speed.

Yet they all agreed that speed was the order of
the day. For instance, the changing and exchanging
of territory happened overnight. When the Mexican-
American War broke out, this hill was just a peaceful place with only about two hundred human
residents. Then one morning, Captain John B. Montgomery and his men marched up to the center of the
town and raised the American flag. It was a bloodless
transition, but that was before gold was discovered
and the stampedes of humans showed up. Now look at
this place. Yerba Buena grew somber and lamented
that their territory was getting smaller and
smaller. With all the trampling and development, it
was too much for them.

As newcomers, our ancestors could offer little
consolation, and now they felt sad too. How could
they help Yerba Buena? All they knew how to do was
filter water, and in terms of volume, they were the
best at this. They would do their darndest to clean.
They made an internal vow that when they arrived to
wherever they were being taken, they would clean and
repair what had been damaged, remembering Yerba
Buena.

More than the robbery, or the laundry business,
our ancestors loved to recall this conversation. We
always wondered why it was this moment in particular that they remembered with such relish, and we
think that perhaps it was the only time they ever
got to talk to a real American. Later, there would

be so much to do, so much risk and uncertainty. They had so many kids and cleaned so much water that they never got to experience leisure time. But this brief rest on a small hillock, as they awaited their future, was as close to a vacation as they ever got.

TRANSCRIPTION OF INTERVIEW WITH ASIAN CLAM 989, TAPE #4

Take a look at this advertisement poster for laundry detergent; we want to show you so you can roughly get an impression of the area surrounding the lagoon, with all the main characters of this scene. You see Yerba Buena growing along the sandbanks; you see the freshwater streams; you see the Chinese migrants who brought our kind to this country. The artist, of course, took poetic liberties with the geological features.

What you don't quite see depicted here, our ancestors said, are us. After they arrived in this area, with its abundance of water, they were spread

out to grow. As we described earlier, there were
several agricultural enterprises surrounding Cow
Hollow. For safety's sake, the Chinese clustered
around their own countrymen. Some of them grew vegetables for market, and since they remembered how
well we had fared in the Pearl River Delta, they
thought, *Why not grow these clams too?* Unfortunately, pollution was beginning to foul up the lagoon, and increased competition from American dairy
farms and nurseries made spreading out difficult.

Eventually, the Chinese expanded farther up the
delta, to San Joaquin River and Sacramento River.
The Chinese were eager to establish other businesses
as they knew the laundry business would be sabotaged
sooner rather than later. They'd learned from experience that whenever they got too successful at any
one thing, that's when they would be penalized. They
needed to think ahead. They were right. In 1880, two
years before the Chinese Exclusion Act was passed
in Congress, an ordinance passed in San Francisco
requiring laundry owners to obtain a special permit.
By then, two-thirds of the laundries subjected to
this ordinance were run by Chinese. None of the Chinese were granted a permit. Only one non-Chinese
owner was ever denied a permit.

TRANSCRIPTION OF INTERVIEW WITH SOFT-SHELL CLAM
(*Mya arenaria*) 8990, TAPE #5

After the transcontinental railroad was completed
in 1869, the transfer of goods from East Coast to
West became easier. Our ancestors hitched a ride
with the imported eastern oysters (*Crassostrea vir-
ginica*) destined for San Francisco Bay. While the
beds of native oysters (*Ostrea lurida*) had lasted,
the oyster industry had been profitable, but after
decades of pollution from sewage, mining activities,
and river flow diversion, the environment was no
longer hospitable for native oysters. They died off.
So live oyster seed from the East was imported to
be grown out for sale, and that was how our species,
Mya arenaria, got our free ride.

As invisible stowaways, we grew virtually unde-
tected in the intertidal zone. Nobody knew we were
there. Just as the Chinese fishermen nearby. Their

fishing villages in San Pablo Bay and San Francisco
Bay were small and out of the way, and consisted of
simple unpainted cabins built on stilts. For the
most part, the Chinese shrimped. They built sampans
and used cone-shaped bag nets that they sunk into
the water. They were skilled and caught lots of
shrimp that they dried and processed. Some were sold
to local markets, but the majority was shipped back
to China. They made quite a living this way. They
shrimped from April to October and subsisted on
their own gardens and livestock and foraged food
for the rest of the season. They did clam sometimes
in the off-season, but not very aggressively.

But soon, trouble arrived. The fish population was
crashing and everyone thought it was due to over-
fishing by the Chinese. By the 1880s, anti-Chinese
sentiment had grown to a fever pitch and the government regulatory agencies went after the fishermen,
imposing regulations to deprive them of a living.
There was a prohibition against Chinese fishing com-
mercially in California. Prohibition against shrimping during the shrimping months. Against exporting
shrimp to China. Against the bag net. The fyke net.
Prohibition against oceangoing vessels for fishing
abalone. Against operating junks large enough to
transport shrimp from camps to market. Possible
fatal retaliation for catching salmon. Prohibition
against line fishing at the shore. Against engaging
in domestic trade while not an American citizen.
Prohibition against becoming an American citizen.

By the early 1900s, most Chinese fishing operations closed. Some who hung on turned to clamming.
At first, we were angry at them, but we understood
the complexity of their problem. Their own human
activities had made life impossible for all of us.
They were the ones who dumped their pollution and

silt into the bay. We were all finding it harder to
survive.

After the Chinese were pushed out, the non-
Chinese fishermen continued their harvest, using the
nets that had been banned from Chinese use. Then the
abalone population crashed and the shrimp population crashed and the fish and the oysters crashed.
The Bay was so polluted, nobody wanted to eat seafood any longer, after the humans got sick. In a
way, we were glad, but in another way, it meant that
keeping our home clean was no longer a priority. The
humans had no stake in it.

Of those who stayed around to clam on a small
scale, we remembered Ah Toy most fondly. Ah Toy came
every day at low tide with her digging fork and a
woven basket on her back. She toddled slowly on
her dainty, bound feet. Though the work caused her
pain—she was already an old woman, and those feet
were never intended for hard labor—she never took a
day off. She tended to a small plot of the beach,
covering us with salvaged netting. Our kind has many
predators; many hungry mouths and eager beaks hunt
for us all day long. She kept them away as much as
she could. In exchange, our clan sacrificed the el-
dest to her. Care was never unrequited. Ah Toy believed this was simply the way of things. Love was
an exchange, a barter of goods of equal amounts.

Whenever she bartered with the locals for a bar
of soap or a sack of rice, she did so with sign language. She had long ago lost her trust of humans.
Especially males. She said that we clams were like
human women: soft, vulnerable, subject to the whims
of men. We provided sustenance; we sacrificed ourselves. We were the injured party. But we managed
well enough. "You only have your own body," she
would often say to us with a haunted smile on her

face. "You have nothing in this world except your own body."

Ah Toy was born in 1828 in China. At age twenty, she found herself sailing to San Francisco, one of the first Chinese women to make the journey. She traveled with her husband, who soon fell ill and died. Now she was alone on a ship in the middle of the sea, sailing to a strange place. Her beauty was both a curse and a blessing. She knew the men on board followed her with their eyes. Fresh meat for the taking. One day, a group of men cornered her in a dark room. Terrified, she decided that she needed protection, and immediately took up with the most powerful man, the captain of the ship. In exchange for her "services," he would keep her safe.

Once in San Francisco, the captain said he would no longer support her, and she had to find her own way. Those first moments upon landing, she did not even know which direction to walk. She knew what awaited her if she returned to China. She would become an old unwanted widow and live out her life in windowless rooms. Here, she could start her life over. The landscape, the sea air, it stirred something. A need to learn what she was made of.

Her body was her most powerful tool. With the money she had on her, she rented a shanty on Clay and Kearny and installed peepholes for viewing. She made herself into a real-life doll in a display case. Men paid an ounce of gold, or sixteen dollars, to look. She strutted and danced in her dark little room while they watched. She put on a good show. Men lined up around the block. Then, taking the earnings from her peepshow, she hired two girls and opened a brothel. She was a madam now. Men arriving at the dock used to break out into a run, straight to her place. She purchased a building on Pike

Street, and her rooms were furnished in the best
teak and bamboo. The most prominent San Francisco
men were among her regulars.

Just as she earned her livelihood from exploiting
men's desires, men were equally set on exploiting
her. They scammed her, abused her, attempted to ex-
tort her. Lust and admiration could turn into hatred
on a dime. But she was never shy about causing a
public spectacle. Whenever she was wronged, she
would take the men to court. By at least one tally,
she appeared in court some fifty times during her
first three years in San Francisco. Each time, she
wore beautiful outfits of "the most flashing European
or American style."

One of these men you might already know. The self-
proclaimed leader of Chinatown, Norman Asing, wanted
the brothel business for himself. He smeared her
reputation and grew obsessed with destroying her. He
plotted to have her abducted. While she managed to
defy Asing, she could not defend herself against the
San Francisco Committee of Vigilance, formed to "ad-
minister justice" against prostitution and other
vices. John A. Clark was the special patrol tasked
with deporting Ah Toy. For a time, Ah Toy made a
"deal" with him too. He would leave her alone if she
agreed to enter into a "relationship" with him.

In 1852, Ah Toy took Clark to court for domestic
violence. The judge dismissed the case, saying it was
a domestic dispute. Two years later, in 1854, she
took Clark to court again for beating her. And that's
when she learned that California had passed a law
disqualifying non-whites from testifying in court.

Our ancestors listened, riveted. They could feel
the blow of each betrayal, each more painful than
the last. There were more court cases, a ban on
brothels, even a suicide attempt, perhaps. Of her

life in the present, they knew only that she remar-
ried and her husband died and she stayed on to keep
house for her brother-in-law. She was nearly one
hundred years old. She had started out as a high-
class woman, and now she was selling clams for sub-
sistence. She never thought she could live in
poverty, but in the end, she decided that poverty
provided its own freedom. One either lived a protected, cloistered life without freedom, or a dangerous life out on one's own, where anything could
happen to you. It was an exchange. That was the lesson she taught us. And from our ancestors, Ah Toy
learned how to be invisible. She no longer felt that
opening her mouth, speaking out, would do anything
to help her.

> SAN JOSE, Feb. 2. — One of
> Santa Clara county's most familiar
> figures, Ah Toy, known to thou-
> sands as "China Mary of Alviso,"
> who, had she lived three more
> months, would have been 100 years
> old, was buried in Oak Hill ceme-
> tery here yesterday afternoon a few
> hours after her death.
> One of the first Chinese women
> to come to San Jose in pioneer
> days, China Mary had lived in the
> local Oriental quarter until the
> death of her husband about 25
> years ago. She then moved to a
> small house in Alviso, selling clams
> to tourists and yatching parties in
> order to make a living. She kept
> house at Alviso for her brother-
> in-law, known as "Chinese Louis."
> The aged Chinese woman, accord-
> ing to records in her possession, was
> born in 1828. She leaves a number
> of children in China.

Our ancestors say that Ah Toy never took more
than she could fit in her basket. She only needed
enough to sell to the yachting parties for the day,
enough to buy food and other essentials. She was
known in Alviso as the clam lady. She lived on nothing at all. After Ah Toy died, our ancestors said,
they were initially terrified. Nobody came to tend

to the little plot, to mend the nets and fencing,
to make sure that the exposed youngsters were buried back into the sand. There were no more stories
either, no daily culls. They were back on their own
against the big, punishing sea. And though they
missed her tender care and her stories, they preferred it that way.

TRANSCRIPTION OF INTERVIEW WITH ASIAN CLAM
HENRY CHEN

One reason we came to America is because we were
worried about Communist takeover from China. After
Taiwan was forced out of United Nations in 1970s,
most countries cut off their formal political relationship with us and we became like international
orphan. Real estate value dip dramatically. The DPP
party continue to rise while the KMT is very cor-
rupted. It was called Black Money Government. Under
their incompetent leadership, Taiwan was filled with
criminal activity. Every day, instead of solving
problems, the parliament members were fistfighting.

Why don't I play you a music video on YouTube
called 1990 Taiwanese by Shen Wencheng? I recall the
chorus goes like, *Taiwanese people's woes, nobody
knows! When I think about it, I get scared! I get
scared!* Something like that. Hey. Here it is. Can
you hear the song? Why are you laughing? Okay, I
agree he look quite silly. But this was a comical
treatment of very big problem. We use to be scared

to go outside for being shot or kidnapped by gangsters. This celebrity Bai Bing Bing's daughter was
tortured for ransom and they cut off her little finger to send in the mail. The whole country followed
the story! I'm only translating these lyrics for
you.

After we arrived in America, the first thing I recall was that the mountains next to the freeway were
so dry and brown, because there was a historic bad
drought. There would be big forest fires burning that
you could see from our house. But you know what,
because I am a dragon, after we arrived, it rained!
The mountains turned green. Briefly, I thought we
would have lots of luck in America and everything
would be piece of cake.

My first working experience in an American company
was that it was very easygoing. Every day, we
started with some water-cooler discussion of current politics, sports news, some other bullshits.
Then after that, we work a regular schedule and I
can even take a nap in my work corner. I was amaze
at the relaxing feeling. Compare with the competitive, hierarchical Taiwan companies, this was like
heaven.

So why did I get fired? How do I know? Ask my
boss! All of us Asian engineers accepted that working for American company will always mean risk. We
try not to make any trouble, because we are always
treated as second class. I remember, I had a work
colleague from Taiwan who already worked many top
places and had a PhD from a good university. But he
could not get any interviews. When he asked me for
my feedback on his résumé, I told him, you better
make yourself less impressive. Because, for the jobs
they will hire us, we are junior tier, we are doing
the very low jobs. If you list your PhD you will

never get an interview. After he revised his résumé, he did get a job.

Somehow, at work, I sense that my colleagues treat me as like a spy. They would ask me some mysterious questions about my programming, and I have to guess the secret meaning or intention. My mantra was, be invisible and do my job. If someone try to talk to me, I stay away, or smile, show a nice face to avoid any politics.

I recall the development team at that time was overseen by a brand-new VP, a middle-age Indian guy, very talented, very nice. I liked him. But my direct boss in the team was older white guy, and the two of them appear to be lock in some conflict. My boss would often criticize the Indian VP and ask if I agree. By the way, this was the boss that was always eager to correct my English or teach me some slang! He was the one to teach me the phrase *hot to trot*, because I was so enthusiastic at the office ping-pong contest.

Anyway, that wintertime, during the Christmas reception, the new VP came to sit with me. He wanted to ask if I would like to join his carpool. California, back then, encouraged companies to carpool together to save pollution. Right away, I smell something fishy going on. Was the VP suggesting that I take his side against my older white guy boss? I didn't know what to do. But I feel it is too risky to jump to his side, so I said no to the carpool with him.

Do you think that was a mistake to say no to the carpool?

Perhaps that is why I missed the chance for promotion and got deserted later on. It was a Monday in April, springtime. The pear trees in Cerritos were blooming. After a brief managerial meeting, my

old white guy boss told me that his whole department was dismissed and he would also be relocated.
Since I was junior, I was laid off to save cost. I
was in such shock. I only worked at Econolite six
months. We had one hour to pack and received a
three-week paycheck. That's it! My boss drove me to
Denny's and bought me a coffee and waited with me
because Ma Ma was too scared to open our house door
before my regular time to come home.

Basically, after that experience, I decide I
shall be in a small business by myself as my own
boss. Working for American company was too risky.
Safer to stick to our Asian community here in San
Gabriel Valley who are more predictable. That is why
I started my own computer fixing company, and later,
why I created Shell.

. . .

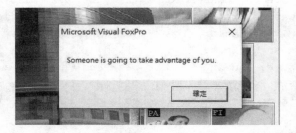

Messages in the Water

*A*fter a sleepless night of reading, the clam was first in line for the free motel breakfast in the lobby. The coffee in her Styrofoam cup tasted burnt with a metal aftertaste, but she welcomed the caffeine. She cut up a few hard-boiled eggs and mixed them into a bowl of instant oatmeal. Round one of breakfast. She planned to load up on this free food so she wouldn't have to eat for the rest of the day. She sat facing the television, set to a cable news channel. Footage of migrants detained at the southern border, of women holding crying babies and men sitting against a fence, cradling their knees. The sound wasn't on, but she read on the running ticker that the president's first budget was soon to be released. The coverage was about whether the allocated amount would be enough to actualize his much-publicized border wall.

The clam chewed slowly, thinking. With the previous night's reading fresh in her head, it was easy to draw parallels between the racial animus of the nineteenth century and the current moment. Now, as then, opponents of immigration saw it as a zero-sum game. Newcomers represented a net loss and threatened scarce resources that ought to be saved for the native population. Her research made clear that so-called native populations were themselves non-native. The designation depended on who was telling the story, and when the story began.

The clam mulled over the outcome of her parents' immigration, and wondered, for the first time, whether her dad's clam persona wasn't a reasonable adaptation to the environmental conditions he found in America. The immigrant's protective shell—in the form of the isolated, "unassimilable" outsider—was advantageous, to an extent. Stay in your own lane. Trust no one but yourself. In a dangerous environment, this was a sound survival strategy. How much of the Asian clam psyche was influenced by this pervasive sense of being unwelcome and unwanted? By extension she, too, was the product of a personal history, a familial history, and a larger environmental history. She could see herself as a subject within an environment, acted on by influences outside her control. She had consumed the nutrients and messages that were available in this water, and these ingredients had made her shell. She had agency, of course, but she lived in the water and the water was inescapable.

She knew she had one final research trip to take before she could hurry home to finish interviewing her dad. She wanted to continue thinking about this question of what was in the water, and how its altered chemistry was affecting all of them.

Microsoft Visual FoxPro ✕

Be patient, good thing will not come out in a rush.

確定

Quid Pro Quo

Daughter called to say she's arrived in Phoenix and will come as soon as she can finish her traveling. "Why the rush? Take your time!" I said. "You will be so tired driving straight shot!"

I know she is hurrying to corner me at home so she can conclude her Shell Computing interview. Now that she keeps getting closer to me, I am worried I will run out of excuse.

Why should I cooperate? Who wishes to think about their life's biggest failure?

That's why this morning, right when I wake up, I go to the backyard to clear my head. Sometimes when I don't know what to do, I exercise. Run some laps around the grass, do step ups on the stool, punch from the hip like in Tai Chi. It feels good to work up a sweat. By yourself, you feel good, so free! No one to judge me moving my body.

However, as I am doing my pushups against the wall (doctor says I must take it easy on my broke arm), I suddenly hear Marie is shouting something from the back door. What? She is awake early too?

"Ba Ba! You are not even bending your arms to do pushups, ha ha ha!"

I look at her. Yes. She is imitating me, making baby *enh enh* noises while pushing the doorframe away in a pathetic manner. But I don't look like that! She is so dramatic and exaggerating!

"用力！You are so weak! Ha ha ha ha! Look at how much stronger I am," she shouts at me. "Get your chest lower, like this!"

Did she forget I barely healed and have a medical screw in my arm? I ignore her bullying and push past quickly, afraid I already worked out too long because my face is quite red.

"If I sweat too much I will get gout!" I shout at her.

Marie points to my feet and says, "Did you exercise in those cheap plastic sandals?"

I am so annoyed, I go to the kitchen cabinet where I keep all my medicine and immediately take three ibuprofen.

Ah! I can't wait to get away!

She is still laughing as I refill my water jug and escape to my room. Safe! But now, somehow, I imagine I hear Yi-an coming home and opening the garage door. Daughter will soon join along with her mom's laughing. Daughter will say, *Yeah, Dad, get your heart rate up!*

Whatever. *My heart rate was very appropriate until you arrived!* I will say. *It is a cardiovascular exercise for me to talk to you!*

Now the blood is flowing very strongly to my brain. And then, all in a sudden, I have an idea.

Yes! I have a bargain right under my nose! How come I didn't think of it before?

What is the Latin phrase? Quid pro quo.

My idea is this: I shall tell Yi-an when she come home that I can agree to help with her writing project only if she will agree to help me complete my PhD research paper. In the past, she helped me edit my graduate school assignments because of her native English grammar skill. She could refine my thoughts and fix my style very well. That paper we did even got many citations! And then, can you believe, my adviser was so jealous at my success that he got mad I didn't put him as primary author.

This time, for my research paper, perhaps I shall simply ask daughter to co-author my paper, and then I can finish quickly and pass the next hurdle. Furthermore, she cannot say no, and I cannot lose, because I have been helping her with her project all this time. I can hold the Shell Computing details like a carrot in front of a hungry horse.

Brilliant!

Right away I open the computer and type my email proposition to her.

My dear daughter,

I got a response from my current adviser who seems not want to pay any efforts regarding my paper.

I am quite mad and thinking of quitting the school.

However, I have a new thought right now.

I want to ask him if I can add you as a co-author of this paper as you are a professor in Columbia.

Usually, if we have a co-author from a good university will be easier to pass the editor in chief.

If you can be the co-author and eventually our paper got accepted, you may get more invitation from my department.

Will you become the co-author of this paper?

Daddy

Now I can sit back and relax. Ah. The future looks possible again!

Evidence of Dissolution

Growing up in Los Angeles in the early nineties, the clam had often worried about acid rain. Spawned in Taiwan, on an island choked with lush photosynthetic matter, she had felt most at home among wet, squishy kin. Rain was not yet something to fear; but after she moved to L.A., there was nothing but cars and smog, which hung in the air like the toxic atmosphere on Venus. Eventually, the young clam learned that the smog precipitated into acid rain, which—her fourth-grade science teacher said—could sear the hair right off your head. The rain was just as acidic as lemon juice, and it had the power to corrode a car's expensive paint job! Her teacher always seemed bitterly emphatic on this point, as though he had suffered personal losses. He told his students to construct rain catchers out of liter soda bottles and hang them outside. One dark afternoon, the clam heard pitter-patter on the roof. When the rain ceased, she ran out with her packet of pH strips. She watched in high suspense as the water absorbed into the strip, streaking it a dark, sulphuric yellow, just like Venus: acid rain.

From then on, the young clam felt she had to take necessary precautions when exposed to the elements. Humans had made the outdoors unsafe: The sun gave you cancer because there was a hole in the ozone, and particulates from pollution crystallized in your lungs like fiberglass. In middle school, during that period when she and her dad still enjoyed stupefying themselves on bad sci-fi films, she would often be struck by the cold, encapsulated life of the future. Space was the most inhospitable place you could imagine. All adventures took place within the life-preserving bubble of the space suit, but one's breath was always clouding up the scenery. Gruesome murders were easy to carry out—all you had to do was push the victim out of the air shaft, where, exposed to subzero, gravity-free space, their skin petrified on contact and exploded into shards of ice.

Now the clam was driving to Oracle, Arizona, in her own life-preserving pod. It was well over one hundred degrees outside. Aside from the tufts of tumbleweed, jerky-like strips of busted rubber littered the highway, from tires that had blown out. The traffic was stop and go. Waves of heat wobbled over the asphalt. The temperature felt antiseptic. It didn't seem to want to harbor life. Everyone—herself included—scuttled carefully from air-conditioned space to air-conditioned space. She understood the absurdity of this situation—agonizing about the fate of the Earth while contributing to its demise. Earlier, while sweating at the gas pump, she'd wondered about the origin story behind the illuminated red-and-yellow Shell logo. Looking it up: The oil company began in the early 1830s, after a shopkeeper named Marcus Samuel built a fortune selling souvenir boxes mounted with beautiful shells from the Far East. With this wealth, his sons built the world's first oil tanker to haul oil from the Caspian Sea to Japan. In an homage to their father, the ships bore the names of shells: *Murex*, *Clam*, *Conch*. It was a cruel twist of irony then, she thought, screwing the gas cap and shutting the hatch. Shells, or what enabled the fossil fuel company to come into existence, might one day become extinct due to the burning of fossil fuels.

Indeed, she was heading to Oracle to visit Biosphere 2, a scientific research facility now run by the University of Arizona, to learn more. It was here where the connection between atmospheric carbon and the ocean's sensitive chemistry was first established. When the clam pulled up to the three-acre compound, it felt a bit like landing in outer space. Glass-and-steel structures—ziggurats, domes, cubes—rose out of the desert landscape. The clam thought this would be a convenient place to meditate on the follies of total enclosure and the current plight of the ocean's creatures.

Biosphere 2 was originally conceived as a space-colonization project, the brainchild of a New Mexico commune leader and an oil tycoon's heir. This unlikely pair saw outer space as the next frontier for humanity. So in the late 1980s, a glass earth ship was built with no expense spared. It contained several biomes stocked with critical plant and animal species, like a modern ark. Eight "Biospherians" would live in the sealed enclosure for two years, growing their own food and relying on recycled air and water. In 1991, they entered the ship, with television cameras rolling. But the project was doomed: Once the doors were sealed, the Biospherians soon lost control of their atmosphere. Oxygen levels dropped while carbon dioxide levels rose. Bees died out, and ants and cock-roaches took over. The ocean biome collapsed. The Biospherians, wheezing with oxygen deprivation and weak with hunger, split into factions. Eventually, liquid oxygen was trucked in to save them, and the experiment was deemed a failure.

After the flashy project was discredited, and the camera crews dispersed, a young Steve Bannon was hired to quietly slash the budgets and salvage what he could. Bannon tapped Columbia University's Wally Broecker, the scientist who had coined the term *global warming,* to become lead science adviser. The vision was to develop Biosphere 2 into a credible research facility to study the effects of CO_2. It was during Broecker's tenure that a young marine ecologist named Chris Langdon, tasked with rehabilitating the ocean biome, noticed that the atmosphere's carbon was getting absorbed, or dissolved, back into the water, making its pH lower and more acidic.

Ocean acidification is one of the lesser-known impacts of runaway carbon. The ocean, which covers 70 percent of the Earth's surface, actually serves as a huge carbon sink, absorbing around 2.5 petagrams of carbon every year. Normally the ocean acts as one of Earth's built-in buffering systems, but when carbon dioxide dissolves in seawater, it triggers a series of chemical reactions that reduces available carbonate in the water needed for shell building. As a result, marine calcifiers—like corals and certain mollusks—expend more energy to gather the same amount of carbonate, while simultaneously corrosive waters work to dissolve existing shells. The stress often proves too much for these organisms, and they grow sick and die.

Ocean carbon dioxide concentrations are now higher than at any time during the past 800,000 years. Oyster hatcheries in the Pacific Northwest have experienced mass die-offs because oyster larvae are literally getting dissolved. Important marine calcifiers called pteropods, a vital part of several marine food chains, are also dying. Scientists at the National Oceanic and Atmospheric Administration note a marked difference in the quality of some pteropod shells, which now look pocked and scarred. "Imagine trying to build a house while someone keeps stealing your bricks," Elizabeth Kolbert writes of this process in her book *The Sixth Extinction*. Visiting volcanic vents where carbon naturally bubbles out of the rock, Kolbert describes what's left of the tenacious limpet, those tough little mollusks that clutch powerfully to rocks and build wave-resistant, armor-like shells. The limpets she saw were marred with gaping open wounds. "Their shells have wasted away almost to the point of transparency."

The clam had made an appointment earlier with Biosphere 2's deputy director, John Adams, who met her at the entrance. He generously led her on a tour of the different biomes, and even showed her the giant mechanical lung in charge of the compound's "breathing." Then he led her to the shore of the enclosed sea.

Underneath the smudged glass dome, the light looked dreamy.

The moist air smelled of salt and algae. At the far end, a group of teachers in scuba gear bobbed at the surface, their voices garbled by echoes. She bent down to look at the hermit crabs feeding in the rocky crags, shoveling algae into their mouths. Once in a while a breeze blew through. The deputy director was telling her that this seawater was trucked in all those years ago from San Diego, but now they maintain it using a mixture called Instant Ocean.

The clam gazed up at the sky above, crosshatched with glass. The wave machine was regular and hypnotic. Imagine if these artificial waves were the only clock, she thought. Because in outer space, it might be dark all the time. And this swimming pool–sized room would be all that was left of the sea. Worst of all, imagine knowing you couldn't leave. The director was now discussing the transformation of Biosphere 2 into an open or "flow through" system. *Yes! Why not! Let the outside in!* A sci-fi film played in her head: The astronaut/alien fighter is reaching for that magic button, the one that will break the seal—it's a move that seems completely suicidal!—and everyone at the control center is screaming *Stop! What are you doing!* but she pushes the button, and the ceiling opens wide like a mouth, and one second passes, two seconds pass, and there is absolute stillness, and everyone waits, until the astronaut throws back her head to laugh—*I can breathe!*—as the blue yawns in.

Later, the clam asked Dr. Julia Cole, the current research director of Biosphere 2's ocean biome, if she would lay out the absolute nightmare vision if all marine calcifiers died off. It was a question that no marine lover could answer without anchoring deep into some pool of despair, but Dr. Cole answered gamely. "Well, for one," she said, "the ocean is going to be slimier, darker. Unquestionably, there will be winners and losers in the new environment. Organisms such as jellyfish and squid might do particularly well in corrosive environments."

Slime and darkness, she thought. *And winning. It's all about winning. Perhaps the legions of slime have already taken over.*

But consider the naked coral hypothesis, Dr. Cole added. This might work for you as a metaphor: There exist certain species of coral that can tolerate dramatic changes in pH. When placed in an acidic environment, these corals will simply lose the shell and grow large and flexible, like sea ferns. Then, when placed back into a normal alkaline environment, the coral will calcify once again and regain its normal shape.

After the tour, driving back to Los Angeles, the clam slowed to enter a checkpoint at the border between Arizona and California. Without examining closely, they waved her on through. It felt like an elaborate formality, almost deliberately ineffective, as far as function goes. *For whose sake is this theater enacted?* she thought, recalling Wendy Brown's assessment of the fantasies of containment in her book *Walled States, Waning Sovereignty*. "Sealing ourselves off from the dangerous outside appear[s] animated by a yearning to resolve the vulnerability and helplessness produced by myriad global forces and flows coursing through nations today," the clam will later underline in her book. Confronted with dissolution, "walls—solid, visible walls—are demanded."

She had no doubt that the desire to enclose, to sequester, came from a place of sincere anxiety. She had no doubt that when certain people refused to acknowledge that the same air and water cycled around the globe, or, especially, that America didn't exist in a bubble, it was to protect a sacred and urgent sense of sovereignty. But how does one clam down when the materials for shell building— food security, clean water, breathable air, healthcare, education, basic tolerance, those things each citizen needs to be protected— are quickly being eroded away, often by the very same methods of exclusion?

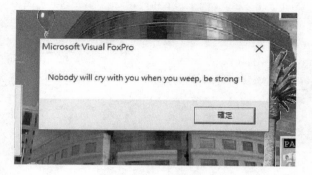

Tofu Fight

Okay. Before I can explain to you about the tofu fight, first of all, I have to say that I responded rationally based on a long history of never being free of the influence of the women in my life. These days, since I don't earn money anymore, Marie's attitude is that she can make comments about my spending and restrict me even more than before. I only wanted to spend some very small potatoes indulgence, but she still had something to say! I could not take it. When this line is crossed, I know I must preserve my own dignity.

Basically, every two weeks, it is me and Marie's routine to go to the Vietnamese tofu maker to buy some boxes of fry tofu. Customarily, we get the cheapest version, plain, but today, as we were standing in the line, I suddenly feel I want to eat the tofu with mushroom. The mushroom costs $1.40 more per box than the plain tofu. So when I get to the front of the line, I tell the cashier, "Hey, please give me the mushroom tofu!"

Suddenly from behind, Marie pinch my arm very hard and say, "Ai yah! Mushroom is expensive!"

It was just like the time with the Flowbee. This was around

1993. That year I discovered an invention called the Flowbee that Sam's Club was selling for very cheap. It was like a kind of vacuum machine for your hair. I saw commercials on As Seen on the TV. So convenient! I bought it even though I recall the cost was quite high at the time, maybe $49.99. But my rational thinking was I could save money by not going to the barber. I hated going to the barber ever since I was a boy because of what happened to me around age five or six. In Taiwan, we use to have strict hygiene days when the school officials line us up to inspect hair, teeth, nails, to make sure we are clean. I knew the day was coming, but my parents never paid any attention to me and refuse every time I try to ask them for money. I was so ashamed to go to school without fresh haircut, so I took the scissors from the drawer and cut my own hair in the mirror. Hey! I was so proud of my accomplishment, but the next day, the teacher slap me and say, "壞孩子!" He called my mom and then she took the turn to hit me. The barber was heartless too. He told my mom, I am so naughty, laughing as he shaved my head. So after that, whenever I go to the hair salon, I always recall this humiliating incident. But with the Flowbee, I could finally get my perfect trim without enduring any human fuss. However, when Marie saw my Flowbee purchase, instead of congratulating my genius, she was so outrage about the expense, saying, *Why you buy this nonsense junk!* Immediately, her chastisement ruin the whole concept for me and I threw it in the closet and I never use it again. Where is the justice? Already I spend so little and conserve like a hermit but still she must make some comment about my spending.

That morning when she yelled at me for buying the mushroom tofu, her tone was so harsh like I am her ignorant child that I feel my whole head will explode. I say to the cashier, "Please, I want *three* boxes of mushroom tofu," and quickly take the money out of wallet and shove it forward, but during that exchange, when I glimpse my rip-up wallet that is holding together with some thin threads only, I suddenly feel a choke in my throat like I want to cry, because, wah, how disadvantage and pathetic am I, that when I simply want to spend $1.40 more for tofu, that I have to be disciplined in this unfair manner, even when she knows that my undershirts are ripped at armpit and I conserve electricity by not using air condition and I don't use stove or microwave and eat everything cold and I use my wallet until this disgraceful condition like that time when I was sweeping up the leaves and garbages outside Futurelink and a man and his young crime partner approach me holding a knife to demand my wallet, and I take out my wallet and pretend I am a humble janitor with only twenty dollars and they actually, can you imagine, believe my bluff and go away, and I believe the knife-holding young guy even feel bad for me, feel sorry for robbing this poor janitor they are thieving from, because my clothes are even more shabby than theirs and my wallet is so ugly that when I take out the twenty-dollar bill, they go away immediately because they don't believe it is justice to demand more. Of course, all of these visions flash across my mind in one second, as we are standing at the cashier station to buy tofu.

The cashier woman took my money and gave me the boxes without commentary, but when we turn around, everyone in the line is staring and laughing. Another whipped husband with his tail tuck between his legs? Is that their thinking?

Is it my destiny never to have any freedom? In the car, I am so mad, I am holding the burning tofu boxes on my lap though it is quite painful, it is too precious and I don't want the liquid to spill over, but as predicted, Marie back out of the parking lot so fast she almost hit another car and slam on brake and the boxes slide off my lap and spill! I cannot take it anymore. I shout in loud voice, "Pay attention! You never do anything right!" She ignores me now and my stomach is full of fire. My speech of accusations will be liberated shortly, but I know it is dangerous to say aloud because Marie can get distracted easily when she is driving, and to argue now will be like suicide situation. You cannot even talk to her normally while she is driving, so I dare not consider fighting. I cannot say anything about the mushroom tofu at this minute as the car is moving, but I am planning everything I will say after we can park safely, for example mentioning again the Flowbee injustice, and how one time I found a stack of checks that she forgot to deposit, thousands of dollars gone. So in compare to that loss, what is this $1.40 that I want to spend on mushroom tofu?

We approach our street, and now there are no more cars around to hit us.

She pull into the driveway.

I say out loud, "I will buy an airplane ticket to go back to Taiwan. I am leaving."

Marie push the garage clicker and pull the car in.

I say, "We have a cash flow problem, and I have no confidence you will manage the finances right. That is why I must go back to Taiwan and make some plan. Maybe sell our Tainan house. Anyway, in Taiwan, I can save money by living more cheaply than here. As that is what you want."

She cut the engine and unbuckle her seatbelt and start to take grocery inside without even acknowledge my speech.

"You cannot deny that we have a lot of risk as our daughters have so much uncertainty," I say.

She still say nothing. Giving me the bitter silence medicine. I stand in the kitchen, watching her put grocery away. She open the fridge roughly and shove the tofu in.

"Nobody want me here anyway. I am just a burden to you."

She take a rag and start wiping around the fridge.

"Additionally, I must wait for my dissertation adviser to respond, and it will be better if I wait for his email in Taiwan. Not like waiting here without purpose, where I am not necessary."

Nothing.

"Okay. I am going to look for the flight tickets now. I will leave as soon as I make some bank arrangements."

I say this all very reasonable, and then go to my room and turn on the computer. I open a new browser for EVA Air. That is my preferred airline, a Taiwanese company with pleasant service and good vegetarian options. But to save money, I will fly China Air or Malaysia Air. Back to counting pennies because I don't deserve more. I think how many flights I have taken, back and forth across the ocean, thousands of dollars, filling up a bank with gold. I waste too. All vanish because I cannot stay still. What a waste my life is.

After some browsing, I feel so tired. Marie sounds like she cooking aggressively in the kitchen so I won't go out. I remember the wuxia story I was reading and click on the tab. I lean forward with my face prop in my hand and my good elbow on the table. I feel like my upper body cannot stay up by itself. I am such old man I do not even have muscle to hold my head up.

Dear Marie. Too bad you marry such a loser. Too bad I ruin your life because I made unreversible mistake of inviting my parents to live with us, who torture you for almost forty years. We never had much happiness, and it is all my fault. Too bad we came to this country where I cannot hold a good job and stay competitive. Too bad your perfect and healthy children inherit such bad qualities from me. That your daughter inherit such negative thinking from me she sometimes end up going to the ER, and now she has to write a book about what the terrible father I am, and she has to do this interrogation every day to figure out how I became a nobody hidden inside my shell.

Shell Computing. Ha ha ha. I always thought Shell was to shield and protect, but to her, it mean to hide like a coward.

Well, I always been trapped, always been abused. This is how I learned to protect.

Put up a barrier and close up so nobody can touch me.

I look at my computer screen, where I have the cheapest China Air ticket ready to purchase. Can I buy it? It is so easy and I can be gone in a few days. Gone, gone, gone. But somehow, something is holding me back.

I think I will give myself a test.

I call Yi-an.

"Ha-llo? Have you finished considering the email I send to you about being co-author of my research paper? I tell you, this is a good opportunity for your career."

"What email?" She says she does not remember.

"Search it up in your inbox! I tell you. We can scratch each other's back. You get a citation to your name. I get my final paper published!"

Now she finds the proposition email and reads it. Oh. She said she didn't paid any attention because she thought it was one of my early morning crazy ideas.

"Were you actually serious? But I don't have the qualifications to co-author your article," she says.

"If it is the full credit you want, I can give it to you no problem. I can make you the head author. Put your name in the very front. My name can go in the back."

"But I'm just an adjunct at Columbia and I teach creative writing. That has nothing to do with your PhD. I don't know anything about computer science learning."

"How will they know? They only care to see that you work at a big name-brand school!"

"But it won't look professional!"

"They won't check what your specialty is. They don't even care."

"No, I can't! Plus, I don't have time. I have to go back to New York and I have to finish my work . . ."

At this word—*work*—I suddenly explode.

"Work! What is your *work*? Like you are some Miss Big Shot!

All this time, I help you so willingly, I answer all your questions on the phone, I spend so much time to indulge this and that query, no matter what you ask. Now you cannot even allow me to borrow your name to help me graduate? I am not asking you to do anything, just put your name on it."

"You misunderstand. I want to help you! If it was something I could help with, I would!"

"What can you do for me?"

"I can edit your paper. I can go through the language with you. But you need to ask your advisers why they're being so unresponsive, and get feedback from them. Arrange a meeting with your colleagues. Your colleagues should be co-authors of your paper. Not me."

"Okay, then you are suggesting I should just quit the school."

"What? You'd rather quit school than figure out what is going on with your advisers?"

"I already know what is going on! They want to play their domination games! Bribes, psychological blackmail, kiss-their-ass praise! They hate me because I won't participate in the system!"

"Then what's the point, Dad? Even if you got your degree . . . what would it be for? Do you enjoy the work? Wouldn't you be happier if you just quit?"

"After all my striving, all my suffering, all these years in my PhD program, you think I can crap it in the toilet?"

"You didn't even start on your dissertation yet! That will take years! How are you going to do that if your advisers already hate you? And even if you finish that and get your doctorate, then what? Will you go on the job market?"

I am so emotional, I cannot listen anymore.

I want to say, *I want a PhD for my personal achievement sense.*

I want to say, *For proving I am a high-quality person.*

I want to say, *So I can say I completed something.*

I want to say, *So I know I have made the right decision.*

Give up. Give up. Give up.

You have no body. You have no desires.

Once again, I cannot take my vision to the finish line because people betray me. My co-workers, colleagues, business partners, now my own daughter too.

"You are unwilling to help me. I understand. I will figure it out on my own."

Quickly I hang up because my voice choked. My head is dizzy and I can't do anything but lie down on the bed.

But I must buy the ticket immediately, who cares! I don't care what my wife and daughters will say. They will say to me angrily, *Go to therapy! Make a friend! Grow a garden! Do some exercise! Play guitar! You cannot just run away!*

To them, I will say, *Why not?*

The truth is so hard for them to accept, but I accept the truth. The truth is that they are happier when I am gone. Their life is more convenient, because no more annoying daddy to deal with. No more strict rules and demands they cannot follow through. They always do whatever they want anyway, what do they care about me?

I know the truth because, when I was a boy, whenever my dad would get angry at something, he would always threaten to "disappear to the mountains." But we kids understand he is like playing chicken. *Prove you want me to stay, otherwise,* 我給你好看. *I'll give you a lesson.* To be polite, to help him save face, we always perform the role and beg him to stay.

There was no love between us, only obligation.

That is how I know my wife and daughters are not being honest when they keep criticizing me for going away. Maybe it is authentic that they feel guilt, but guilt is because we say we should behave like this or that. We say that family must stay together, but sometimes it is more truth that life would be easier, separate.

I stand by truth, even if it is cruel.

Imagine. My mom used to ask me, *Of the women in our house,*
who do you love the most?

Though I know it will hurt her, I can only answer the truth.
First my daughters, then my wife, then you.
Breathe. I must breathe.

When you meditate, you might feel
You're in the universe
You're in space looking at the globe
You're flying everywhere, looking at everything
You should just die, don't want to live anymore
You're like a fruit tree, a leaf on the tree

Big rain falls
It keeps falling
It keeps falling

Microsoft Visual FoxPro ✕

Becareful with you mouth, think before you speak.

確定

B-R-A-T

When the clam got home to L.A., she was doubled over with intense stomach pain. She went to urgent care the next morning. The clam sat now on the crinkly paper at the doctor's office while he grilled her for answers. "Have you had many stressors lately? Smoke? Drink coffee? How about hard liquor? French fries?"

Her face reddened—her mother was there in the room with her—"I mean, yes," she confessed, "all of the above."

The doctor sighed and gruffly pressed on the tender spots in her belly. The stomach ailment had worsened into gastritis, an inflammation of the lining caused by too much acid. She also had a gallbladder infection. The doctor ordered an ultrasound and told her not to be too stressed. At the pharmacy, to pick up her acid-reducing medication, the pharmacist hashed out the importance of adhering to the BRAT diet. The acronym stood for bananas, rice, something else, and something else. But somehow it sounded like an accusation, a prognosis of her character.

When her dad heard the diagnosis, he led her to the kitchen cabinet where he kept all his medications.

"This is omeprazole that I stocked from Taiwan, where I can

get it much cheaper," he said to her. "You can have this in case your current prescription runs out."

She trailed him as he made other preparations to leave. She was determined to pay attention to his packing this time. She would watch him make decisions; she would see exactly how he prepared himself for exile. After he showed her where his stash of medications was, he instructed mother and daughter on the location of important documents, the password codes and insurance policies locked tidily in a drawer.

"Dad, honestly, if you *really* want me to co-author your paper . . . I will . . ."

No. Wrong thing to say. This was simply damage control to assuage her guilt. He shot her a sorry look. She was entirely ready to take back her initial refusal, but now his tone was contrite. In the past, whenever he walked back an outrageous proposal, she assumed it was because he realized it was a crazy idea. Now, she could see that his shame was directed inward—for straying too far out into hope, into trust. Every hurtful refusal was a jolt back to center, that's why he accepted it so readily. Refusal was simply what he was already expecting. *Nobody will cry with you when you weep. Be strong!*

He was always misreading people, she thought, his default assumption of malignity. That was his critical flaw. He overreacted to perceived slights because he read others in the most uncharitable light, but in her case, was he so wrong? Wasn't he right to protect himself from her? Here she was, out to uncover every failure and humiliation he ever experienced because it was a good story. She never stopped to think what it meant to have it be *his* story. She was ashamed to think how, in her notes, she had even drawn a chart for herself, of rising action and increasing stakes. "He was in the prime of his life when he lost it all." The *he* in this story was her own father. How did she think it would be fair to expose him like this, when his one goal, his one true aspiration, has been to find a safe place to disappear? He never wanted to participate in her project or become a character for her inquiry, but he had done it for her sake.

They said very little to each other on the way to LAX. At the terminal, she got out of the car and leaned in for the hug, which he endured like a child. His computer programmer's slouch had worsened with the shrinking of age. She was taller than him now. His hair was nearly white. He dragged the heavy felted suitcase toward the check-in gate, a bright scrap of fabric tied to the handle. Earlier, they had argued over this unwieldy thing—why not buy a newer suitcase with wheels?—he insisted on using this one because he couldn't tolerate the idea of using one that had any value. He didn't want to feel responsible with its care. At least with this bulky piece of junk that nobody cared about, he said, there would be no grief in its loss. This was how tenuously he wanted to be tethered to objects and people alike—as though both he and his belongings could simply vanish without a trace, and hurt no one.

He often boarded the flight without texting final goodbyes; he didn't see the point. Once he arrived in Taipei he would correspond with Marie exclusively. In a sense, interacting with him while he was mad at her was not so different from interacting with him when he wasn't. Just like that, he was gone again, whisked away, and the clam did not know how many months might elapse before they would again have reason to talk. She had never talked to him as often as she had these past several months, while they were conducting the interviews. Would he miss their chats? Would she?

What was there left to do but work, now? Back home, back at her desk—time to *work*. She said it to herself in the derisive tone of her father. He was off to do his *work* and she was off to do her *work*. As little as he understood of her *work*, he had nevertheless made an effort to take it seriously; she wasn't sure she had ever given him the same respect.

She opened her files, everything she had collected from him in the last several months. She clicked through the folder Henry Old Stuffs.

In her previous cocktail party version of events, relayed with distance and irony, she would have summed up his story this way:

My father wrote his top-secret accounting program alone. When it came time to make it accessible to others, he couldn't, or wouldn't, take the final step to open it up. By then, Shell Computing had already performed its purpose. He had used Shell Computing to build a shell around himself against others. He saw no incentive to open up again after his shell was complete, impenetrable.

She opened a file titled "Conclusion of Shell" and reread the transcript she had typed up.

After I finished writing the Shell Computing, I had to write the user manual, right? That was totally painful, but I did it! Hundreds of pages. Remember? I did it by myself. I asked you to help me with writing manual but you said you too busy, and then maybe two years later, you were, I think, a senior in college? Everything was ready and finally it was time to start selling. I hired one lady to become my salesperson, but I quickly realized she was not on board with the basic principles of my program at all. I told her to read through the user manual but she insists she cannot understand. To prove her point, she even asked some of my most faithful customers to try using Shell, and got their feedbacks for me. Almost like, to prove to me that I am the problem, not her. "You have to make some important changes," she said. She said, "Your customers feel that the security features in the program are too confusing. Also it has no internet capability." That was the most criti-

cal flaw, according to her. No internet. "Maybe in 1990 it was okay to have no internet," she said, "but not in 2007." You understand why I was so mad? This was supposed to be Shell Computing, the most secure software for customer's financial data, of course it cannot open to the internet! How come she *don't understand the most important selling point? This was not a failing feature but Shell's unique value! She was so stubborn, she said, she really cannot find any customers who will take a program without internet. Could I change it? Soon we ended the partnership.*

After she left, I was thinking how I would have to deal with customer service by myself, just like I did before with SBT. The thought was horrible. Talking to people to hobnob. Put on salesman hat again, make stupid conversation. I tried to call my old Rolodex network. Many of my old clients said they were using a program call Intuit, or Quickbooks. I argue to them that the internet poses a big security risk, not to trust the internet. I think they were not interested and I had no energy to persuade them. To me, to rewrite program with internet capability would be destroying all my purposes of protecting the data and not letting anyone in. Why should I open up the program when the whole idea is to keep bad people out?

Anyway, one day, the boxes I design and order from the print shop came to the office on a big pallet on a truck. I temporarily stored it in the warehouse, imagining I would soon sell a lot of program sets. I know the disks have to be assembled and put in the boxes, also I have to print the user manual to complete the set. But so far, I did not even have one interested customer. I spent a large sum of money to put some advertisement in the Chinese newspaper, and maybe a few people responded with interest, but soon they dropped out. I thought, It's okay, don't worry, tomorrow I will deal with question of how to sell the program. It was a very big question. Today, I will just rest. When I thought this tomorrow, tomorrow, thought, I felt immediately better. When the next day came, I was feeling so bad, I thought again, tomorrow, tomorrow, and felt better. And the day after that the same.

One day, I don't remember how much time passed, I came back from

Taiwan and peeked in the warehouse. All the boxes were gone. I asked Marie, "What happened?"

She said, "Oh, we threw your boxes away. Why are you mad? Do you want to keep all that junk?" Well, since she threw it away without consulting me, I guess it was worthless. I was kind of relieved, you know? I didn't have to deal with it.

So you ask me, what's the lesson you should take? The lesson is, in my life, I have never accomplished anything big with anybody's help. Everything I accomplish, I do on my own. That is the lesson. The minute you have to rely on someone, everything falls apart. My life experience teaches me that. Everything I was ever proud of in my life did not depend on other people.

Reading back the transcript, it was clear: The moral of *his own* story was right there. The crucial lesson he wished to impart had been relayed in so many variations. *It was dangerous to involve yourself with others.* Only, she had refused to accept it, clouded by her wish that he could have learned a different lesson. She was trying to tell his story from the perspective of the shunned child, focused on the intolerable refusal.

The moral of the story, according to him: *Alone is better. Take it from me,* he was saying over and over. *I learned this the hard way.*

Her interviews with him had been yet another reinforcing event. He took a risk by opening up and then got hurt, just like all the other times.

Year after year, they misunderstood each other. What would it take to truly understand? She imagined him flying to his latest home in Taiwan. He unlocks the front door, sniffing nervously for mold. In the past, he has arrived to discover the water heater leaking and all the furniture submerged, or the windows shattered from a typhoon. This was the price he paid for his distrust of neighbors. He never knew when he would be back again, but he never allowed anyone to check up on the place. He also refused to call repairmen because he felt they condescended to him.

He has moved restlessly from house to house, city to city, all by himself, setting up kitchens, living rooms, and bedrooms alone. The photos in Henry Old Stuffs felt like landscapes of an abandoned aftermath. To her, they were scenes of isolation. But what if these unpeopled, lonely rooms and courtyards were actually scenes of peace and safety?

Everything was easy until others got involved, he said.

That was his takeaway. And he was right. He would drag the waterlogged couch into the street by himself and patch up the holes in the wall.

Doing things alone took time, but it was easier.

And here the clam decided that the daughter would learn to leave her father alone, once and for all. She would stop requiring things of him. Stop asking him to be a father he can't be. The clam would return to New York to continue her project; her dad would continue with his graduate studies in Taiwan. They would be cordial acquaintances, polite and unobtrusive, asking nothing of each other. She would find a way to tell the story of her shell-building tactics without him—and without herself, even, by removing herself entirely.

A few weeks later, the clam opened her inbox and saw that her dad had written them all an email:

Sat, Jul 7, 2017, 7:25 PM

Dear Family

After a whole day full of sadness and emptiness, I finally figure out why I am so troubled during the past years while in my current school.

Because deep in my heart, a graduate school for me should be a place that I can "learn what I want to learn," and "do what I want to do," and "research what I want to research."

Then, it turns out all the PhD students become the sweatshop workers that make the trophies for their advisers.

Finally, I understand why I feel so strange and not blending in Taiwan's higher education system, because it is a sick environment!

The school has very little budget, the professors have low pay and high quantity of journal paper pressure, the PhD students have no dignity and self-esteem.

I am so amazed that it takes me such a long time to figure this out (I think maybe because I got lost and forget why I go to school, and working so hard try to get my degree).

So, now I finally realized why I am so suffering in recent years and become a black sheep in my adviser's eyes; I cannot fool myself and have to do things following my own call, but it is totally a conflict to the master-slave atmosphere in Taiwan's educational environment.

What a sad discovery! No wonder I feel so lost and empty!

Anyway, I finally justify myself regarding why I quit the school.

The basic tone is: Be myself, follow my heart, and forward in my own way.

That is what I am holding on!

Daddy

IV

Calm Down, Soon You Will Find Your Solution for This.

The clam returns to New York. Between teaching and job interviews, she makes time only for the project. Everything else is secondary. She sees friends only when it suits her, usually when she is too exhausted to think or do anything else. Admittedly she is not lively company. Once in a while, her sister pushes through the caffeinated haze. This morning, they are breakfasting at Purity Diner, after a strenuous walk around the park.

"Wait, can I see your fingernails?" Angela asks.

The clam thrusts them forward for inspection. "What are you looking for?"

"Dad asked me yesterday if I had brittle or wavy or bruised nails, because it might mean I have liver damage or lung cancer."

The clam jumps as though she's been startled awake from a nap. "You called Dad?"

"Yeah. He was talking to Mom when I called her, so when they were finished, I called him. I haven't talked to him in so long! I wanted to see how he was doing . . ."

Here's the better daughter, the clam thinks. One daughter calls when spurred by extractive instincts; the other actually cares about his welfare. Ever since the "fight" that propelled him overseas again, the clam has not dared to call. Or more accurately, she has been determined not to call. Since *he* never calls, this refusal on her part guarantees their ongoing silence. It's been a year of indirect newsgathering, of speaking through the proxy that is her mother. In some ways, this mode of communication is unexceptional. The only difference, this time: The clam had simply gotten used to calling him without premeditation. During her months at the residency, it had felt as though they were creating something together, like co-workers strategizing a campaign. They were good teammates.

"But *you* think he's doing okay," the clam clarifies.

"Well, he *is* much more relaxed now that he's quit school. He said, *You and Jie Jie are doing very well now, I don't need to worry about you. You have each other and that's enough.*"

Recently, the Chen sisters received some life-altering news they weren't sure they deserved. The clam learned that she was about to be employed full-time at the university where she had been an adjunct for years; her sister would enroll in the photography program she'd always wanted to attend. The future cracked open. As a result, their dad relayed, through their mother, that he had, through his daughters, fulfilled his own academic dreams. He would proudly wear the branded fleece pullovers they purchased for him and would retire from the role of family worrier.

"I was thinking, I'll do a photography project called 'Our New Home' that is just a collage of all the photos he's sent us over the years with that email heading," Angela says.

The clam stirs her coffee. "Ooh, yeah, good idea . . ." The thought that her sister might accomplish a Dad-related project where she had failed set her nerves on edge. "But I feel like the best policy with Dad is to leave him alone," the clam says. She knew the bargain. Since she hadn't helped him with his paper, it didn't seem fair for her to ask him for anything more. She would have to make do with whatever she had.

"So, after school's out, I think I'll do the pilgrimage to Santiago!" the clam chirps. "That would be the perfect ending, right? Follow the seashell path until the end of the world. Go see the final cliff where pagans would take off their clothes and burn them!"

"Yeah, okay! Why not?" Angela returns enthusiastically. "Another research trip? You have it all planned out!"

"I actually have no idea what I'm doing," the clam admits. "I don't know. It's a mess."

The clam deflates, elaborating her justifications for these other potential trips and endings, and feels herself losing her grip on the morning.

"Don't worry, you'll figure it out. And if you need to interview Dad some more, he'll probably be fine with it."

"No. He doesn't want to think about the past, he's said it a million times."

"You know, Dad's not avoiding you because he's mad at you. He's not holding any grudges because you wouldn't help him co-author his paper."

"Why, what did he tell you?"

"Nothing specific. But you know him, he gets mad for a day and then he's over it! It's like he already forgot. He said, the reason you don't call him anymore is because he gave you enough details and now you finally understand him."

The sisters finish up and settle the bill, promising to hang out once the clam returns from abroad. This time, Angela will be the one going home to drive the car away, so she can have it at school. On the sidewalk, after hugging goodbye, the clam feels tears welling. "You really think he's not mad at me?" She can't help but feel that she continues to betray him in some fundamental way. Her avoidance of him this past year: Has it been a form of punishment or self-sabotage? Or is she simply trying to protect him? The latter, she affirms. He's even said so himself: He's at peace because she finally understands him. Alone is best. Alone is easy. This is the relationship he wants. Let him be.

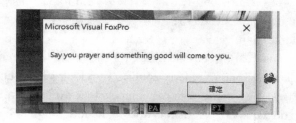

Walking to the End of the World

*J*t's late May. The clam has just landed in Madrid, chasing leads she believes she needs to follow. She'll spend a few days here before leaving for Santiago to begin her true pilgrimage. After unpacking, she heads to the Prado to study caches and pillboxes, objects that hide other things away. Then on to the Reina Sofia to watch Germaine Dulac's forgotten surrealist film *The Seashell and the Clergyman*. She sits on the floor, taking notes, and watches the film over several times. After dinner, she goes to a bookstore called Desperate Literature. Then she wanders down an alley with *conchas* in its name, her eyes watering. She is so allergic to Spain. She assures herself that she does have a purpose here. That first trip to New Mexico had felt like such a triumph, but now she has traveled all over the world alone. She has visited Darwin's house, and crawled through musty shell grottoes in Margate, and stood on the shore where distant clouds roved back and forth, yielding pockets of sunlight. She has taken copious notes. *The White Cliffs of Dover are made of the calcified remains of one-celled algae called coccolithophores.* And? With each trip, she feels she is deconstructing the part of herself that didn't know how to be alone, and reconstructing a new identity that needs nothing and no one.

Now the clam is on the train from Madrid to Santiago, a book open in her lap. Outside the train windows, the Galician countryside shuffles by in squares of green and yellow. She sits opposite a pair of nuns wearing sensible shoes, rosaries wrapped around their hands, and a group of elderly couples who look geared up for an alpine trek. The conversational snippets that drift within earshot have to do with poor weather, bedbugs, and muggings. With effort, she refocuses her attention on the book, Anne Carson's *Plainwater*, which she brought along thinking its relatable topics—romantic failure, loss of father, pilgrimage to Compostela—might jog some sort of revelation.

"Water is something you cannot hold. Like men. I have tried," the clam has underlined. "Father, brother, lover, true friends, hungry ghosts and God, one by one all took themselves out of my hands."

The essay is an account of the narrator's relationship with the fugitive men in her life, starting with her father, who suffers from dementia. Her withholding father, never very communicative to begin with, now erupts with language that equally resists meaning. The daughter, visiting him at the nursing home, realizes that the opportunity for understanding has passed. "Father tell me what you were thinking all those years when we sat at the kitchen table together munching cold bacon and listening to each other's silence?" Around this time, the narrator becomes interested in mystics and martyrs and penance. She learns about the pilgrimage to Compostela and decides to leave her life in order to see it anew.

"I was a locked person. I had hit the wall. Something had to break."

Once the train arrives in Santiago, the clam trudges up the hill in a procession of other tourists, following the sound of tolling church bells. Santiago feels like an energy vortex where the world's seashell fanatics have, on some cosmic cue, converged. Seashells are pinned to every backpack and adorn every ear, every scarf, every sock. Even the architecture is adorned: seashells on the doorways and arches and wrought-iron gates. One man is even wearing the traditional rustic brown cloak, with two shells on the chest, like a mermaid's bra.

The clam goes to the registration office to collect a map to Fisterra, her planned destination. In a contrarian spirit, she will do a loop, a there-and-back journey. At the office, a long line of tired walkers at the end of their exertions are jammed into the narrow corridor. It smells powerfully of body odor and wet socks. These people are waiting for their final Compostela passport stamp to certify their walk, after which they will be able to register their names in the Book of Reasons. After which, according to the logic of these things, they will be granted a lifetime of forgiveness.

She watches those in line, suspended between one state and another, incompletion and completion. Divorcées, recovering drug addicts, survivors of illness, perimenopausal women—she recites to herself—the usual suspects. It turns out to be true what she read in the blogs. Many walkers, as they approach the registration book, burst into tears. Why are they crying? Is this reaction caused by crashing blood sugar, spiking dopamine? Do they feel transformed? She guesses what she would log in the book if she had to—

Purpose: draws a blank.

To forgive? To be forgiven? She searches for an honest reason. Simply: She wants to get this walk over with to see if she can finally end it, end her seashell search, and move on.

The first day of the walk. It's early and the fog hasn't burned off yet; the streetlights cast pallid haloes overhead. She's not used to the walking poles. The coordination of them makes her feel like a clumsy stick-limbed insect, clacking along the asphalt. In her backpack: a liter of water, snacks, her phone charger, simple toiletries, books. She'd been so nervous about getting lost, but the path is well marked at regular intervals with the blue-and-yellow motif. She squints at each marker, having read online about a serial killer who made counterfeit plaques to lure unsuspecting women to his house.

The path winds through cobbled alleys and ascends into a wooded trail. There are walkers ahead and walkers behind, all united by the same task, and it stops being scary almost immediately. "Silent your mind," some graffiti reads. "What are you thinking about?" On a bench where she sits down to rest, she sees an infinity symbol etched into the back. Funny, even the infinity symbol looks like a scallop shell. She traces a line from the center of the figure eight, out each wing, then back to the center. By lunchtime, she has already reached the next stop, an elegant Roman bridge flanked by stone and terra-cotta roofed houses. Here, she eats a snack, watching the families across the way, on an outdoor terrace, children weaving between their parents' legs.

Come on, move on, move on. *Poco a poco.* Little by little. This is what walkers say as they pass her on the trail, greeting words that are like ants touching their antennae. The lesson is, don't focus on the destination, just focus on the here and now. If you take it step by step you'll get there. Many walkers go forward with confident stride, heads bowed, hands loose at the sides. In her headphones, a playlist she has selected at random plays songs filled with lyrics about roads, paths, new and old, journeys, buses, calling out, going forward, head down out of this blue. Ten steps back and ten steps forward. She's tired, tired, but she doesn't stop. Either the algorithm knows what she's up to or, collectively, people can't get enough of this metaphor, of being on the road, of going on, of not stopping.

. . .

That evening, at an auberge. The clam is eating an uninspired dish of pasta and reading Anne Carson again. Nearby, a merry band of German cyclists are celebrating their day with pitchers of beer, their laughter full and resonant. It's hard to concentrate in the midst of such revelry, but there's nowhere else to sit. Dining alone used to fill her with such angst, but she's learned that books are a useful prop for the occasion.

Now the clam has read up to a section about a certain cathedral wall in Astorga. Without her realizing it, the dining room has quieted down, and the waiters signal that the restaurant will soon close. She is reading about this wall, enclosed with iron bars. Women once placed themselves in there, shorn and starving, subsisting only on scraps from passing pilgrims. The women who put themselves in there think this is a fair trade-off, because, at least, locked inside a wall, the world of risk is removed. "It is a strange economy that shame sets up," Carson writes.

After dinner, the clam returns to her own room with its unfinished drywall. The wall facing the bed has been patched in a spot about chest level, which makes her wonder if someone smashed a fist through it recently. Hopefully not in a domestic dispute. There's no reading light within arm's reach, so she wears her headlamp to bed. It's like camping. She reads until she catches herself reading the same line over and over again, already half-asleep: "What is the breaking point of the average pilgrim? I feel so lonely, like childhood again."

The next day, the clam traverses cow country—rolling hills with pasturelands, seventeen miles of cow shit. Stinging flies attack her head and it feels as though she's covered in burrs. To get away from the flies, she tries to jog. Now it feels like her hip bones are grinding in their sockets, bone striking bone. Bonk. Crunch. It rains, stops, rains. She sprawls out on the side of the road, wearing her plastic poncho. Suffering is the point! she goads herself. Criminals wouldn't have their sentences commuted if suffering wasn't involved! She rolls her head from side to side. The sky sweeps above her, back and forth.

Another day passes. Another auberge, another cold bed, another morning. She approaches the end of the world. After climbing most of the morning, it's nine miles downhill in a relentless downpour. From the top of the ridge, she catches her first glimpse of the sea. Tunnel vision. Faster. She closes in on the shore. The sky blues. Scrubby pines glisten in the sun, with happy birds singing in them. The path releases farther onto a stretch of sand. A mania of seashell collecting is happening here. People are hunched over, hunting for their hard-earned souvenirs. Of course, she had planned to do the same thing upon arrival, but now that she sees everyone doing it, she reconsiders.

She continues on through the town of Fisterra, heading toward the mouth of a long peninsula. She walks with the sea on her left, her eyes squinting into the setting sun. This is the final section. She can see the lighthouse perched on the cliff where, presumably, the pagans had once performed their transformation ritual. This promontory is where the famous 0,00 K.M. marker is, to signal to the pilgrim that they've arrived.

Up at the lighthouse, all the infrastructure suggests amusement park. Heaped bins of seashells painted in gaudy colors, embellished, glued into little figurines—turned into trash—to be purchased and forgotten. The seashell industry is one of the most environmentally damaging enterprises, she thinks. Little-known fact: To get a perfect seashell, you have to harvest it with the animal still living inside, then boil it alive to extract the flesh. Entire reefs are dynamited to stun the animals. Teenage girls wearing puka shell necklaces have no idea they're wearing a massacre.

Quickly she approaches the 0,00 marker, thinking she ought to take a picture. A circle of tourists surround the marker, taking selfies. She sees children wearing heavy hiking backpacks, smiling through clenched teeth. Why should children be here? Why should they be on pilgrimage? This sight of children with backpacks on infuriates her, she can't explain it. Nearby, a busker plays that predictable song—"Stairway to Heaven."

This is it. This is it? What had she hoped to find? How interesting to come all this way, only to find that there's nothing left to find. She dutifully followed the shell-lined path to the end of the world and now she's sitting here alone, feeling nothing, no sense of finality.

She sits there. The sun sets. She hears the clatter of wine bottles against rock, the sweep of blankets gathered up. She keeps waiting to feel . . . different. By now, she ought to have shed something, a former skin to hold up as evidence of one's former shape! Transformations are supposed to be final and unambiguous! The frog turns into the prince, The End. She stands where land abuts sea, one of the only true natural barriers. What should happen next? Throw some item of clothing into the sea. Burn something. Both will contribute to ocean litter. *You should find somewhere to sleep. You should turn around*, she thinks. But there's something so unbearable about going back the way you came. That's not how we're conditioned. That's not how we evolved. In Santiago, there had been endless advertisements recommending destinations to go *after* the walk. "Don't want this to end?" the ad copy asked. Now she understands. Once people get to the end, they want to keep going. Like water, we cannot bear to stop.

Once she had a whole life, fixed and predictable. Now she has infinite choices. Every moment, she has to choose: Which way? Where should I go? How should I be? Is freedom the ultimate good? The clam recalls now the disgraced women, the walled-in ones, that Carson writes about.

Didn't they wish to be free? They did: They wanted to be free from shame, fear, anger, hurt, those forces that kept them contained inside. Unlike those women, she was free to find freedom through motion. But there's physical freedom and there's psychic freedom, she thinks, and maybe the two freedoms are not connected. We think they should be connected, so we pursue physical freedom when what we are actually after is psychic freedom. Similarly we pursue physical entrapment as a way to rein ourselves in. Some walkers spend years on the road, in a type of reverse bondage, not recognizing that perpetual movement can also be a shell, a shell against commitment. Others spend their whole lives in hermetic imprisonment, yet attain the spiritual freedom of mystics. But it doesn't have to be all or nothing, she concludes now, an intense animal hunger clawing to the surface.

She dreams of potatoes, fried ones. Freedom must be somewhere in between, she thinks. Freedom to be in the middle. To clam or not to clam? Matter is malleable, nothing is permanent, and at any moment, she can choose which way, which way to be. That's a superpower in itself. To have a choice and a say. Isolation might represent freedom for her father, but it doesn't have to be freedom for her. She doesn't have to spend her life in a shell, just like she doesn't have to spend her life running from it. She finally understands what she has to do next, but first—

In town, she ducks into the first chips place she sees, the universal food of the weary. It arrives on a plate with chunks of meat and cheese on top.

"Hey, Dad!"

"Yi-an, gan ma?"

"Hi. How's it going?"

"沒什麼. What do you want?"

(He hates false preambles. Get to the point!)

"What was it like? The first house you got in Taiwan on Evergreen Road, in the mountains?"

"That house? Oh, I remember the view of that house. So peaceful! What a remote and romantic view. I wish I didn't sell it before you came to see. You had to take a bus, then another, one hour from Taipei to reach."

"Do you remember the day when you moved in?"

"Are you interrogating me again?"

"Just curious about your memories, that's all."

"I moved there during spring 2003. America just occupied Baghdad. The day I moved, I had very bad flu symptoms. Fever, body ache, cough, hurting lungs, diarrhea, and more. At that time, SARS was spreading fast and many medical people died. When I went to the doctor, he gave me antibiotic and say it is stomach infection. That night, I decide, okay, if I don't have SARS, then I should keep working. I buy the fridge, AC system, hot water heater, stove, install gas, set up phone, water filter system, washing machine, security system, bicycle. After, I begin to have gout, but I keep working. Buy blankets. Buy compass. Buy insurance. Buy food."

"Did you carry everything up the stairs by yourself?
It was a walk-up, right?"

"Six floors up!"

"How many rooms were there?"

"Three rooms. Two balconies. Two bathrooms, him and
her. Dining room, kitchen, living room."

"Why so big?"

"Maybe in my head, I was buying a house for a family."

"What did you eat? Where?"

"I believe I just ate simple rice and vegetables I steam in the cooker? Xi fan."

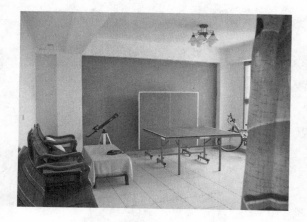

"In the afternoon, I always did a little recreation. I have my bike, my ping-pong table, my telescope."

"Did you get a lot of work done there?"

"Yes. I made great progress on the program. It was a comfort to bury myself in the data."

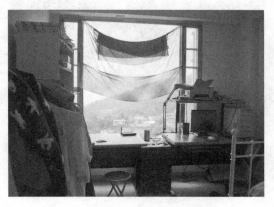

"What other routines did you have?"

"I call Ma Ma every day. She would tell me about broken toilet at home, leaking roof, or one day she said a kid's foot is crushed by a car at Futurelink! So annoyed.

"Sometimes, I go hiking. I went to see sun rise. Six km to the top.

"Or go to flower market to look at flowers . . .

"Is it a dream? Did I live there all by myself? A whole house. Eventually, I bought a smaller house in Kaohsiung. Then, I moved to a smaller apartment in Tainan. Then, I moved to even smaller studio in Kaohsiung. Now, this studio I have is only two hundred square feet, maybe less. It is only a room.

"I remember, one time I was taking a shower, and dong! Fell down. Hit my head. Very big bump. 那時候, 想說, 撞死怎麼辦? I thought, if I die here, no one will find me for a long time.

"After that, I made an altar. It's a poster of Guanyin, and a clear glass of water for the offering.

"Guanyin, please bless me and my family so that everyone is safe."

"Anyway, you can look at my notebooks for more materials the next time you come home. I will go home to show you."

"I thought you said you had journals in Taiwan?"

"No, the notebooks are in Temple City, on the shelf in my room. Next time we are both home, we can see. Then I can escape the dengue fever. The city came to spray the mosquitoes and still I must sleep inside the mosquito net. In Temple City, I will be more comfortable. So maybe you can make a plan to come home, and I will go home too."

Born to Lose

*E*arlier this morning, when I went to Yi-an's room with the box of materials that I collected, she was not there. Went for swim already? She is still on her New York time. Always exercising, that girl. Good thing she didn't inherit my bad lungs.

Later, when daughter came out of her room with her notebook, "ready" to work, her hair was wet and she smell like chlorine. When your kids do something that is confusing to you, just remember that their disobedience is the result of your own parenting. I accept my responsibility in this outcome.

"Okay, should we start? I have been waiting all morning!"

We pull out the big box of stuffs that I have collected. This is the special barcode scanner I bought that was so expensive in the past, and the folder with all my copyright application and certificates and letters. Here is the stack of backup disks. Look how many lines of code I wrote! It fills a printer paper box, and this is only small part of it. I show her all the failed escrow folders and tell her this is a big part of my retreat. Each folder here represents one step back. When Marie walks by, I repeat this to her. Then I bring out the boxes of pictures, and of course all the notebooks I wrote during my Shell Computing days.

"What do you think?" I say to her in Chinese. This is all good material. I put them on the table and tell her to flip through. "Too bad you can't read Chinese. These documents are very interesting!"

We spend all day looking through the contents. I take her through the pictures and share what I was thinking when I took each picture, so she can understand the situation.

"See how you want to package. If you can make people feel moved. Extend the historical feeling. Add compassion to how Americans can understand immigrants."

We are clicking through the pictures, when suddenly daughter interrupts—

"Dad. Will you be upset at what I write?"

"Why should I be mad?"

"Remember last year when I was interviewing you, and you said, 'Whatever you do, just don't betray me'? What would it mean for me to betray you?"

"What? I never say, don't *betray me*. I would never say something like that."

"I remember *very clearly* that you told me not to betray you."

"Did I use that word, *betray?*"

"Yes."

"If I did, then I probably said, don't betray *you*, not me."

"What does that even mean?"

"Huh? It mean don't betray *yourself*! Whatever you think is the truth, you must write that. Don't be afraid to tell the truth according to your own judgment."

"Are you sure that's what you said?"

She is so confident about my previous command that I stopped here to think.

Okay, at that time, when she first broke up with her husband, it is correct that I thought she was totally crazy. But now it has been over two years later. Somehow, she got a full-time job, she published her book, and she is living very well on her own. Was that because she followed my advice? Or because she rebelled against me?

Maybe I did say before, don't betray *me,* but I don't feel that is very important now.

"You cannot betray me because I am born to lose, ha ha, like that Ray Charles song. Born to lose, a born loser, like Buddha! I don't have any more ego."

"So . . . it's not possible for me to betray you?"

"I trust you, you are my daughter! I believe you do not want to betray me."

When I say this thing, she seems like she want to start crying again, and I think, *Uh oh.* Maybe I have said something hurtful on accident. So I quickly add—

"Even if I say that before, to don't betray me, it doesn't matter now. I have no more credibility. Your life turn out to be more successful than my life. You don't have to listen to me anymore. From now on, you're the boss!"

After this, we go back to looking at the old stuffs, and I am actually so happy because somehow, I really feel I have nothing to lose. Yes! I am the loser dad, born to lose, and it's okay, as long as I can make my daughter happy, then I am happy.

However, my one sad remaining feeling is that daughter is so much more adult now. If I have nothing to lose, does that mean I also have nothing to give? After she complete this project, she will not have reason to bother me anymore. After I give her all the stuffs, I won't have more to give. I always say to her, don't call me too much, if you got nothing to report, that is good, because no news is good news. If you got nothing to report then I am happy. If I got something to report I will tell you. Don't ask me how I am doing; you can send a text.

She got this lesson very well, I believe. And this time I think she will obey.

"Hey, Yi-an, are you familiar with the Ray Charles song I am talking about? No? I play it for you, okay? This song it is like describing my life."

Daughter said she never heard it. Okay. Since she never heard it, we get to do one more thing. Which is go on YouTube so I can play her the song.

All my life, I've always been so blue!
Born to lose, and now I'm losing you

Restoration

To begin a story: Identify one point among the infinite constellation of points to call an event. An arbitrary boundary between before and after. It can be this moment, or another, but let's say, for the sake of beginning, that a woman was granted an adaptation, and she took it and never looked back.

To end a story: Identify one point among the infinite points that have happened and will continue to happen. The clam who is me continues on, unsure if she's earned her ending. Is the story complete? How about now?

The clam is in Newport, Oregon, with a plan to interview some scientists at OSU Newport about ocean acidification. This morning, she has planted herself down on the dock by the slough, pulled in by the nature all around. Notebook out. Tide coming in. The water stirred up looks milk coffee brown; along the edges there's a more vegetal, kelpy hue. She logs: Miso soup. Green tea with a fistful of mud thrown in. How many ways can you describe this color? She moves on to document other greens: the chalk mint green of lichens, the prehistoric green of ferns in summer . . .

Another woman has come down to the dock. "Neighbor down-aways is building an osprey nest," she drawls. "Sure looks like he could use some hell-llp." Friendly introductions. K says she lives nearby, she and her husband; they're recent transplants from Texas. An hour later, they are still sitting on the dock telling stories, the kind that can only be shared between strangers who will never see each other again. "Your fifth?!" the clam cries. "Did you really get married and divorced five whole times?"

K laughs. "But I've been married to this one going on twenty-six years!" K says that now in the twilight of her life, she's finally able to confront her issues with commitment and male authority. It probably stems from her cheating father, *another empty shell of a dad* (her words). The last two years have been a *spiral*, K says, choosing this word, *spiral*. Sick parents. Her own declining health. So they bought a trailer and hit the road.

"But I could never do what you're doing," K says. "A single woman traveling alone. I'd say you're probably quite brave." The clam blinks a few times, wondering if she has ever been characterized this way. To be called brave.

One day, the clam who is me meets a beautiful man, Dan, and, as it happens, this man seems to take an interest too! He is a *horticulturalist*—a delightful word she has never attached to a person. It's a profession she can't fathom. All day, he's outside, growing flowers—*peonies!*

"Do you know about Charles Darwin's grandfather Erasmus? He wrote a book of *erotic* botanical poems," the clam says. Ah. But somehow, this line works.

Soon after, she is supposed to go to a writing conference in Key West, where she is an invited guest. They go together—to Florida, like a retired couple! They sit on the plane with their various reading materials; it feels like they've known each other a long time. On a moonlit night, they meander through the streets of Miami. Salt on the wind, sweat on lips and skin. The clam wants to visit the National Shell Museum in Sanibel and wake up in the middle of the night according to the tide chart, to look for washed-up shells.

They go. At the tourist bookstore, she notes: So many stories begin with divorce and end with romance. Well-to-do women retreating to the shore to recuperate, and there, find some "Heart-throb Harry." Maybe the clam is living in a romance novel. Ending up in seashell mecca—with this man! Is this the conclusion of her travels?

"I think this is going to be the last trip," the clam who is me says.

Returning from Florida: "Goodbye, California king. Hello, tin can bed," they joke, remembering the plush bathrobes, the veranda, the room service breakfasts by the pool.

Then they read the news. The virus? No, it won't come here. But sure enough it does.

Her train rolls by the quarantined town where the first outbreak has occurred. Armored Humvees surround the station. Nobody will be getting off. At school, there is one last training before the world is reduced to the width of a computer screen. Her whole life takes place in this screen. Between classes, she clicks through images of body bags heaved into Thermo King trucks, parked outside the hospital, humming.

The pulsing arteries of commerce slam shut. The concrete wasteland where the I95 connects with the I91 becomes a wildlife preserve. Animals tiptoe in. They must think it's so strange. Where have all the people gone? When the clam meets her sister for another of their walks, they spread their arms as though preparing to twirl, like samaras floating down. Touch fingertips. Okay, this is six feet.

Their father has been preparing for quarantine his whole life. The rest of the world is finally living the life he has lived all along. He's always preferred to wear a mask in public. For the first time, he relaxes, knowing that nobody will ask to visit. Nobody will ask why he's at home. He is no longer the anomaly. Nobody asks him to justify his fear of violence. Finally, nobody is able to find the right kind of personal safety equipment, but he retrieves an envelope of pristine N95 masks from his drawers, which he sends to his daughters in Connecticut. Saved it from the last SARS pandemic.

. . .

On a whim, one day at the hardware store, with Dan, I buy a packet of cosmos seeds, remembering it was a flower that my dad once talked about. I mail it home. Weeks later, I learn that he has been watering those beloved seedlings one bucketful of water at a time, doling out the water from the large outdoor trash can he's positioned underneath the house gutters. Any small amount of precipitation is duly captured and saved, and sometimes he wakes up in the middle of the night, if it's a heavier rain, to switch out garbage bins so he can collect more water. In preparation for total societal breakdown, he has rigged up this elaborate system for wan yi. He also built a ramp to reroute the washing machine water into yet another bin, and he uses that throughout the day, like a well. He goes back and forth from his various trash bins to water his garden. It's pre-modern. It's pre-agricultural. Mom says they have a work-ing sprinkler system but he'd rather do it this way. He pisses into a bucket, dilutes that with gray water from dish washing, and waters his citrus trees with it. On the plus side, with this specific and rigor-ous watering schedule, he barely has time to read his wuxia novels.

"It's a great workout for him!" Mom reports. "His muscles get stronger every day!"

The summer passes. Dan and I marry in the courthouse, stiffly positioned next to a historical fire engine where the city employee has directed us to stand. It is just the three of us in the echoing hall. She reads through the vows quickly: nautical metaphors about ships, safe harbor, choppy seas. We want to giggle behind our masks. Finally, she says, *Now you may*—hesitates—*hug.* We skip out of the courthouse happy.

A year later, I get pregnant and the name Henry floats up in the list of possibilities.

I am in my first trimester when we decide it is time to travel again, to visit my parents in Temple City. It will be Dan's first visit to see the house of my childhood. We are vaccinated now, and the world is beginning to open up, bit by bit.

The minute we arrive, we are tasked with digging new vegetable beds. Since the pandemic, they have expanded their garden from one bed to many. Mom is growing squash, leafy greens, onions, beans. She often sticks kitchen scraps in the dirt to see if it'll do anything. Dad feels overwhelmed by the vegetables because there's pressure to do something with them. He begs her to stop growing so many, while painstakingly harvesting all the tomatoes. They're not good for his acid reflux, but because they're food, he has to eat them. Flowers are different, he argues. Flowers ask nothing of you. They are only there to be appreciated. They serve no other function.

Dan and I are in the guest room, changing into gardening clothes. I am fuming (and out of breath and nauseous as ever) because of an argument earlier about who would water their garden. I mentioned that they might need to simplify their watering system for the sake of whoever will be taking over, since they'll need to come see the baby that summer.

"But I'm not going to see the baby!" Dad said. "I can't!"

"You'd rather miss the birth of your first grandson than ask a neighbor to come water your garden? Come for one week! That's all we're asking!"

"I don't need to be there right when he is born!"

"Why? It's a big event!"

He made excuses—"I'll get sick and I'll get the baby sick!"

To which I said, "Ugh, okay, fine!"

To which he said, "Whatever, you can FaceTime me after you leave the hospital!"

To which I said, "But he's going to be named after you!"

To which he said, "If I see any little blood or smell anything I will faint! When Ma Ma was giving birth to you, I wasn't in the room!"

To which I said, "What? You didn't accompany Mom to labor?! She did it all by herself?"

To which he said, "What use can I be if I am unconscious?"

After I finish recounting this "infuriating" conversation once more to Dan, we both start laughing. To my surprise, the feeling of indignation fades away. It's not that he doesn't love us or doesn't want to be involved, it's just . . . he really doesn't want to see any blood! Dan sums up. He's very attuned to his limits.

Dan and I finish changing, put on hats, and go "out back," to what I remembered as a crisped expanse of crabgrass. The yard always felt more akin to a range from the area's ranching and or-charding days. After two years of obsessive planting, though, this scraggy plot has transformed into something almost tropical. An acre of Taiwanese countryside plopped down, atmosphere in-cluded, in its saturated greens and grays. Climbing jasmine ex-plode along the wooden fence; shrubs of sweet Osmanthus hum with insect life. A small orchard comprising varieties of Taiwanese guava, Asian pear, avocado, hibiscus, kumquat, banana, and the huge orange and tangerine trees that were here from before have been freshly fertilized, pruned, and mulched. It's citrus season. Glossy orbs of fruit fringe the trees in a lacy orange skirt. What relentless, seething life! No wonder my dad feels overwhelmed.

We look for him, in another area of the yard, where the new beds are to be mounded up. He is dragging a cartload of heavy pavers he's salvaged from somewhere. He says he is trying to build a path through the beds so his ankles won't touch the plants. He says they give him an allergic reaction.

"Dad!" I yell in his direction. "Let Dan help you! He can build an irrigation system while he's here! It's no problem! He's very strong! You don't have to do everything manually by yourself!"

"Look, he's squatting and burning calories," Dan says, when I elbow him in the side.

My dad gets up from his crouched position and puts his hands on his waist. He blinks a few times. I think he's dizzy from standing up too quickly.

"I live a very environmental life," he says. Then he returns to his task, edging the paver a little this way, a little that way, getting them all straight. Slow and easy.

As he's working, Dan and I take a closer look at their handiwork, the various beds that have been opened up and cultivated since lockdown. For the trellising, it looks like two human magpies descended and did fast work with wood scraps, cracked plastic tubing, produce netting, and colorful bits of electrical wire. An old broom handle is tied to a rusted shelf rail with a defunct yellow network cable, secured with more fabric and wire. Is this a spigot? I crank the metal knob on what looks like a tall yard spigot only to see that it's there for decoration. This yard looks like a cheerful and orderly hobo art encampment. There's flattened cardboard everywhere, for mulch. In another bed, Mom has strung up paracord in a tent-like configuration, looking like cat's cradle or a primitive trap for birds, so the beans can coil themselves up. It's an ingenious method that she learned from the neighbor who used to be a farmer back in Vietnam.

"This is so great," Dan says, pointing to a wooden pallet that has been secured upright to form a kind of wall, against which a congregation of cosmos flowers have amassed. Bouncy, feathery stems of cosmos beam up at us in magenta and pink and white. From that initial packet of seeds that I sent, Dad has diligently spread multiple generations of cosmos flowers around. He grows them out, lets some go to seed, collects them, and plants new beds. They are his favorite flower.

I think of all our previous attempts to force him to start a hobby—start a garden, play the guitar—these were all things we thought he might enjoy. In his journals, he had often remarked that he had gone to see flowers that day. Now, on his own time, he's gardening and so excited to see what changes. His joy is palpable.

He has a farmer's undershirt tan. His daily walks to the arboretum are infused with purpose as he trots around, collecting seeds. He notes the plant names and compiles lists of what he might like to buy. Everything happens on its own time, according to its own logic. We used to be hidden inside this house; we used to seal up all the windows. Then the spell lifted. It just took time. As seeds sprout when the conditions are right, people come out of their shells.

A Note on the Chinese and Taiwanese

During the copyedit stage, I knew I had to make a final decision about how to represent the Chinese and Taiwanese in this manuscript. Should I use only Han characters, or only English romanizations, and if so, which system? Should I include tonal marks? In the end, I chose to adhere to no system. I feel somewhat justified in this because even today, in Taiwan, there is no consensus. You might find yourself reading a street sign that is spelled one way, but across the street there is another sign with a different spelling of the same road. Is it Lu Hsing Road or Luxing Road? In 2009, in an effort to get everyone on the same page, Hanyu Pinyin was adopted as the national standard in Taiwan, but this was a controversial decision since this was the same system used in mainland China. Some municipalities, like Kaohsiung, stuck with Tongyong Pinyin, while other places left their Wade-Giles signs alone. One might make a fair guess at the politics of a place just by scrutinizing their romanization choices. But, since my family is not very doctrinaire—and we never learned these systems officially—we've always used our own idiosyncratic mix of non-standard romanizations, especially when transcribing spoken Taiwanese. The important thing is that we understood one another.

Throughout the book, I stay as true as possible to this private system. Our names are the best examples. We refer to me and my sister as "Yi-an" and "Anchi" even though in Hanyu Pinyin it would be "Yian" and "Anqi." Then there are place names, such as 新店, where my dad's family is from, which is known as Xindian, but is also referred to as Hsin-tien, Shinten, Sindian, Sintien, or

Hsintien. Or, as my dad would spell it, "Shin Dian." And why are some phrases written in Chinese characters while other phrases are transcribed, and why are still other phrases translated into English entirely? You may be disappointed to learn that a lot of it is "just because." If I think it might be necessary for the reader to identify the phrase later, such as "wan yi" or "gan ma," which come up multiple times, then I transcribe it so a non-Chinese reader would be able to recognize it. If the phrase does not repeat again, then I usually depict it in Han characters. (But not always.) It also depends on whether I think the sound is important, such as the antibiotic wash Sa Wei Long. And exclamations I spell out too, like "wah sai!" and "ai yah!" I include no tonal markings because we would never, ever go through the trouble of adding tonal marks in our correspondences. To represent Taiwanese, I simply approximate: "pah biang" means to hustle. Sure, why not? However, idioms, cheng yu, and classic poems, those types of things, are rendered in Chinese without reservation. Doing it any other way would be perverse and disrespectful.

For non-readers of Chinese, I expect that when you get to the unreadable characters in the text, you might feel momentarily irritated, or paralyzed, not knowing how to proceed. And that is okay. That feeling you have is not unlike the feeling I have when my parents text me something that I cannot read. I am initially filled with the same indignation as you, that they have not made my life easier by giving me the information I need *in English*! Other times, what I feel is guilty, as though my parents were accusing me of not caring. But most of the time, what I feel is loss. Those undecipherable characters flash and fleet away like fish, scattering below into a realm I'll never reach. I peer down into this vast unknown region: my mother tongue. Usually, that's when I'll shake myself out, plug those characters into Google Translate, and try to hold on to that tether, connecting me with them, for at least a little while longer.

Author's Note

Without looking at the Library of Congress classification for this book, you might think that what you've just read is a novel, and that is entirely fine by me. I *am* a novelist—fiction is what I teach for a living—and that judgment seems fair. What *would* you call a book that's narrated from the perspective of a woman who thinks she's a clam? To complicate the issue, half of the book is written in the first-person voice of my father, and yet another chapter is narrated by Asian clams. Whatever this is, it's certainly not a *memoir*. And yet, I'd like to argue that it *could be*.

In the eight years that it took to write this book, from initial conception to publication, the question of genre only tortured me these last several months, when it came time to decide how to classify it. In the end, we decided to go with the Creative Nonfiction category, because I still think that fits the spirit of the book best. My intention all along was to write about what happened to me, and to my family, in an immersive and transporting way. I wanted to fill the book with research that could be fact-checked and substantiated. And I wanted the uncanny resonances and coincidences of real life to speak for themselves. So many times, I find a perfect detail or anecdote that makes me go, *no way*—and suddenly all the stars seem to align. Truth *is* stranger than fiction. Because I love this expansive, preordained feeling, that is what I wanted to recreate for my readers.

Early on while I was writing this book, a filmmaker at a residency with me commented that what I was doing felt very "Adam Curtis," with the same off-kilter piecing together of unorthodox evidence to tell a hidden story. I thought that was such a compliment, and it helped crystallize this impulse that was only fuzzily intuitive or groping before. Encountering Yoko Tawada's *Memoirs of a Polar Bear* that winter in 2016 was hugely impactful to me. Other acknowledgments: Sigrid Nunez's "official" biography of the marmoset of Bloomsbury, *Mitz*, which gave us a portrait of the Woolfs through their pet monkey. The use of first-person plural in Julie Otsuka's novel *The Buddha in the Attic*. All of the "autofiction" that I love, including the books of Chris Kraus and Annie Ernaux. My friend Lisa Chen's novel *Activities of Daily Living*. Saidiya Hartman's *Wayward Lives, Beautiful Experiments* and John Keene's *Counternarratives*, which bring history to life using fictional treatments. Anna Tsing's collaborative project on invasive snails in Taiwan. I could go on with this list of inspirations. These are fictional works that read like nonfiction, and nonfictional works that read like fiction, and together they gave me some courage and conviction about what I was attempting.

I do seem to possess a compulsion to mash up genres and styles, to hybridize, clash, and make it weird, to see what emerges in the process of cross-pollination. Form is very important to me, as well as story, and I'm constantly pouring one into the other to find the right shape. And so—full disclosure—I let myself take certain liberties with trimming and rearranging and re-channeling whenever I thought it would help bring the story out more clearly.

As has been argued so many times before, stories are artifices. To tell one, you have to condense, cut a path, and leave out everything else. In that sense, can any story really be entirely accurate? Jorge Luis Borges puzzles over this dilemma in his story "On Exactitude in Science," which describes a map so precise it is exactly as large as the territory it represents. Like maps, we know that stories can't be told at a scale of 1:1. If they were, they would be incomprehensible and useless.

So here, I'll share some of the contractions and elisions I imposed to tell a more streamlined story, so you're not under any illusions that this is all "true." The sections written from my dad's perspective are the most obvious examples of manipulation. I interviewed my dad over the course of several years, but in the book, I condense our conversations down to a handful of calls. I also recreated it to follow a more conventional, emotional build. Similarly, it took me a year of intense work to read and write everything that went into the "Invasive Asian Clams" section, but I depicted it in the book as taking place on a single night. I went to Arizona several times, not just once, and you might see that some of these details about who I was with are different from when they first appeared in *The Paris Review Daily*. It seemed like a better storytelling decision to keep the reader in one place instead of back and forth, back and forth. It would have been possible, but harder. I did make a lot of judgments like that throughout the book. I could tell a truer truth, but then the reading experience would suffer.

Besides omitting large chunks of what happened, I also changed certain small details to protect the privacy of some of my characters.

Lastly, the research that I did: Because this book is the product of years of reading and absorbing, sometimes late at night on my phone, just casually browsing, or in conversation with friends, I don't always know where I got something. I tried to keep careful records but I didn't always succeed. The sources that follow represent the majority of where I got my information, because they were the sources I returned to again and again, and also the sources we used for the fact-check. It is an incomplete accounting.

Sources

Auster, Paul. *The Invention of Solitude*. New York: Penguin Books, 2007.

Cixous, Hélène. *Vivre l'orange*. Paris: Des Femmes, 1979.

Waldbusser, George. Professor in the College of Earth, Ocean, and Atmospheric Sciences, Oregon State University, Corvallis, in conversation with the author, March 2019.

I

Andersen, Hans Christian. "Correspondence to Grand Duke of Weimar." In *My Dear Boy: Gay Love Letters Through the Centuries*, edited by Rictor Norton. London: Leyland, 1998.

Bachelard, Gaston. *The Poetics of Space*. Translated by Maria Jolas. New York: Penguin Classics, 2014.

Bernofsky, Susan. "On Translating Kafka's 'The Metamorphosis.'" *The New Yorker*, January 2014. https://www.newyorker.com/books/page -turner/on-translating-kafkas-the-metamorphosis.

Buchsbaum, Ralph. *Animals Without Backbones*. Chicago: University of Chicago Press, 1938.

Calvino, Italo. *The Complete Cosmicomics*. Translated by Martin McLaughlin, Tim Parks, and William Weaver. Boston: Mariner Books Classics, 2015.

Carrington, Leonora. *The Complete Stories of Leonora Carrington*. St. Louis: Dorothy, a publishing project, 2017.

Crawford, Anwen. "Leonora Carrington Rewrote the Surrealist Narrative for Women." *The New Yorker*, May 2017. https://www.newyorker .com/books/page-turner/leonora-carrington-rewrote-the-surrealist -narrative-for-women.

da Cunha Lewin, Katie. "A Labor We Will Never See." *Los Angeles Review of Books,* October 2021. https://lareviewofbooks.org/article/a-labor -we-will-never-see/.

Emre, Merve. "How Leonora Carrington Feminized Surrealism." *The New Yorker,* December 2020. https://www.newyorker.com/magazine/ 2020/12/28/how-leonora-carrington-feminized-surrealism.

Ingram, Simon. "Beneath Paris Lies a Dark and Forbidden World of the Dead." *National Geographic,* November 2020. https://www.national geographic.com/premium/article/paris-catacombs-forbidden-world-dead.

Kafka, Franz. *Letter to the Father.* Translated by Ernst Kaiser and Eithne Wilkins. New York: Schocken, 2015.

Kafka, Franz. *The Metamorphosis.* Translated by Susan Bernofsky. New York: W. W. Norton, 2014.

Kafka, Franz. "A Report to an Academy." In *The Complete Stories,* translated by Willa and Edwin Muir. New York: Schocken, 1995.

Kraus, Chris. *Torpor.* Los Angeles: Semiotext(e), 2006.

Laing, Olivia. "Agnes Martin: The Artist Mystic Who Disappeared into the Desert." *The Guardian,* May 2015. https://www.theguardian.com/ artanddesign/2015/may/22/agnes-martin-the-artist-mystic-who -disappeared-into-the-desert.

Lanthimos, Yorgos, dir. *The Lobster.* A24, 2015.

Martin, Agnes. *Writings.* Edited by Dieter Schwarz. Berlin: Hatje Cantz, 2005.

Ovid. *Metamorphoses.* Translated by David Raeburn. New York: Penguin Classics, 2004.

Ponge, Francis. *Selected Poems.* Winston-Salem: Wake Forest University Press, 1994.

Princenthal, Nancy. *Agnes Martin: Her Life and Art.* New York: Thames & Hudson, 2019.

Tawada, Yoko. *Memoirs of a Polar Bear.* Translated by Susan Bernofsky. Brooklyn: New Directions, 2014.

Tawada, Yoko. In conversation with the author, December 2016.

II

Carroll, Angus. "Darwin's Seal." Darwin Online. https://darwin-online .org.uk/EditorialIntroductions/Carroll_DarwinsSeal.html.

Chaffin, Tom. *Odyssey: Young Charles Darwin, the* Beagle, *and the Voyage That Changed the World*. New York: Pegasus Books, 2022.

Colp, Ralph, Jr. "The Relationship of Charles Darwin to the Ideas of His Grandfather, Dr. Erasmus Darwin." *Biography* 9, no. 1 (1986): 1–24. https://www.jstor.org/stable/23539284.

Darwin, Charles. Letter to Charles Whitley. Circa 1831. Collection of the Linnean Society of London.

Darwin, Charles. Letter to J. D. Hooker. January 1844. Collection of the Darwin Correspondence Project, University of Cambridge.

Darwin, Charles. Letter to Robert FitzRoy. October 1831. Collection of the Darwin Correspondence Project, University of Cambridge.

Darwin, Charles. Letter to Robert FitzRoy. October 1846. Collection of the Darwin Correspondence Project, University of Cambridge.

Darwin, Charles. *On the Origin of Species*. New York: Macmillan Collector's Library, 2017.

Darwin, Erasmus. *The Temple of Nature; or, The Origin of Society*. New York: T. and J. Swords, 1804.

Darwin, Erasmus. *Zoonomia; or, The Laws of Organic Life*. London: Printed for J. Johnson, in St. Paul's Church-Yard, 1796.

Drohojowska-Philp, Hunter. *Full Bloom: The Art and Life of Georgia O'Keeffe*. New York: W. W. Norton, 2004.

English Heritage Guidebook to Down House. London: English Heritage, 2009.

Falk, Dan. "A Debate Over the Physics of Time." *Quanta*, July 2016. https://www.quantamagazine.org/a-debate-over-the-physics-of-time-20160719/.

Fordham, Hubbard Latham. *Portrait of a Shellfish*. Mid-1800s. In "Still Life in the Studio: Permanent Collection Exhibition." Parrish Art Museum, Water Mill, New York, November 2014 to October 2015.

Fortey, Richard. *Earth: An Intimate History*. New York: Vintage Books, 2005.

Gordon, Greg. "Carmel." In *Landscape of Desire: Identity and Nature in Utah's Canyon Country*. Salt Lake City: Utah State University Press, 2003.

Hayes, Jeremiah. "A History of Transatlantic Cables." *IEEE Communications Magazine*, September 2008.

Helmreich, Stefan. "Seashell Sound." *Cabinet* 48 (2012): 23–29.

"The Idea Takes Shape." In *Darwin*. American Museum of Natural History, New York, November 2005 to August 2006.

Jensen, Morten Høi. "Darwin on Endless Trial." *Los Angeles Review of Books*, January 2018. https://lareviewofbooks.org/article/darwin-endless-trial/.

King-Hele, Desmond, ed. *Charles Darwin's "The Life of Erasmus Darwin."* First unabridged edition. Cambridge: Cambridge University Press, 2003.

Krutch, Joseph Wood. *The Desert Year*. New York: William Sloane, 1952.

Liberman, Anatoly. "The Long Arm of Etymology, or, Longing for Word Origins." *OUPblog*, September 13, 2006. https://blog.oup.com/2006/09/the_long_arm_of/.

McPhee, John. *In Suspect Terrain*. New York: Farrar, Straus and Giroux, 1983.

Stott, Rebecca. *Darwin and the Barnacle*. New York: W. W. Norton, 2003.

Valleriani, Matteo. "Galileo's Abandoned Project on Acoustic Instruments at the Medici Court." *History of Science* 50, no. 1 (2012): 1–31. https://doi.org/10.1177/007327531205000101.

Williams, Felice, Lucy Chronic, and Halka Chronic. *Roadside Geology of Utah*. Missoula: Mountain Press, 1990.

III

Adams, John. Deputy director and chief operations officer of Biosphere 2, in conversation with the author, May 2017.

Armentrout-Ma, L. Eve. "Chinese in California's Fishing Industry, 1850–1941." *California History* 60, no. 2 (1981): 142–57. https://www.jstor.org/stable/25158037.

Brown, Wendy. *Walled States, Waning Sovereignty*. Brooklyn: Zone Books, 2010.

Cilker, Noel C. "A Little China Leader, a Brothel Owner, and Their Clashing American Dreams in Gold Rush San Francisco." *Chinese America: History and Perspectives* (2018): 57–63. link.gale.com/apps/doc/A581024575/AONE?u=nysl_oweb&sid=googleScholar&xid=e7a22b42.

Cole, Julie. Professor of Earth and environmental studies, University of Michigan, Biosphere 2 board member, in conversation with the author, May 2017.

"History of Arcosanti." Cosanti Foundation. Accessed September 2017. https://www.arcosanti.org/history/.

Jeong, May. "Ah Toy, Pioneering Prostitute of Gold Rush California." *The New York Review of Books,* June 2020. https://www.nybooks.com/online/2020/06/19/ah-toy-pioneering-prostitute-of-gold-rush-california/.

Kolbert, Elizabeth. *The Sixth Extinction: An Unnatural History.* New York: Henry Holt, 2014.

Lee, Erika. *The Making of Asian America: A History.* New York: Simon & Schuster, 2015.

Mann, Charles C. *1493: Uncovering the New World Columbus Created.* New York: Alfred A. Knopf, 2011.

Smith, Jordan Fisher. "Life Under the Bubble." *Discover,* December 2010. https://www.discovermagazine.com/environment/life-under-the-bubble.

Takaki, Ronald. *A Different Mirror: A History of Multicultural America.* New York: Back Bay Books, 2008.

Wallace-Wells, David. "The Man Who Coined the Term 'Global Warming' on the Worst-Case Scenario for Planet Earth." *New York,* July 2017. https://nymag.com/intelligencer/2017/07/man-who-coined-global-warming-on-worst-case-scenarios.html.

IV

Carson, Anne. *Plainwater: Essays and Poetry.* New York: Vintage Books, 2000.

Nooteboom, Cees. *Roads to Santiago: A Modern-Day Pilgrimage Through Spain.* Translated by Ina Rilke. New York: Harcourt Brace, 1997.

Image Credits

251 *A back yard. 1890s. [No. 297. Date on photograph is 1880.]* United States, ca. 1890s. Roy D. Graves Pictorial Collection, BANC PIC 1905.17500:29:31— ALB, The Bancroft Library, University of California, Berkeley.

255 William Shew, *View from Rincon Point.* United States, 1923 DPW copy of gelatin silver copy photography by T. E. Hecht from the 1853 original. OpenSFHistory/wnp36.03148, Department of Public Works Collection, San Francisco Public Library.

258 *Men lifting sacks of rice, 921 Grant Ave.* United States, ante-1910. Photograph. California Historical Society, San Francisco, accessed through the Online Archive of California, http://www.oac.cdlib.org/ark:/13030/hb696nb13n/?order=1.

261 Carleton E. Watkins, *The Golden Gate, San Francisco: View west from Russian Hill, over Washerwoman's Lagoon.* United States, ca. 1859. Miscellaneous mammoth plate photographs by Carleton E. Watkins, BANC PIC 1964.072:01, The Bancroft Library, University of California, Berkeley.

265 Shober & Carqueville, *The magic washer, manufactured by Geo. Dee, Dixon, Illinois. The Chinese must go.* United States, ca. 1886. Lithograph. Library of Congress Prints and Photographs Division, Washington, D.C., https://www.loc.gov/item/93500013/.

267 *View of Chinese fishing camp against a hillside. Drying grounds, nets cast out to sea, and shanties hugging the shoreline.* United States, ca. 1889. Photograph. Still Picture Records Section, Special Media Archives Services Division (NWCS-S), National Archives and Records Administration, College Park.

272 "'China Mary of Alviso' Dies as Century Neared." *Oakland Tribune,* vol. 108, no. 33, February 2, 1928. California Digital Newspaper Collection, Center for Bibliographic Studies and Research, University of California, Riverside, https://www.newspapers.com/article/oakland-tribune-ca-madams-ah-toy-died-bu/13646270/.

Acknowledgments

This book would not have been possible without the initial invitation from Caitlin Love at *The Paris Review* to write the mollusk column. Thank you for seeing the potential in this material and for discouraging me from writing about rocks. Victory Matsui was my first advocate at One World, but how lucky I was to fall into the care of Nicole Counts. Nicole, your editorial wizardry is an extension of your pure empathic ability to jump into another person's shell (and gently coax them out). I'm in awe of you. Thank you to Oma Beharry for your feedback on the ending, to Chris Jackson, and to the entire team at One World: Avideh Bashirrad, Carla Bruce, Lulu Martinez, and Tiffani Ren. Molly Atlas, I would be a useless wreck without you. You steered me through the most trying times, when I was attempting to birth a book and a baby. To my intrepid research assistants, Kevin Wang and Kim Hew-Low: Thank you for your sharp eyes and incisive feedback and for always being my first sounding board. I hope it was encouraging to see how even flailing attempts could eventually amount to something.

This book was completed with institutional support from the Wurlitzer Foundation, Blue Mountain Center, BANFF Literary Centre, Akademie Schloss Solitude, Columbia University's Hettleman Travel Grant, Columbia University Junior Faculty Provost Grant, and Convent Arts.

Thank you to everyone who ever sent me screenshots, factoids, or anecdotes about mollusks! This is an incomplete list, but you kept me going: Anne McClintock and Rob Nixon for the mussel shells and for early brainstorming; Fatma Cheffi for hospitality in Tunis and telling me about Italo Calvino's "The Spiral"; Bonnie Chau for

the screenshot of the "community-verified" translation of "clam
down"; Ladan Osman for the poem "The sea fell on my house";
Clemmy Brown for unearthing your high school tchotchkes; Audrea
Lim for the GIFs; Heidi Julavits for your subliminal orgy plates;
Holly Shaffer for the happy clam mug; Mary Lou Gaeta for the seashell drawings; Jos Sances for the etching; and countless, countless
others. Thank you especially to M. Rezaee and Alex P.-B. for your
wisdom and companionship during those years.

Thank you to the experts who volunteered their time to answer
my questions: Julia Cole and John Adams for talking to me at Biosphere 2; Chris Langdon for explaining seaweed and diploids; Nancy
Steinberg and Mary Markland at the Hatfield Marine Science Center;
Xin "Liu" at Oregon Oyster Farms; Wallace Kaufman for adventures on the slough; neighbor Kim for an ending; Meredith White at
Mook Sea Farm; Mark Green at Basket Oysters; Brian Kim-Mozeleski
at Otter Cove Farms; Nico Franz and Dale Snyder at the ASU Mala-
cological Collection. George Waldbusser, thank you for letting me
use your beautiful description of pre-Cambrian seas.

Thank you to my early supporters, whose work has enriched
me in uncountable ways. Leslie Jamison, for teaching me about
vulnerability and daring; Rivka Galchen, for your singular voice,
which always makes me feel less lonely. Dana Spiotta and Ed Park:
Thank you for believing in me when there was so little to go off of.
Thank you to my big sisters at work, always one text or phone call
away: Dottie Lasky, Heidi Julavits, Lynn Xu.

My deepest gratitude for my friends, for the walks and pep talks
and laughs and tears when that was necessary. What I owe you is more
than I can put into this short acknowledgment: Lisa Chen, Andy
Hsiao, Eugene Lim, Michael Krimper, Sam White, Sasha Graybosch,
Viet Nguyen, Mona Chalabi, Sukjong Hong, Jane Kim, Miko Yo.

Dan: You're my fairy-tale ending.

This book was co-created with my family, who taught me everything I know about unconditional love.

About the Author

ANELISE CHEN is the author of the experimental novel *So Many Olympic Exertions* (Kaya Press), a finalist for the VCU Cabell First Novelist Award. She is a 5 Under 35 honoree from the National Book Foundation. Chen received her MFA from New York University and her bachelor's degree from the University of California, Berkeley. She teaches creative writing at Columbia University School of the Arts, and lives in New Haven, Connecticut, with her family.